Language in Education
Theory and Practice

More than Meets the Eye

Foreign Language Reading:
Theory and Practice

Marva A. Barnett
University of Virginia

A Publication of **CAL** Center for Applied Linguistics

Prepared by the **ERIC** Clearinghouse on Languages and Linguistics

PRENTICE HALL REGENTS Englewood Cliffs, New Jersey 07632

Library of Congress Cataloging-in-Publication Data

Barnett, Marva A.
     More than meets the eye : foreign language reading : theory and
practice / Marva A. Barnett.
         p.   cm. -- (Language in education ; 73)
     "A publication of Center for Applied Linguistics, prepared by the
Clearinghouse on Languages and Linguistics."
     Bibliography: p.
     ISBN 0-13-601345-7
     1. Language and languages--Study and teaching. 2. Reading.
I. Center for Applied Linguistics. II. ERIC Clearinghouse on
Languages and Linguistics. III. Title. IV. Series.
P53.75.B37   1989
407--dc20   89-8710
                                                              CIP

Language in Education: Theory and Practice 73

This publication was prepared with funding from the Office of Educational Research and Improvment, U.S. Department of Education, under contract No. RI 88062010. The opinions expressed in this report do not necessarily reflect the positions or policies of OERI or ED.

Production supervision: *Arthur Maisel*
Cover design: *Photo Plus Art*
Manufacturing buyer: *Mike Woerner*

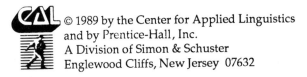 © 1989 by the Center for Applied Linguistics
and by Prentice-Hall, Inc.
A Division of Simon & Schuster
Englewood Cliffs, New Jersey 07632

Printed in the United States of America

10 9 8 7 6 5 4 3 2 1

ISBN   0-13-601345-7

Prentice-Hall International (UK) Limited, *London*
Prentice-Hall of Australia Pty. Limited, *Sydney*
Prentice-Hall Canada Inc., *Toronto*
Prentice-Hall Hispanoamericana, S.A., *Mexico*
Prentice-Hall of India Private Limited, *New Delhi*
Prentice-Hall of Japan, Inc., *Tokyo*
Simon & Schuster Asia Pte., Ltd., *Singapore*
Editora Prentice-Hall do Brasil, Ltda., *Rio de Janeiro*

Language in Education: Theory and Practice

ERIC (Educational Resources Information Center) is a nationwide network of information centers, each resposible for a given educational level or field of study. ERIC is supported by the Office of Educational Research and Improvement of the U.S. Department of Education. The basic objective of ERIC is to make current developments in educational research, instruction, and personnel preparation readily accessible to educators and members of related professions.

ERIC/CLL is the ERIC Clearinghouse of Languages and Linguistics, one of the specialized clearinghouses in the ERIC system, and is operated by the Center for Applied Linguistics (CAL). ERIC/CLL is specifically responsible for the collection and dissemination of information on research in languages and linguistics and its application to language teaching and learning.

The ERIC Clearinghouse on Languages and Linguistics (ERIC/CLL) publishes two monographs each year under the series title, *Language in Education: Theory and Practice*. ERIC/CLL commissions specialists to write about current issues in the fields of languages and linguistics. The series includes practical guides, state-of-the-art papers, theoretical reviews, and collected reports. The publications are intended for use by educators, researchers, and others interested in language education.

This publication can be purchased directly from Prentice Hall Regents and will be available from the ERIC Document Reproduction Service, Alexandria, Virginia.

For further information on the ERIC system, ERIC/CLL, and CAL/ Clearinghouse publications, write to ERIC Clearinghouse on Languages and Linguistics, Center for Applied Linguistics, 1118 22nd Street, NW, Washington, DC 20037.

Acknowledgments

Writing such a book as this entails more than meets the eye. I could not have completed the project without a great deal of help, and I wish to express deep appreciation to the following people:

My husband, Jon Guillot, for his unflagging support through the agonies of composition and for his clear eye for style; my mother, Marva T. Barnett, for her impeccable editing skills, honed through work with hundreds of technical writing papers; my father, John R. Barnett, for his confidence and understanding; all foreign and second language reading specialists, for their theories and research that continue to provoke thought and experimentation; the University of Virginia, especially Vice President and Provost Paul Gross, Director of the Center for Advanced Studies, W. Dexter Whitehead, and the Committee on Summer Grants, for generous research leave time and summer grants; Professor Brenda Loyd for her statistical brilliance and constant amiability; Professor Jim Deese for his belief in the project; Renée Severin, for her help with reading strategy experiments and valuable ideas; Whitney Stewart, Jeanne Rennie, Charles Stansfield, Kathleen Marcos, Quang Pho, Minh Pho, and the rest of the staff at ERIC Clearinghouse on Languages and Linguistics, for ongoing editorial assistance and encouragement; the anonymous reviewers of the manuscript, for their intelligent suggestions; our graduate student teaching assistants, for their effective administration of reading experiments; and, finally but perhaps foremost, my students, the instigators of it all, for their confusions and insights when reading French.

M.A.B.

To Guill

About the Author

Marva A. Barnett (Ph.D., Harvard University) is Associate Professor and the Director of the Required Courses Sequence in the Department of French Language and Literature at the University of Virginia. She works on language curriculum development, teaches French language courses, and trains and supervises graduate student teaching assistants, offering a week-long Orientation/ Workshop and a methods course.

Professor Barnett received her B.A. from Westminster College, Salt Lake City, Utah, and her M.A. from the University of Maine at Orono. After completing her doctorate in the area of seventeenth-century French literature, she spent one year as an assistant professor at Purdue University and two years at Indiana University. There she developed her expertise in language methodology, became better acquainted with the field of second language acquisition, and participated in the writing of *En Route*, a first-year French textbook.

Professor Barnett is also the author of *Lire avec plaisir: Stratégies de lecture*, a practical application of her research in foreign language reading strategy use. She is the author of articles published in *Modern Language Journal, ADFL Bulletin, Foreign Language Annals*, and *The French Review*.

Although she has specialized in studying how students learn reading, she is also interested in the writing process and has presented papers at conferences of the International Association of Applied Linguistics, the American Council on the Teaching of Foreign Languages (ACTFL), the Northeast Conference, the Seminar East of the Association of Departments of Foreign Languages (ADFL), and the Modern Language Convention. She also serves as a consultant on language pedagogy and on working with students who have language learning disabilities.

Table of Contents

LIST OF FIGURES

LIST OF TABLES

LIST OF APPENDICES

A Background Knowledge Questions: "Prisonnier de guerre"

B "Prisonnier de guerre" par Joseph Kessel

C Propositional analysis of the first five paragraphs of "Prisonnier de guerre" and Four Student Recalls

D Background Knowledge Questions: "Clint Eastwood sur les traces de Reagan"

Background Knowledge Questions: "J'ai vécu dans la maison de l'An 2000"

E "Clint Eastwood sur les traces de Reagan" "J'ai vécu dans la maison de l'An 2000"

F Strategy-Use Choices: "Clint Eastwood sur les traces de Reagan"

Strategy-Use Choices: "J'ai vécu dans la maison de l'An 2000"

G Pilot Study Comprehension Questions: "Clint Eastwood sur les traces de Reagan"

Pilot Study Comprehension Questions: "J'ai vécu dans la maison de l'An 2000"

H Questionnaire to Elicit Perceived Strategy Use

I Selections from Think-Aloud Protocols
"Clint Eastwood sur les traces de Reagan"
"J'ai vécu dans la maison de l'An 2000"

J How to Analyze Text Structure

K Basic English Prefixes

Introduction

BACKGROUND

To teach foreign or second language reading well, we need to know as much as possible about how the reading process works and how to integrate that knowledge effectively into our reading pedagogy. Researchers and teachers are fortunate to have at their disposition numerous resources from colleagues studying first language learning. With interdisciplinary insights from such diverse fields as psychology, sociology, education, and theoretical and applied linguistics, second and foreign language researchers and theorists have a new awareness of the mental processes underlying language use and a deepening respect for the complexities of these processes. For instance, from the advent of artificial intelligence research, we have the beginnings of computer simulations of learning processes. We also recognize how expectations defined by readers' cultures influence what they understand when reading. We are delving into reader strategies and exploring how we can help weaker readers use more effective strategies for comprehending. We are aware that reader purposes and approaches to written texts vary, depending on many factors, including text types, readers' language abilities, cognitive development, interest, and readers' willingness to take risks in predicting and guessing meanings. We recognize the heterogeneity of readers. We are comparing what we know and hypothesize about the first and second language reading processes and, as a result, are expanding our pool of knowledge. As the growing science of second language acquisition establishes appropriate research tools and experimental models (cf. Beebe, 1988; VanPatten, Dvorak, & Lee, 1987), we are less willing to overgeneralize and oversimplify than in the past. Research in second and foreign language reading is coming of age.

From the era of the grammar-translation method, reading skill has generally held an important place in foreign/second language study and teaching, with the exception of the era of the audiolingual method. Now, however, we see reading in a different light: as

1

communication, as a mental process, as the reader's active participation in the creation of meaning, as a manipulation of strategies, as a *receptive* rather than as a *passive* skill. Reading is a primary means of language acquisition. For Krashen (1981), comprehensible input is vital for language acquisition, and reading is an inimitable source of such input. Within the proficiency framework established by the American Council on the Teaching of Foreign Languages (ACTFL), reading and listening are valued as receptive skills in which the reader or listener actively *produces understanding* (Byrnes, 1985). Also, somewhat indirectly, the intense emphasis on *oral* skills early in the proficiency movement provoked increased, reactive attention to reading (Hummel, 1985). Within traditional programs, moreover, reading is still valued as essential to appreciating target language literature. Reading is the skill adults can most easily maintain and improve independent of established language courses. The main reason people around the world study English as a foreign language is to read(Carrell, 1988a). Finally, within the educational system and the nation at large, literacy is a momentous issue; better understanding of the second language reading process and developing students' reading skills in a foreign language may help us address this larger concern. For many reasons, then, foreign/second language reading is currently a popular focal point for language learning/acquisition research.

SECOND AND FOREIGN LANGUAGE READING:
SOME DIFFERENCES

As reading theory and research mature, specialists increasingly distinguish between the circumstances of people learning a *second language* from those learning a *foreign* language. The term *second language reading* suggests a diverse learner population, because it usually refers to learning another language while living in a community dominated by that second language and culture (e.g., students of English as a second language (ESL) [cf. Dubin, Eskey & Grabe, 1986; and the work of Barnitz, 1985; Carrell, all works listed; Clarke, 1980; Devine,1981, 1984, 1987; Hudelson, 1981,1984; Perkins, 1983]). These learners may range from childhood age well into adulthood, representing varying levels of cognitive development; they come from many different cultural backgrounds; they have divergent first language educational backgrounds; they may or may not be literate in their first language; they are surrounded by the second language in their daily lives; they may learn to converse with second language speakers before they begin to assimilate the complexities of reading; they may well be dependent on learning the second language for their financial survival.

Almost equal diversity is shown by the population of learners labeled EFL (English as a Foreign Language), that is, students studying English in their native environment (cf. the British journal, *Reading in a Foreign Language*; Alderson & Urquhart, 1984, and the work of Bensoussan 1984, 1986; Cowan, 1974,1976; Laufer & Sim, 1982,1985; Nuttall, 1983). Frequently, EFL students differ from ESL learners only in that they do not live in an English-speaking environment. A specific category of both EFL and ESL students is that which includes learners of English for Specific Purposes (ESP), (cf. Pugh & Ulijn, 1984; Cohen 1984, 1986, 1987; Ulijn, 1977, 1980,1981,1984), which includes English for Academic Purposes (EAP), (cf. Dubin, Eskey, & Grabe, 1986, and the work of Laufer & Sim, 1982,1985). ESP and EAP researchers and theorists customarily concentrate on adults learning to read English for professional purposes, in technical or specific academic fields.

American foreign language (FL) reading specialists typically work with a different kind of student: American adolescents or adults learning a foreign language in a U. S. academic setting. Thus, although at some schools children may study a foreign language at an early age, references to foreign language reading normally assume that the learners are adolescents or adults (cf. the work of Barnett, 1986, 1988; Bernhardt, 1984, 1986, 1987, 1988; Hosenfeld, 1976, 1977, 1979, 1984; Lee, 1986, 1987, 1988; Phillips, 1975, 1984, 1985; Swaffar, 1981, 1985, 1988). Rather homogeneous in nature, foreign language learners typically demonstrate characteristics that can distinguish them from second language learners: because of their age, they have a reasonably high level of cognitive development; most of them have lived for some time in the United States and have a US cultural and educational background; they are usually first language literate; they do not often encounter the foreign language outside the classroom; their foreign language reading abilities may well outstrip their foreign language speaking abilities; they may not have an immediate, practical purpose for learning a foreign language. Because more has been published about second language than about foreign language reading, and because I teach American students French and study their learning processes, my orientation is toward foreign language reading. Of course, research on second language reading offers substantial insights equally appropriate to reading in a foreign language. Theory, whether derived from foreign or second language reading situations, is commonly termed *second language reading theory*.

Focus of this Volume

With the increase in second and foreign language reading research and theories and the concomitant pressure to bring new ideas into the classroom, a review and analysis of the possibilities is necessary. This volume is intended to provide an overview of the field, to provoke thought about future directions for investigating the second or foreign language reading process, and to suggest productive reading pedagogies. Colleagues who want to teach reading better, to learn more about the reading process, or to undertake their own experimentation should find this book worthwhile.

In Part I, pertinent first language theory and research are noted with an eye always to the impact they have had —or may have— on second language reading theory. Reading models presented will include both *bottom-up* and *top-down* varieties, and *interactive* combinations of the two, with a glance cast toward current consideration of the interrelationship of the reading and writing processes. Part I then summarizes and examines second language reading theory and research, including the role of schema theory and reading within the ACTFL proficiency movement. There is a review of studies conducted to ascertain determining factors in second or foreign language reading; some researchers find that good first language readers transfer their skills to second language reading; others assert that linguistic control of the second language matters more than first language reading skill. Finally, a discussion follows of the relative importance of reader characteristics versus text characteristics, with special emphasis on the role of strategy use in reading, including a replicable design for experimentation on the use of reading strategies. For this section, the term *reading strategy* includes the numerous problem-solving behaviors readers employ in order to understand texts: e.g., skimming, thinking about the title, rereading, and guessing word meanings from context.

Part II focuses on classroom applications and is dedicated to the teacher who is considering better ways to teach reading in another language to adolescents or adults already literate in one language. After an analysis of general pedagogical principles following from reading research is an exploration of a reading lesson plan designed to help students interact with texts. References to other effective pedagogical models for teaching reading are included. Part II then discusses methods of analyzing readers' processes, choosing appropriate reading texts, motivating students through self-selected reading, moving beyond reading comprehension to literary analysis, adapting textbooks when necessary, and testing reading.

Part I

Reading Theories
and
Research Results

1

What Do First Language Reading Theory and Research Mean for Foreign Language Readers?

"I usually have a pretty good idea about what I'm going to read before I actually begin. You know, Agatha Christie is pretty predictable."

"Maybe, but there's no way you can know exactly what's coming next. I'd rather not think about it and be surprised."

"Yeah, I don't like illustrated books because they give away the plot."

"Neither do I, but that's because the pictures never match what I imagine is happening."

"But what about the photos in *Time* or *Newsweek*? They help me understand."

"I try to get the gist of what I'm reading as quickly as possible."

"What do you mean 'gist'? Everything I read is important, and I need to understand it."

"But what about the words you don't know? Don't you have to guess what they mean? That's what I do."

"I wouldn't dare guess. I look them up."

"I look them up, too. What a great way to learn new vocabulary!"

"I don't think any of that makes sense. If there are too many big words, I just stop reading. Why bother?"

"Right! About all I read is the TV schedule."

As admittedly unlikely in most circles as such a conversation is, most language teachers and researchers have heard—or made—similar comments, and we can glean a great deal from such a hypothetical exchange. First, in first or second language reading, individuals vary in their reading styles, in the strategies they use to comprehend, and in their level of awareness of their own reading processes. Some predict text content from the title or illustrations or from what they already know about the topic or the author. Others plunge immediately into the text with little conscious thought about what they might find there. Some readers (usually considered less efficient) concentrate on most of the words in the text, whereas others look for the main idea, central facts, or general tone. Some visualize scenes described or actions taking place. Reading styles and techniques employed depend, too, on the context in which a reading is undertaken and on the reader's purpose in reading a particular text; most good readers read differently depending on whether they have picked up a newspaper, novel, or research journal. Finally, reading proficiency must depend to some extent on the individual's general language proficiency and world experience. A physician reads the *New England Journal of Medicine* with more ease than might a lawyer. How much of a person's reading style is taught? How much is natural inclination? How much is under the reader's control and could be modified? Should we presume to say that a single reading process exists for all readers?

GENERAL CONSIDERATIONS

In order to address these questions, first language learning professionals long engaged in explorations of the reading process have proposed a variety of theories. In order to conceptualize and disseminate these hypotheses about the mental activities involved in comprehending written text, first language reading specialists have created reading process models—prose and graphic representations of the theorized processes. Some theorists base their models on existing data; others first conceive of a logically consistent model and then devise experiments to evaluate it (Samuels & Kamil, 1984). A model provides an imagined representation of the reading process that not only provokes new ideas about reading but also provides a paradigm against which aspects of the reading process may be tested.

Naturally, many second language researchers wonder about the relationship between the first and second language reading processes. In recent years, second and foreign language experts have given considerable attention to first language reading models (Bernhardt, 1986c). This chapter will (1) review principal issues in first and second language reading, (2) briefly summarize some of the first language models most frequently discussed in the literature on second and foreign language reading, and (3) consider what insights they may give us into the second language reading process, recognizing that first and second language reading are alike in some ways, but different in others.

Many of the major issues in reading addressed by first language reading models are equally central to the second language reading process. For ease of discussion, these may be divided into questions of text characteristics and reader traits. Important elements in a text include the following: letters or characters, also referred to as graphics or features; the phonological component, that is, letter and sound correspondences; words as individual entities; the lexicon or vocabulary, that is, words perceived as embodying meaning; semantics, the meaning of groups of words together; syntax or grammar, how words function in relation to each other; and sentence, paragraph, and text structure. Of course, an important aspect of any text characteristic is the way the reader responds to it. For example, also at issue with respect to the phonological component is the extent to which the reader encodes words phonologically, that is, understands them through their sound. Other influential reader characteristics include these: prior knowledge about or experience with a text topic or structure (often termed a *schema*); general language proficiency and ability to decode vocabulary and syntax; cognitive skill, as evidenced in an ability to predict, guess from context, and infer; memory; and attention. Depending on their view of reading, specialists include these facets of reading to a greater or lesser extent in their individual models.

It is important to remember, as Samuels and Kamil (1984) and Kamil (1986) emphasize, that models are usually partial rather than complete, that they are often subject to later revisions, depending on research conducted, and that they are not programs for reading pedagogies. Moreover, it is difficult to compare reading models for several reasons: they are somewhat limited by the period in which the work was done (e.g., the era of behaviorism or of cognitive psychology); they have different origins and foci; they are based on research with different types of readers (older versus younger, stronger versus weaker) performing different types of tasks in different contexts. As a result, models cannot be generalized to fit all conditions.

Neither can they always apply directly to second or foreign language learning. Whereas first language readers normally speak the language with some facility before they learn to read it, foreign language learners may advance more quickly in reading than in speaking; they may, in fact, visualize spoken words in written form (Brooks, 1984). On the other hand, learners of English as a second language may acquire facility with spoken English but be unable to read either in their first language or in English. Moreover, most first language reading models analyze the processes of proficient readers (Samuels & Kamil, 1984). The issue of reading in a second language arises most frequently, of course, with beginning or with nonproficient readers.

Still, a study of first language reading theory provokes for second language reading specialists precisely that question of how first and second language reading differ. Is the role of phonological encoding the same for readers who are not proficient speakers of the language? What is the importance of cognates for readers who have a wide first language vocabulary? How do cultural differences inherent in texts written in different languages affect the reading process? These are but some of the reflections sparked by a perusal of first language reading theory. After a review of the most frequently cited models, there is a discussion of the implications of each model type for second language theorists.

TYPES OF READING MODELS

Although some first language reading models cannot be categorized, those most frequently referred to in second language literature fall into one of three general categories: *bottom-up, top-down,* or *interactive.* A new type of interactive model, that of *reading/writing* models, offers additional insights for second language reading. Models vary in the emphasis placed on text-based variables (e.g., vocabulary, syntax, rhetorical structure, cultural content) and reader-based variables (e.g., background knowledge of the world and texts, cognitive development, interest and purpose in reading, strategy use).

In *bottom-up* reading models, the reader begins with the written text (the *bottom*), and constructs meaning from the letters, words, phrases, and sentences found within and then processes the text in a series of discrete stages in a linear fashion. The incoming data from the text must be received before the higher-level mental stages of understanding transform and recode the data. Following an information-processing approach to comprehension, bottom-up models analyze reading as a process in which small chunks of text are absorbed, analyzed, and gradually added to the next chunks until they become meaningful. Clearly, these are text-driven models of comprehension. Bottom-up models (e.g., Gough, 1972; the original LaBerge-Samuels, 1974; Carver, 1977-78) have not been favored by second language reading specialists (Bernhardt, 1986c), but they may provide insights into the approaches of less proficient second language readers.

Although *top-down* models also generally view reading as a linear process, this process moves from the *top*, the higher-level mental stages, *down* to the text itself. In fact, in these models (including the *psycholinguistic* models), the reading process is driven by the reader's mind at work on the text (*reader-driven* models). The reader uses general knowledge of the world or of particular text components to make intelligent guesses about what might come next in the text; the reader samples only enough of the text to confirm or reject these guesses. Strictly top-down models are rare, having quickly given way to interactive models, but two of them have had great consequence in second language reading theory: those of Goodman (1968) and Smith (1971, 1982).

Interactive reading models do, as their label implies, theorize an interaction between the reader and the written text. Like top-down models, they are reader-driven. They are not linear but rather cyclical views of the reading process in which textual information and the reader's mental activities (including the processing of graphic, syntactic, lexical, semantic, and pragmatic information) have a simultaneous and equally important impact on comprehension. That is, as in top-down models, the reader uses his or her expectations and previous understanding to guess about text content but, as in bottom-up models, the reader is still dependent upon what is in the text. Text sampling and higher-level decoding and recoding operate simultaneously. Because of their influence on second language reading theory, interactive models are treated in depth here. Included are the models of Rumelhart (1977a), Stanovich (1980), Rumelhart and McClelland (1986), the revised LaBerge-Samuels

(1983), Kintsch and van Dijk (1978), Just and Carpenter (1980), and Anderson and Pearson (1984).

Finally, a recent innovation in first language reading models derives from a renewed interest in writing. Although many are not yet explicit, these models hypothesize a close relationship between the reading and writing processes and sometimes describe reading as a composing process. The composing model of Pearson and Tierney (1984) is a good example of a reading/writing model.

First Language Reading Models and Implications for Foreign Language Reading

Bottom-Up Models

Gough. Gough's (1972) model of the first language reading process is a detailed description of how a reader processes text from the first moment of looking at the printed words until the time when meaning is derived from the words. Using eye fixation research findings, Gough hypothesizes that the reader's fixation on the text leads to the formation of an icon, a representation of the visual stimulus of the print. Supposing that this icon takes in about 15 to 20 letters and spaces, Gough suggests that it will become *legible* in about 100 milliseconds, allowing the reader to recognize the lines, curves, and angles as the familiar patterns of letters. The reader then creates a new icon from the next fixation (see figure 1).

Fluent readers identify letters quickly, and Gough argues that readers do read letter by letter, serially, from left to right. To be meaningful, however, the letters must make sense in the mental lexicon, a dictionary of words and meanings stored in the human brain. Gough offers no definitive explanation of this process but submits that the reader maps print onto a string of systematic phonemes, processes the words serially from left to right, and stores them in primary, short-term memory. When the contents of primary memory are understood, the sentence goes into what Gough calls PWSGWTAU, the *Place Where Sentences Go When They Are Understood.* Just how a sentence is understood is under debate, according to Gough; but he posits a wondrous mechanism, which he dubs Merlin, to interpret the sentence. If Merlin fails, the eye fixation is continued or an eye regression occurs for further processing. Then the primary memory is cleared so that new items may be entered into

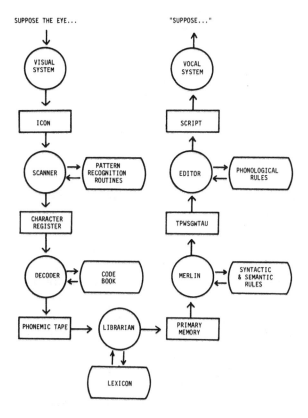

Figure 1
A Model of Reading from P.B. Gough, " One Second of Reading,"
appeared originally in J. F. Kavanaugh & I. G. Mattingly, (Eds.),
(1972). *Language By Ear and By Eye: The Relationship Between Speech
and Reading*, (p. 345). Reprinted by permission from The MIT Press.

it, and the process recommences. Clearly, Gough's primary focus is on the letter and word level of the text. In fact, the reader's process of comprehension remains somewhat mystical in Gough's presentation.

LaBerge and Samuels. The original LaBerge-Samuels (1974) model, explained here as an often-cited bottom-up view of reading, has undergone several revisions. In later versions (Samuels, 1977; Samuels & LaBerge, 1983), the addition of feedback loops allowing later processing stages to influence earlier ones makes it fall into the *interactive* category, although LaBerge and Samuels still do not delve into the question of comprehension as do Kintsch and van Dijk, (1978), Rumelhart (1977a), or Pearson and Tierney, (1984). LaBerge and Samuels (1974) emphasize the role of attention in processing information and the importance of automaticity in the reading process. In sum, they presume that readers probably can attend to only one thing at a time while reading but that they may be able to process many things at once as long as only one requires attention. A skill or subskill is automatic when it can complete its processing while attention is directed elsewhere. In a basketball analogy, where ball handling by an experienced player is automatic, LaBerge and Samuels point out that the subskills of dribbling, passing, and catching, as well as the transitions between them, must be automatic as well. For fluent reading, the processing at each stage from visual perception to meaningfulness must be automatic. Skilled readers, therefore, can allocate their attention to comprehension, whereas beginning readers need more attention for decoding.

Like Gough, LaBerge and Samuels assume that the reader's understanding depends on what appears in the text and that the reader performs two tasks when reading: decoding and comprehending. For LaBerge and Samuels, decoding is going from the printed word to some articulatory or phonological representation of the printed stimulus. Comprehending is deriving meaning from the decoded material (Samuels & Kamil, 1984, p. 197). Figure 2 shows the five components of the processing system (visual memory, phonological memory, semantic memory, episodic memory, and attention) and the feedback loops.

Note that visual word codes can feed directly into word meaning codes or be processed through phonological word, or word-group,

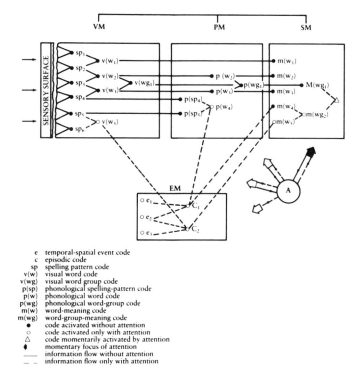

e   temporal-spatial event code
c   episodic code
sp   spelling pattern code
v(w)   visual word code
v(wg)   visual word group code
p(sp)   phonological spelling-pattern code
p(w)   phonological word code
p(wg)   phonological word-group code
m(w)   word-meaning code
m(wg)   word-group-meaning code
●   code activated without attention
○   code activated only with attention
△   code momentarily activated by attention
◆   momentary focus of attention
____   information flow without attention
_ _   information flow only with attention

Figure 2
Information Processing Model from Laberge & Samuels originally
appeared in L. M. Gentile, M. L. Kamil & J. S. Blanchard (Eds.), (1983).
Reading Research Revisited, (p. 42). Reprinted by permission from
Merrill Publishing Company.

codes. The model therefore allows for some variety of processing routes from letters and words to meaning but nevertheless does not allow a higher level to modify analysis at a lower level (until the feedback loops were added). The theory of automaticity says that as letters and word patterns become familiar, less attention will be needed to process them, and reading will become more fluent. Certainly, LaBerge and Samuels take the reader into account more than does Gough; still, the reader's primary function seems to be to process words from the printed page.

Carver. Carver (1977-78) presents what he calls a theory of reading comprehension and *rauding*. The term *rauding* links reading and listening comprehension (auding) and refers "to those frequently occurring language comprehension situations where most of the thoughts being presented in the form of sentences are being comprehended as they are being presented" (p. 13). For Carver, the sentence is the unitary expression of a thought; the primary purpose of most reading and auding is to comprehend the thoughts of the writer or speaker. His model falls into the bottom-up category because, during rauding, words are checked successively to determine whether a complete thought is being formulated and because, according to this model, readers say each successive word to themselves. Carver hypothesizes that this internal articulation aids comprehension; he thus attributes a major role to phonological encoding. His theory refers only to "typical reading situations" which do not include skimming, scanning, studying, or memorizing. Such specificity limits the applicability of this model to general second language reading.

Implications. Carver's model may, however, be helpful in determining how second and foreign language reading differ from first language reading. Foreign/second language readers frequently read material without understanding it, and the role of internal speech during second language reading is questionable. In general, the history of bottom-up models in second language reading theory is checkered. Because it was initially in favor, bottom-up reading process theory underlies much early work in second language reading. In the late 1960s and early 1970s, second or foreign language reading was viewed principally as a decoding process: the reader attempted to reconstruct the writer's intended meaning by recognizing the letters and words as meaningful units (Rivers, 1968; Plaister, 1968; Yorio, 1971). Many early pedagogical suggestions focus on the role of vocabulary in reading; the specialists making these suggestions implicitly assume that foreign language readers process meaning from words in the text.[1]

With the advent of Goodman's top-down view of reading as a psycholinguistic process, the bottom-up view of reading fell into disfavor. Yet the text-driven nature of bottom-up models may have more to say about weak second and foreign language readers than has been acknowledged (Eskey, 1988). Readers who do not expect target language texts to make sense, who read words individually, and who do not think about what words mean together may well be using a bottom-up approach to reading. Mentalistic data offered by Hosenfeld (1977b, 1979) and Cohen and Hosenfeld (1981) (discussed in detail in Chapter 3 of this work) provide some insights into individual students' processing strategies. Thus, bottom-up models are regaining favor in second language reading theory. They are now viewed as part of the interactive reading process. Finally, some specialists emphasize text types rather than reader characteristics (see Chapter 2 of this monograph).

Top-down Models

Goodman. The theories of Kenneth Goodman and Frank Smith are prime examples of top-down views of reading and have, so far, been more often cited in second and foreign language reading literature than any other first language models (Bernhardt, 1986c). In fact, second language reading is still referred to as a *psycholinguistic* process, a term used by Goodman (1968, p.15) to define reading as "an interaction between reader and written language, through which the reader attempts to reconstruct a message from the writer." Though revised through the years and restated in Goodman (1975), the original Goodman model of 1967, referring to reading as "a psycholinguistic guessing game," has also had a strong impact on first language reading instruction (Kamil, 1986). This model argues that readers use their knowledge of syntax and semantics to reduce their dependence on the print and phonics of the text and specifies four processes in reading: predicting, sampling, confirming, and correcting. First, readers make predictions about the grammatical structure in a text, using their knowledge of the language and supplying semantic concepts to get meaning from the structure. Then, they sample the print to confirm their predictions. They neither see nor need to see every letter or word. The more highly developed the readers' sense of syntax and meaning, the more selective the readers can be in sampling. After sampling, they confirm their guesses or, alternatively, correct themselves if what they see does not make sense or if the graphic input predicted is not there (see Figure 3). As Goodman writes, "In all this it is meaning which makes the system go" (1967, p. 98), but the model does allow the reader to move from print to sound to meaning when necessary.

Although the generality of this model makes it hard to verify in a scientific sense (Kamil, 1986), Goodman and his colleagues have accumulated an impressive amount of unambiguous data using what they call *miscue analysis*. Having children read aloud moderately difficult stories they have not previously seen, these researchers then analyze the children's misreadings as miscues, with the assumption that "oral miscues reflect the psycholinguistic process of constructing meaning through predicting, sampling, confirming, and correcting" (Goodman, 1981, p. ix). The children then retell what they remember of the story, thus providing an indication of how much they comprehended. In his research, Goodman has found that readers often do not correct misreadings if they make sense. If readers do have difficulty, they look for something to fit the grammatical structure before they check the graphic cues.

Smith. Like Goodman, Smith (1971) emphasizes the role of meaning and of the reader's need to predict when reading: "Reading is less a matter of extracting sound from print than of bringing meaning to print" (p. 2). Extrapolating from research on eye fixations, he cites four distinctive and fundamental characteristics of reading: (1) Reading is purposeful: people read for specific reasons or with specific goals; (2) Reading is selective: logically, readers attend only to what is necessary to their purposes; (3) Reading is based on comprehension: the reader brings certain prior knowledge (what Smith calls *nonvisual information)* to a text and adds to it, whether in support or contradiction, the information and ideas gathered from the reading; (4) Reading is anticipatory: the interaction of this prior knowledge, the expectation of comprehending and the purpose in reading lead readers to anticipate text content.

Proficiency Level 1

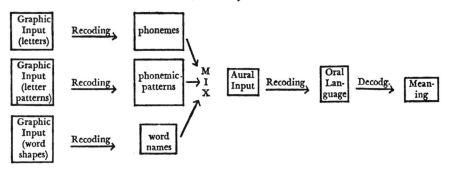

Proficiency Level 2

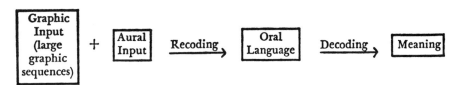

Proficiency Level 3

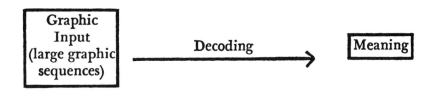

Figure 3
Proficiency Level 1, Proficiency Level 2, and Proficiency Level 3 from
K. S. Goodman, (Ed.), (1968). *The Psycholinguistic Nature of the
Reading Process*, (pp. 17 - 19). Reprinted by permission from Wayne
State University Press.

Although Samuels and Kamil (1984, p. 187) argue that Smith's theories are less a model of reading than "a description of the linguistic and cognitive processes that any decent model of reading will need to take into account," Smith's clear view of first language reading has had a tremendous impact on second language reading theory. In fact, in terming reading *anticipatory*, Smith himself anticipates the interactive models of reading in which text and reader characteristics together influence what a reader comprehends. Both Goodman and Smith give the reader a central role in understanding what he or she reads.

Implications. As noted earlier, second language reading theory has gleaned much from top-down views of reading, particularly from the psycholinguistic perspective. When many adult second and foreign language learners are already more or less proficient readers in their native language, their ability to make predictions about a text and their relatively wide-ranging general knowledge have been assumed to play a large role in their reading comprehension. Goodman's *predicting* reader and Smith's *anticipating* reader seem a fitting mold into which to place the intelligent and cognitively skilled adult second or foreign language reader. From a different point of view, that of the second language learner not literate in a first language, these models based on work with children learning to read also present a certain logic.

Looking back, we may say that the influence of Goodman's and Smith's work led to a new era in second language reading theory. As Bernhardt (1986c) points out, seminal research in second language reading has been done within the psycholinguistic framework[2], and Coady's *psycholinguistic* model (1979) is one of the earliest in second language reading. In addition, many second and foreign language pedagogical models claim affiliation with psycholinguistic principles and advocate developing readers' anticipatory strategies[3]. Prereading, or previewing, activities have been frequently suggested as necessary to activating learners' predicting skills and/or expectations. Recently, however, second language theorists have seen that a purely top-down concept of the reading process makes little sense for a reader who can be stymied by a text containing a large amount of unfamiliar vocabulary.

Interactive Models

Interactive models of reading respond to the question of how vocabulary skill relates to comprehension: although they allow that higher-level processing stages influence lower-level stages, they still recognize that comprehension also depends on the printed text. Second language researchers have lately taken more note of interactive reading models, so much so that Bernhardt suggests a *paradigm shift* from a psycholinguistic to a conceptually based perspective (1986c).

Rumelhart. Rumelhart (1977a), one of the first to argue against the linear processing presumed by bottom-up models, suggests that "reading is at once a 'perceptual' and a 'cognitive' process" (p. 573). Citing numerous experiment results, Rumelhart demonstrates the influence of syntactic, semantic, lexical, and orthographic information on the reader's perception of print. For example, to explain the guiding power of semantic knowledge over word perception, Rumelhart summarizes experimentation that reveals that a subject can decide more quickly if a letter string spells a word when a pair of words are semantically related, as in bread-butter or doctor-nurse, than if they are unrelated, as in bread-doctor or nurse-butter. Thus, still following an information processing perspective, Rumelhart's model emphasizes many different types and directions of processing, depending on text context and available information sources. For a graphic representation of the model, see Figure 4.

According to Rumelhart, the reader looks at the words and spelling that are registered in a visual information store (VIS). The feature extraction device pulls out the critical features of these words (with the successful reader sampling only enough of the text to continue) and moves them into the pattern synthesizer. The pattern synthesizer is where all the reader's previous knowledge about the language spelling patterns, syntax, vocabulary, semantics, and context come together to interpret what has been read. "Thus, all of the various sources of knowledge, both sensory and nonsensory, come together at one place and the reading process is the product of the simultaneous joint application of all the knowledge sources" (Rumelhart, 1977a, p. 588).

In general, the understanding of each of these levels of knowledge or analysis is influenced or partially determined by a higher

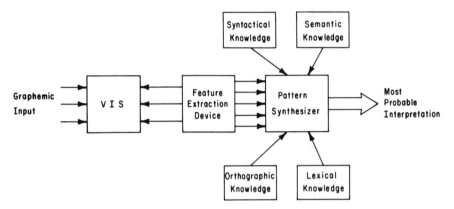

Figure 4
A Stage Representation of an Interactive Model of Reading from
D. E. Rumelhart, "Toward an Interactive Model of Reading," originally
in S. Dornic (Ed.), (1977). *Attention and Performance VI*, (p. 588).
Reprinted by permission from D. E. Rumelhart, Mental Health
Research Institute.

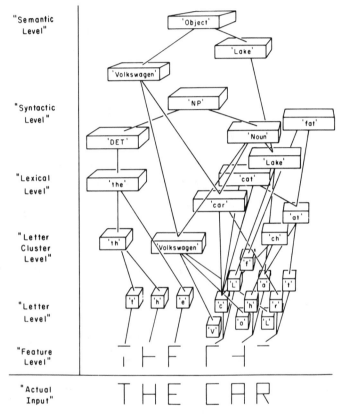

Figure 5
The Message Center Well Into the Processing Sequence from
D. E. Rumelhart, "Toward an Interactive Model of Reading," originally
in S. Dornic (Ed.), (1977). *Attention and Performance VI*, (p. 588).
Reprinted by permission from D. E. Rumelhart, Mental Health
Research Institute.

level of analysis. See Figure 5 for the hierarchy Rumelhart establishes.

Rumelhart also hypothesizes about how each of these knowledge sources works. At the feature level, the reader uses language knowledge to recognize letters and extracts only as much information as necessary. Similar processing is at work at the letter level, where the reader presumably takes into account letter frequency; more featural evidence is needed to postulate a *z* than an *e*. At the letter cluster level, the reader looks for letter sequences that form units in the language and hypothesizes from the lexical level. Rumelhart characterizes the lexical and syntactic levels, like the others, as both bottom-up and top-down; the quality of lexical and syntactic hypotheses depends on the quality of the evidence on which they are based. At all levels, "a convergence of top-down and bottom-up hypotheses strengthens both" (p. 598). Finally, Rumelhart considers the complex semantic level as perhaps the most difficult to characterize yet assumes that it works much like the other levels, evaluating the plausibility of hypotheses at both the lexical and syntactic levels. For second language readers who bring adult experiences and knowledge of first language structure and semantics to a foreign language text, such a theoretical interaction of knowledge sources makes sense.

Stanovich. Stanovich (1980) adds a new feature to the interactive Rumelhart model by suggesting that strength in one processing stage can compensate for weakness in another. According to Stanovich, problems in both the bottom-up and top-down models can be alleviated with his interactive-compensatory model. That is, bottom-up models do not allow for higher-level processing stages to influence lower-level processing. And top-down models do not account for the situation in which a reader has little knowledge of a text topic and, therefore, cannot form predictions. In sum, Stanovich declares, "Interactive models assume that a pattern is synthesized based on information provided simultaneously from several knowledge sources. The compensatory assumption states that a deficit in any knowledge source results in a heavier reliance on other knowledge sources, regardless of their level in the processing hierarchy" (1980, p. 63). In the opinion of Samuels and Kamil (1984), Stanovich has made a unique contribution to reading models: his theory explains the apparent anomaly found in many experiments in which poor readers sometimes show greater sensitivity to contextual constraints than do good readers. Poor readers may be thus using strong syntactic and/or semantic knowledge to compensate for less knowledge of orthography or of the lexicon. Evidently, efficient second language readers might use first language skills and strategies to compensate for linguistic weaknesses.

Rumelhart and McClelland. Rumelhart and McClelland et al. (1986), working with a number of colleagues, also expand upon Rumelhart's original interactive reading model. By constructing, with computer simulations, what they call *parallel distributed processing* (PDP) models, Rumelhart and McClelland explain how the mind processes information. These models of human cognition recognize that many different pieces of information and processes exist in the mind at once, all playing a part, constraining others and being constrained by them. PDP models "assume that information processing takes place through the interactions of a large number of simple processing elements called units, each sending excitatory and inhibitory signals to other units" (I, 10). As in Rumelhart's (1977a) model, these units may represent possible hypotheses about letters in a particular display or ideas about the syntactic roles of words in a sentence. In these cases, the signals relate to the strengths associated with the various hypotheses, and the interconnections among units stand for the constraints known to exist between the hypotheses. Thus, the mind considers numerous options at once in order to direct muscles to perform a physical function, like turning a knob, or in order to comprehend written text. Rumelhart and McClelland apply PDP models to information processing in general; the concept is appealing in terms of second language reading because it takes into account the myriad functions necessary for understanding meaning through a foreign language.

Kintsch and van Dijk. In their model, Kintsch and his colleagues emphasize comprehension to the exclusion of word identification, though they assume the latter must exist. The most nearly complete version of this model, published by Kintsch and van Dijk in 1978, assumes the following: (1) multiple micro-processing of the elements or propositions in a text; (2) a drive toward text reduction (i.e., finding the gist or *superordinate proposition*, sometimes involving the use of inference); and (3) the use of memory and reader schemata (what the reader knows of the text structure and expects to find there) to generate a new text built from the processed propositions. The original set of propositions comes from the interpretation of the surface structure of the text discourse and/or inferences from known facts the reader interpolates to make the sequence coherent. Whereas other models seem to hypothesize one text (that of the author), Kintsch and van Dijk see the reader as creating another text, one that mirrors the author's version in varying degrees.

The semantic structure of the text itself is considered in terms of its microstructure and its macrostructure. The former term refers to the local level of the discourse, including the structure of the individual propositions; the latter indicates the global meanings that characterize the text as a whole. *Macrorules* are the semantic mapping rules that organize propositions into appropriate levels. For a text to be coherent, the textual propositions must be connected and logically supporting at the macrostructure level. Then the reader can put the propositions and necessary inferences in short-term memory; because of memory limitations, however, the reader must process the text in chunks, and also in cycles, with some important propositions appearing in several chunks of recalled text. The short-term memory buffer (a holding pool stocked with text propositions recently encountered) is reader-driven, varies in efficiency, and crucially influences processing of text meaning. The model assumes that this cyclical process of proposition interpretation and storage is automatic and puts little demand on capacity but does recognize that certain types of propositions will be more difficult to process than others. Thus the reader's goals, directed by reader schemata for each text, are particularly important since they control the way the text is transformed into macropropositions containing the gist of the text. Clearly important in view of reader purposes, the Kintsch and van Dijk model may promise other future directions for work in foreign and second language reading, such as research on the extent to which efficient foreign/second language readers reconstruct their own text from the printed text.

Just and Carpenter. Like the Kintsch model, the Just and Carpenter model (1980) accounts for comprehension processes but bases that understanding upon studies of reader eye movements. Using special equipment, Just and Carpenter have recorded and analyzed what a reader's eye does as it scans the text: location and duration of fixations; time, speed, and acceleration of movement; frequency and characteristics of regressions. Their studies support their assumption that a reader attempts to interpret content words immediately upon seeing them rather than delaying interpretation until more words have been read. They have shown that the amount of time an eye fixates on a word is a direct index of the amount of processing time that word requires. Just and Carpenter define five processes (see Figure 6): (1) seeing the next word and extracting its physical features; (2) seeing the word as a word and comparing it to the mental lexicon; (3) assigning a case (e.g., nominative, objective) to the word; (4) relating the word to the rest of the words; (5) wrapping up the sentence when complete.

The model is interactive in that any of the stages in Figure 6 can affect the processing of the other stages. The serial nature of word recognition and comprehension in this model may help explain the word-for-word reading styles of some second language readers.

Anderson and Pearson. Although less a model of the reading process than an exploration of the interworkings of the schemata and memory that readers must use to comprehend, the Anderson and Pearson (1984) schema-theoretic view of mental processes parallels in many ways the schema-based theories of second language reading that will be explained in Chapter 2. Readers' schemata are the abstract knowledge structures already stored in memory, whether it be knowledge relating to the text topic or to the text structure (sometimes called general or background knowledge). Anderson and Pearson use as an example the schema of a ship christening, including various parts, or *slots:* a celebrity blessing a ship, a ship in dry dock. In their article, Anderson and Pearson attempt to determine what sort of knowledge is abstracted from texts to become a general concept and how much knowledge remains tied to memory of specific instances. They conclude that "during language comprehension, people probably rely on knowledge of particular cases as well as abstract and general schemata" (p. 269).

They also argue that an adequate account of schemata structure will include information about the relationships among components and that inference must play a major role in a complete theory

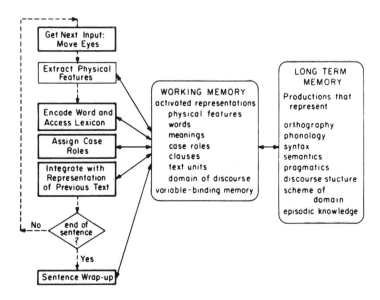

A schematic diagram of the major processes and structures in reading comprehension. (Solid lines denote data flow paths, and dashed lines indicate canonical flow of control.)

Figure 6
From "A Theory of Reading: From Eye Fixations to Comprehension," in M. A. Just & P. A. Carpenter, (1980). *Psychological Review, 87,* 329 - 354. Washington, DC: American Psychological Association. Reprinted by permission from the authors.

of schema activation. According to their theory, any one of four kinds of inferences can occur either when textual information enters or is retrieved from memory. Inferences may be involved in any of the following situations: (1) deciding which schema should be activated for the text; (2) deciding into which schema slot any textual item best fits; (3) assigning default values to any slot (that is, imagining what element lacking in the text is necessary to complete the schema); and (4) drawing logical conclusions based on lack of knowledge within a schema (for example, deciding that because a text describes Prince Charles as drinking from a bottle of champagne, he is not christening a ship). For Anderson and Pearson, two questions remain: (1) Given the large number of possible inferences, which will a reader make during comprehension? (2) Do readers make inferences when encoding the information or when retrieving it? The enigma of inferencing has equal import for second and foreign language reading.

A reading/writing model: Pearson and Tierney. A relatively recent phenomenon in first language reading theory is the consideration of the similarities between the reading and writing processes (cf. research by Shanahan, 1984, Chall & Jacobs, 1983). For Pearson and Tierney (1984), reading is the active process of negotiating meaning between a reader and an author, both of whom create meaning (see also Tierney & Pearson, 1983, for another description of their model). With their *composing* model of reading, Pearson and Tierney develop the premise that "reading is an event in which thoughtful readers act as composers" (p. 147). Their model, depicted in Figure 7, assigns to the reader four interactive roles (planner, composer, editor, and monitor) and views comprehension as the act of composing a new version of the text for an inner reader. Thus this model also postulates a reader-driven reading process.

As planner, the reader creates goals, mobilizes knowledge or prior experience appropriate to the text, and decides how to align him or herself with the text, that is, to what extent to agree with the author. As composer, the reader searches for coherence, often needing to fill in gaps in the text with inferences. The editor stands back, in effect, from the planner's and composer's activities and examines their developing interpretations. Good editing behaviors include rereading, annotating the text page with reactions, and questioning

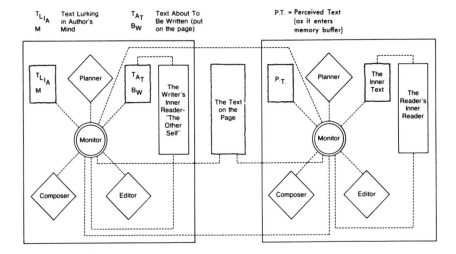

Model of the reader as writer

Figure 7
From P. David Pearson & Robert J. Tierney, "On Becoming a Thoughtful Reader: Learning to Read Like a Writer," in A. C. Purves & O. Niles (Eds.), (1984). *Becoming Readers in a Complex Society. Eighty-third Yearbook of the National Society for the Study of Education, Part 1.* Chicago: University of Chicago Press. Reprinted by permission of the Society.

which particular version of the text is the most desired one. Finally, the monitor directs the work of the planner, composer, and editor, deciding which role should dominate the process at any particular moment. The monitor determines when the model of meaning can be turned over to the inner reader. Although Pearson and Tierney do not cite in this article the work of Kintsch and van Dijk, the concept of reconstructing text for the comprehension of an internal reader is integral to both models and potentially useful in understanding the second language reading process, where cultural differences between reader and author may lead to a reader text very different from that intended by the writer (see the section on schema theory in Chapter 2 of this volume).

Implications. The influence of interactive, reader-driven models on second language reading theory has become pronounced in the last five years, with a spotlight on schema theory.[4]

The reader is seen as an active participant, and all of the reader's knowledge and previous experience play a major role in reader comprehension. The fact that the text cannot be ignored makes the interactive view appealing, as does Rumelhart's view that the impact of each processing stage can vary (Devine, Carrell, & Eskey, 1987). The reader seen as an active participant in written communication who seeks meaning purposefully (Smith, 1971, 1982; Rumelhart, 1977a, 1977b; Rumelhart & McClelland et al., 1986; Kintsch & van Dijk, 1978) and reconstructs text for an internal reader (Kintsch & van Dijk; Pearson & Tierney) has also become a part of second language reading theory (Swaffar, 1981; Bernhardt, 1986b). An emphasis on using strategies to glean meaning from text (like those suggested by Pearson and Tierney) has become central to second language reading theory and foreign/second language pedagogy.

Two features of reader-driven first language theory make especially good sense in terms of foreign and second language reading but have so far received little attention: reader variables and the role of inference. Clearly, individual readers have different characteristics that must be taken into account (Hatch, 1974). Although we have some data on the impact of linguistic development on a reader's comprehension,[5] little experimentation has been done on the relationship between comprehension and such variables as reader vocabulary development, interest, or purpose in reading. If applicable to second and foreign language reading, the Stanovich interactive-compensatory model would imply that readers who do not know much vocabulary, for instance, could rely on knowledge of the text topic to understand; it could also guide teachers in choosing reading texts for readers at varying levels of proficiency. Similarly, the LaBerge-Samuels view of the attention needed for decoding by beginning first language readers may help us understand the lack of reading automaticity on the part of poor second and foreign language readers.

Inference, an integral part of the models of Kintsch and van Dijk, Just and Carpenter, Anderson and Pearson, and Pearson and Tierney, is another potentially intriguing aspect of the reading process; second and foreign language readers who are low in language proficiency may use inference more than first language learners do. If so, which schemata do they activate for their inferences? How much confidence do they have in the facts they infer?

CONCLUSIONS

Probably because first language theory and research are extensive and well-established, second and foreign language reading specialists often look in that direction for insights and possible approaches. Following so often the processes and models of first language research, second and foreign language work should, with the benefits of hindsight, be able to correct some of the scattergun approaches to learning how readers really read. Moreover, the different situations, motivations, and perspectives of foreign/second language readers mean that first language reading theory may not completely apply to the second language reading process. When we compare first language reading models to what we know of second language reading, we find basic differences which raise questions and suggest studies. First, unlike first language readers, most foreign/second language readers do not have a fully developed phonological system when they begin to read. Therefore, the bottom-up models that depend on the reader's encoding of the text into phonological symbols or internal speech cannot apply directly to the second language reading process.

Second, while beginning first language readers are normally young children, the foreign language learners most often the subject of inquiry and pedagogical suggestions are adolescent or adult learners already literate in one language, although some research on children as second language readers is available. Many second language learners are also first language literate. Most foreign and many second language readers generally have relatively highly developed first language vocabularies, syntactic knowledge, topical and rhetorical schemata, and varying first language reading strategies. Still, for both second and foreign language readers, the cultural differences and distance inherent in any target language text can make the activation of appropriate schemata difficult; analyzing and overcoming this phenomenon has engaged a number of second and foreign language reading specialists. Both schema theory and the extent to which first language reading expertise has an impact on foreign and second language reading are central issues in the following chapter.

2

What Do Second Language Reading Theory and Research Tell Us?

No fully defined model of second language reading yet exists; nevertheless, certain generally accepted theoretical principles have emerged. Attention to the *process* of how the mind functions during reading rather than to the *product* of reading (for instance, comprehension test results) governs most second language reading theory. Involving a complex interplay of reader and text variables, the foreign/second language reading process is most generally considered analogous to first language models of *interactive* processing; the reader interacts with the text to create meaning as the reader's mental processes interact with each other at different levels (e.g., letter, lexical, syntactic, or semantic) to make text meaningful (Carrell, 1987c; Rumelhart, 1977a). Obviously, the reader is central in this process, and most second language theorists today regard the reading process as primarily *reader-based* or *conceptually driven*; that is, they believe that reader purposes, cognitive skill, language proficiency, strategies, and background knowledge and schemata contribute more to comprehension than do the graphic, syntactic, and semantic symbols of the text itself (cf. Bernhardt, 1986b; Carrell, 1988b). Yet, because the text as the entity to be comprehended must enter into consideration, specialists also study the impact of *text variables*: typology, structure, grammar, vocabulary, and cohesion.

The focus on individual readers' abilities to cope with specific texts and textual elements makes readers' *strategies* integral to a study of the second language reading process. A catch-all phrase that summarizes reader behaviors, the term *strategies* refers to the problem-solving techniques readers employ to get meaning from a text. Moreover, since readers use strategies to divine meaning where text is unclear to them, strategy use may resolve many second and foreign language reading difficulties noted by researchers. Readers use strategies in varying ways: to activate appropriate schemata, to guess meanings of unknown words, to follow unfamiliar syntax, t decide what to glean from texts. From a theorist's point of view, then, strategies enter into most of the other questions about foreign/ second language reading. From a teacher's point of view, knowing about reading strategies is crucial since they are eminently teachable. (For a summary of research, see Chapter 3.)

Research Issues and Problems

Perhaps because there is no single generally accepted theory, research on second and foreign language reading follows several different directions, selectively borrowing aspects of first language reading theories, as explained in Chapter 1. For example, some researchers emphasize the role of reader schema and background knowledge, whereas others refer to reading as a psycholinguistic process and explore how readers interpret the syntax and semantics of a text. Still others determine text readability by analyzing text structures, and they consider reader characteristics to be secondary. Differences between first and second/foreign language reading are also fundamentally at issue; compared to first language readers, foreign/second language learners are disadvantaged because of the greater tax imposed on short-term memory by the relatively unfamiliar linguistic code of a new language. Thus, to manage the foreign code, efficient readers may use the comprehension strategies that they usually employ in first language reading. Still, because written texts are inextricably bound up with the culture in which they originated, the reader must deal with the target language cultural schemata of the text. Individual researchers have chosen to emphasize one or more of these diverse aspects of the process.

In addition, the complexity of the reading process has inspired a variety of research techniques. Connor (1987) argues that the *multimodality* of first and foreign/second language reading research designs, which result from researchers' varied backgrounds, is an asset to the field. Psychologists prefer experimental studies with treatment and control groups; linguists use descriptive case studies and textual studies; anthropologists work with ethnographies. Second and foreign language reading researchers gain multiple insights by examining the reading process with tools as diverse as cloze passages, miscue analysis, eye-movement studies, recall protocols,

, protocols (See note for elaboration of these terms
.ices.)[1] Possible future research routes include several
.tions: exposing the text on the screen bit by bit (Johnston,
.owing the reader to vary the size of the text-window
.oerg, 1984, cited in Connor, 1987); and gathering learner data
.a microcomputers (Garrett, 1987). Such diversity is indeed healthy;
we need an assortment of methods to analyze a process as complex
as reading. Yet this heterogeneity does impede comparisons and
summaries of published studies, and some aspects of second and
foreign language reading research may seem to lack directional
coherence (cf. Lee, 1988b). We must always remember, too, that
reading comprehension processes are invisible and that our evidence about what is taking place can be no better than secondhand
(Casanave, 1988).

In his 1984 review of first language reading research, Kamil
similarly laments a lack of long-range reading studies that he
attributes to pressure on young scholars to produce sizable dossiers
of work quickly. Promotion and tenure criteria may equally restrict
second language acquisition specialists, who seem to avoid long-
range studies and who tend to work alone. Is there a fear that sharing
one's ideas before they are ready for print will be the first step
toward losing credit for them? Is the relative youth of the field and
general lack of support for research programs leading to a divergent
collection of reading research data—to a scholarly tower of Babel?
Perhaps wider realization that American citizens must be more than
monolingual to compete in an international market and intellectual
environment will increase support for research into second language learning/acquisition. Certainly, we need more coherent reading research (such as the congruous work on schema theory) and
longer-term studies, as well as more experiment reports that permit
replication by presenting fully the instruments used. (Chapter 3
includes one such replicable experimental design.) Moreover, we
must construct reading models that propose verifiable hypotheses,
and test those few models that now exist (cf. Bernhardt, 1986c; Lee,
1988b).

In an effort to organize contemporary second and foreign language reading research, this text summarizes research questions
examined by a number of reading studies. Within the reader-based

view of foreign/second language reading, questions arise:

Can second and foreign language reading be seen as a psycholinguistic process? How vital is the role of reader schemata (content/topical, formal/rhetorical, and/or cultural) in reading comprehension? How effective are other reading strategies, and can they be taught? (Because the answer to this question involves in part a replicable experimental design, it appears in Chapter 3.) Are the first and second language reading processes similar, and does first language reading skill transfer to second and foreign language reading? What is the impact of readers' control of language on their reading proficiency?

Those who emphasize a text-based view of foreign or second language reading ask the following questions:

What is the importance and role of text type? Can we determine the difficulty, or readability, of individual text? Is text vocabulary a determining factor in reader comprehension? Which is more important for the reader to control: syntax or semantics? What makes a text cohesive, and how does cohesion relate to coherence and comprehension? The investigation of these few questions comprises the main thrust of much current second language reading theory and research and, hence, of this chapter. Related pedagogical suggestions appear in Part II.

FROM THE PSYCHOLINGUISTC PERSPECTIVE

Coady's Psycholinguistic Model

A relatively early model of second language reading—and one of the few so far extant—Coady's (1979) *psycholinguistic model* is an avowed attempt to apply Goodman's and Smith's first language theories to reading English as a second language. Coady postulates that comprehension results from the interaction of conceptual abilities, background knowledge, and process strategies. Although he does not cite Rumelhart, Coady lists individual process strategies quite similar to Rumelhart's levels of knowledge sources:

- Phoneme-grapheme correspondences
- Grapheme-morphophoneme correspondences
- Syllable-morpheme information
- Syntactic information (deep and surface)

- Lexical meaning and contextual meaning
- Cognitive Strategies
- Affective mobilizers

According to Coady's model, the beginning second language reader first acquires the more concrete process strategies (e.g., syllable-morpheme information) and uses them to understand, whereas the proficient reader prefers the more abstract strategies, using syntax and semantics more frequently and "sampling" the text, as in Goodman's model. Coady also notes the individual nature of the reading process: process strategies are "paths to comprehension which readers must travel but not necessarily in the same manner or to the same degree" (p. 8). He suggests that a reader shifts processing strategies to match different types of text or to accomplish different reading goals; readers also have the capacity to decide that a particular combination of skills is not effective and try something else. In this way, Coady's work foretells current interest in the individual reader's use of strategies to comprehend.

General Applications of the Psycholinguistic Theory

Especially in the late 1970s and early 1980s, reading specialists frequently applied first language psycholinguistic reading theory to second and foreign language without offering a formal model or second language research data to support their hypotheses. Their work represents an initial effort to grasp the complexities of the reading process and sometimes affords surprising insights which, as we will see later in this chapter, are borne out by current second and foreign language reading research.

Eskey (1976) recognizes the complexity of the reading process, arguing that an adequate description would necessarily account for three spheres. In the sociolinguistic sphere, the text and reader would be related respectively to a particular universe of texts and a particular society of readers; Eskey's concept here foreshadows current focus on the importance of cultural schemata. In the linguistic sphere, texts would be related to the functions and forms of a given language, and the reader to his or her functional knowledge of that language. Finally, in the psycholinguistic sphere, Eskey brings the reader and text together in the mind of a single human being. Although he does not detail how this reading process works, Eskey underscores the need to consider the reader and text together.

Saville-Troike (1979) focuses on the importance of sociocultural meaning for many different sorts of second language reading, including imaginative and scientific/technical writing. First, she cites the difficulty that idiomatic expressions pose for language learners who have no appropriate experience; in illustration, she notes that a Chinese who has never seen the gesture will not understand "to shrug something off." She also demonstrates that word connotations are sociocultural; in English, the referentially synonymous pair *smile* and *leer* are hardly synonyms. Finally, she discusses the importance of readers' ability to separate what the writer asserted from what he or she presupposes the reader knows. Such awareness of culturally loaded text is still a central issue for those subscribing to schema theory.

From a similarly psycholinguistic perspective, Robinett (1980) uses Wardhaugh's (1969) definition of first language reading to discuss the role in second language reading of meaning, visual clues to spelling, probabilities of occurrence, contextual-pragmatic knowledge, and syntactic and semantic competence. Her *probabilities of occurrence* follow from Smith's first language theory of predictability within text and foreshadow the interactive view of the reader who brings meaning to the text. Her *contextual-pragmatic knowledge* is another way to refer to readers' cultural schemata.

Rizzardi (1980) also applies to foreign language reading Smith's theory that readers use nonvisual information to understand a text. Viewing a reading passage as a cohesive unit, she explores the need for readers to follow grammatical connectors (e.g., personal pronouns, demonstrative adjectives), lexical connectors (e.g., synonyms, general words used to avoid repetition), and conjunctions, as well as the need to make preliminary assumptions about the content of the written text. Such approaches are now considered vital reading strategies.

Thus, although much early work on second language reading theory was highly derivative, many of its hypotheses reappear in the more research-oriented theory of late. In addition, psycholinguistic reading theory has been the directing impulse for researchers who examine the relationship between first and second language reading, and the role of syntax and semantics in the reading process.

How Vital are Reader Schemata in

Reading Comprehesion?

Schema theory presently guides much second and foreign language reading research; it is probably the most thoroughly explored theory (for summaries, see Carrell, 1984c, 1988b; Carrell & Eisterhold, 1983). As explained in Chapter 1, *schemata* (singular, *schema*; also called *scripts*) are a reader's existing concepts about the world, "knowledge already stored in memory" (Anderson & Pearson, 1984, p. 255). They constitute the framework into which the reader must fit what she or he understands from the text. If new textual information does not make sense in terms of a reader's schemata, the material is comprehended in a different way or ignored, or the schemata are revised to match the new facts. First language comprehension is viewed as the interaction of new information with old knowledge (Anderson & Pearson, 1984). According to advocates of this theory, reading is an interactive process in which the author's perspective, points of view, allusions, or arguments are all interpreted through the reader's experiences, perspective, cultural orientation, and biases (cf. Bernhardt, 1984b).

Rumelhart (1977b) clearly shows how even a short passage can activate a reader schema.

Mary heard the ice cream man coming down the street. She remembered her birthday money and rushed into the house. (p. 265)

American readers, at least, immediately use their own experiences to infer that Mary is a child who heard the bell of a truck which toured residential neighborhoods selling ice cream and cooling snacks in the summer (when children are not in school), that she wanted some ice cream, that the house was her home, and that in order to buy some ice cream she went inside to get the money she had received for her birthday. From the bottom up the reader gets the facts of the situation; from the top down she or he activates appropriate memories of similar experiences and adds a great deal to the actual text; the final result is an understanding that goes beyond the written text itself. The "ice cream man" schema is a relatively simple one, and Rumelhart goes on to make two other points: (1) schemata can differ in the amount of detail with which they account for a situation, and (2) ordinarily, not just one schema but a set of interrelated schemata is needed to account for a situation. Thus, it can be hard to define exactly how schemata are operating in any particular act of comprehension. Furthermore, individual readers probably activate schemata differently, and to a greater or lesser extent (see Bransford, Stein, & Shelton, 1984; Carrell, 1988c).

Readers have schemata, or concepts, relating not only to a text topic or content (*content schemata* or *background knowledge*) but also to text structure or rhetorical organization (*formal schemata*). Examples of content schemata are a ship christening (examined in detail by Anderson and Pearson, 1984), an office party, a barn, a murder mystery. Research shows that readers who are familiar with the content of a passage, whether written in their first or second language, understand and recall more than do readers less familiar with text content (see the specific studies cited below). Formal schemata, knowledge of how texts are organized, are equally important because they define reader expectations about how pieces of textual information will relate to each other and in what order details will appear. Different types of texts have different conventional formal schemata. Consider the varied reader anticipations involved in understanding a fairy tale, a newspaper article, an experimental study. Fairy tales, for instance, normally follow a chronological sequence (Byrnes & Fink, 1985); journalistic prose usually answers who, what, when, where, why, and how questions and includes many different types of scripts (Zuck & Zuck, 1984b). The reader's ability to recognize textual organization and to create expectations on the basis of a standard rhetorical structure determines to a certain extent his or her facility in arranging the text information in memory.

Not only are schemata of two sorts, they are also more or less culturally determined or culture-specific. To what extent readers' culture defines their schemata is the subject of ongoing research (for a summary, see Steffensen & Joag-Dev, 1984). Imagine how Rumelhart's *ice cream man* example might be interpreted by a reader who had never seen or heard an ice cream truck, had eaten ice cream only out of a dish, or had never given or received money as a birthday present. It is obvious that culture plays a central role for many text topics: American football, the Tour de France, university life, wedding practices. For text structures, the impact of culture is less outwardly evident but apparently still present. For example, Kaplan (1966) finds that culture-specific rhetorical patterns appear in ESL learners' free writing in English; Arabic-speaking students develop paragraphs not in a linear English fashion but with a complex series of parallel constructions like those found in the King James version of the Old Testament.

The issue of whether (or which) schemata are cross-cultural or culture-specific is still unresolved for both first and second language reading (Bensoussan, 1986; Carrell & Eisterhold, 1983). Kintsch and Greene (1978) argue that storytelling conventions differ from culture to culture; Mandler et al. (1980) take the opposite stance. Carrell (1983a) suggests that we may not yet safely generalize about universality nor about specificity of culture in schemata. Moreover, she recognizes that content schemata may vary for individuals within the same culture (cf. Hirsch, 1987). Even 90 American high school students demonstrate *high* and *limited* knowledge of baseball, certainly a cultural phenomenon (Levine & Haus, 1985). Findings relative to culturally defined schemata enter into the following summary of the role of content and formal schemata in reading comprehension, as well as into Bernhardt's (1986c) constructivist model of second language reading.

Research on Content Schemata

Much of the research exploring the influence of reader schemata on reading comprehension focuses on content schemata, frequently referred to as background information. Perhaps since researchers must, by the nature of the question, work with subjects of different cultural backgrounds, the cultural aspects of a text are often interwoven with content per se. Nevertheless, experiment results tend in the same direction; foreign and second language readers who already have or who are given appropriate background knowledge about a reading passage understand and recall more of the passage than subjects with less background knowledge, whether that knowledge is culturally defined or not.

Experimental designs and purposes vary. Omaggio (1979) and Lee (1986), concerned in part with visual stimuli, assert that pictures depicting different aspects of text content activate foreign language readers' schemata for better understanding. Omaggio's American students reading French did best with a scene from the beginning of the story, apparently because it enabled them to activate suitable schemata early. Lee (1986) replicates Carrell's (1983b) experiment which followed Bransford and Johnson's (1973) first language design; unlike Carrell, he found that having a title and picture page improved comprehension for foreign language students when the topic was familiar ("washing clothes") but not when it was novel ("balloon serenade"). He hypothesized that since the subjects probably did not have a schema of a balloon serenade, an unusual occurrence, the picture was of no more help than was the text. Lee argues that he was able to find a significant effect for background knowledge because his students wrote their recall protocols in their native language, English; he asserts that Carrell's conclusion that second language readers do not use background knowledge derives from their inability to express themselves well in English, their second language, in their recall protocols.

Giving subjects pertinent information or having them experience relevant cultural practices has similar results: subjects recall more of the text (Johnson, 1982), perform better on a test of unfamiliar vocabulary (Adams, 1982), or perform better on both an objective post-test and a written recall (Floyd & Carrell, 1987). Floyd and Carrell conclude that cultural content may be and must be explicitly taught. ESL students from a particular discipline (e.g., engineering, liberal arts) perform better on cloze tests in their own discipline than do students from other disciplines (Alderson & Urquhart, 1985). American subjects who know about baseball answer textually explicit questions about a Spanish baseball article significantly better than do subjects with limited knowledge (Levine & Haus, 1985).

Research that directly compares reader comprehension of texts with familiar and unfamiliar cultural content also indicates that readers recall more and make more correct inferences after reading texts set in their own culture than those from another culture (Carrell, 1981; Johnson, 1981; Steffensen et al., 1979). Although we do not yet know whether the impact of culturally different texts comes from content or formal schemata, or from a combination of the two (Carrell, 1983a), students faced with unfamiliar cultural content may mistranslate or misinterpret according to their own cultural perspective (Bensoussan & Rosenhouse, 1984; Bernhardt, 1986a; Johnson, 1981; Laufer & Sim, 1982; Parry, 1987; Steffensen et al., 1979). Different assumptions about meaning and comprehension held by members of oral and literate cultures is an even more complex issue (Field, 1987; Parry, 1987).

Research on Formal Schemata

Carrell's work dominates research on how readers' expectations about the rhetorical organization (their formal schemata) affect comprehension. Inspired by Meyer's (1975, 1977, 1979) findings that first language readers process and recall certain types of rhetorical organization of expository prose differently from other types, Carrell (1984a) studies advanced ESL students' reading processes and cautiously submits three conclusions. First, the tightly organized comparison, causation, and problem/solution types of organization tend to aid recall of text ideas more than does a loosely organized collection of descriptions (cf. Hinds, 1983): English speakers find specific aspects of Japanese rhetorical structure difficult. Second, readers from different native language groups seem to find certain English discourse types more or less facilitative of recall, possibly because of interference from preferred native rhetorical patterns. Texts of different cultures have been found to indicate different configurations of rhetorical thinking, e.g., Oriental paragraphs are generally circular, whereas English logic is mostly linear (Kaplan, 1966, 1967). Finally, if ESL readers possess an appropriate formal schema for a particular text and if they organize their recall protocols according to that formal schema, they retrieve more information. Since 75% of the subjects failed to use the discourse structure of the original text, however, Carrell hypothesizes that they could not successfully identify the rhetorical organization of the text they read and may not possess the appropriate formal schema (see also Carrell, 1983b, 1988c). Explicit training in recognizing and analyzing the four expository text types can facilitate ESL students' reading comprehension, as measured by quantity and quality of information recalled (Carrell, 1985).

Not only expository schema but also narrative schema (story structure) influences reading comprehension (Carrell, 1984b). Intermediate ESL students of varying first language backgrounds recalled significantly more from stories with conventional narrative organization (one well-structured episode followed by another) than from stories violating standard story schema. Moreover, the subjects who read these interleaved stories, in which different parts of each story were intermingled, tended to write recalls reflecting normal story schematic order rather than the temporal order of presentation in the story they read. Much more work needs to be done with narrative formal schemata; whereas some formal schemata may be universal, it is likely that several different types of narrative schemata also exist both within and across different cultures (Carrell, 1983a).

Results of a study on the interaction of content and formal schemata for high-intermediate ESL students show, not surprisingly, that when both form and content are familiar to a reader, the reading is relatively easy; when both form and content are unfamiliar, the reading is relatively difficult (Carrell, 1987a). The interaction of text and reader schemata is the focus of the experiment; unfamiliar content causes the reader more difficulties than does unfamiliar form. Still, rhetorical form proved to be more important than content in the comprehension of the top-level episodic structure of a text and in the comprehension of event sequences. Thus, form, content, and culture play significant but different roles in text comprehension.

Bernhardt's Constructivist Model

The impact of reader schemata on reading comprehension is essential to Bernhardt's recent (1986c) constructivist model of second language reading (see Figure 8). Based upon recall data generated by intermediate, university-level American readers of German, French, and Spanish, this model defines an interaction of text-based and extratext-based components but emphasizes the latter. The reader recognizes words and syntactic features, brings prior knowledge to the text, links the text elements together, and thinks about how the reading process is working (metacognition).

To illustrate the model, Bernhardt discusses how readers interpreted *Grösse* (size) and *Geldstück* (money) in a German text about a scientific experiment examining poor and affluent children's perceptions of money. *Grösse*, a cognate, had appeared in students' textbooks, yet only two subjects recalled it as *size*; others reconstructed it as *more important, sum, various denominations,* and *value* (Bernhardt, 1983). Bernhardt attributes this response to the fact that

47

the American money schema involves amount and denomination rather than physical size. Thus, most of the students wove meaning from the text to match their concepts of the topic.

Constructing her reading process model from recall data like the above, Bernhardt notes that text-based components include word recognition (like that of *Grösse*), phonemic/graphemic decoding (recognition of words based on sound or visual mismatch, for instance, mistaking *Geld* for *Gold)*, and syntactic feature recognition (interpretation of the relationships between words). Extratext-based components are intratextual perceptions (the reconciliation of each part of the text to preceding and succeeding elements), prior knowledge (whether the text makes sense with respect to the reader's schemata), and metacognition (the extent to which the reader is thinking about the reading process, indicated by question marks and notes in the recall protocols).(See figure 8.)

Interactive and multi-dimensional, these components work in a circular fashion and in different ways for individual readers reading particular texts. Although Bernhardt has not yet explored precisely how each component part of her model operates, the model contains the aspects of the reading process researchers believe are determining factors: the look and sound of words, how they function in relation to each other, what they mean, and how the reader understands them and creates meaning from expectations and from reading the text as a whole.

How do First and Second/Foreign Language Relate?

Questions comparing first and second or foreign language reading generally revolve around two interrelated but separable issues: the reading process and reading skills. Some researchers investigate whether first and second language reading processes are similar or whether there is, in fact, a universal reading process. Others wonder whether individuals' reading skills transfer from their first language to a second. Researchers ask whether good first language readers are also good second language readers. In this section, there is a review of research results on each of these questions.

In a summary of research comparing first and second language reading processes, we must recognize at once certain obstacles. Matching equally challenging first and second or foreign language

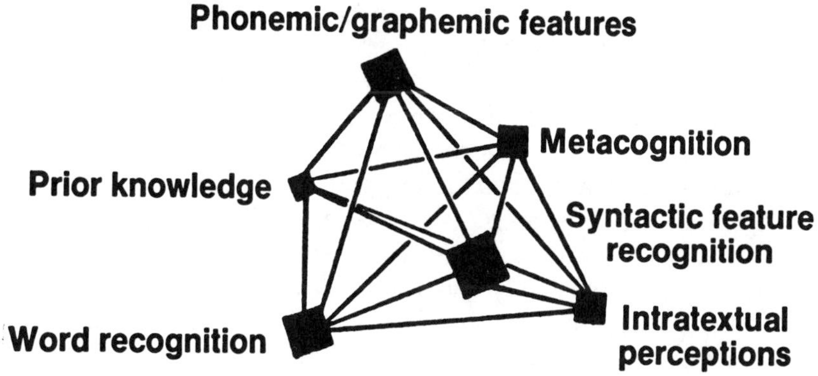

Phonemic/graphemic features

Metacognition

Prior knowledge

Syntactic feature recognition

Word recognition

Intratextual perceptions

Figure 8
The Constructivist Model. A model of the interaction of text-based and extratext-based components in L2 text reconstruction from E. B. Bernhardt, "Reading in a Foreign Language." The figure originally appeared in B. H. Wing (Ed.), (1986). *Listening, Reading and Writing: Analysis and Application*, (p. 103). Northeast Conference REPORTS. Reprinted by permission from the Northeast Conference on the Teaching of Foreign Languages.

texts, especially for beginning and intermediate readers, can be complicated; difficult second language texts normally become simplistic when translated into the first language (Kern, personal communication, May, 1988). Defining subjects' first language reading proficiency is another hurdle. Most subjects in the following studies are adult language learners assumed to be literate in their first language. A look at any society, however, shows wide variation in adult reading proficiency.

Furthermore, comparison of studies is problematic because they differ in research methodologies, hypotheses tested, and readers' levels of expertise (cf. Lee, 1988b). Subjects' first and second languages vary from study to study: Americans read Spanish, French-Canadians read English, Dutch read French. Results are not always analogous; foreign and second language learning situations are rarely comparable. On the other hand, partially because of the relatively advanced state of second language acquisition research in the field of English as a second language, English is usually the subjects' first or second language in reports disseminated in the United States. Thus, we rarely encounter comparisons of reading in non-Indo-European languages and languages with a non-Roman alphabet (see Jew, 1986). A quick perusal of the professional literature shows relatively few studies comparing reading in alphabetic languages and in ideographic languages like Chinese or Japanese (e.g., Biederman & Tsao, 1979; Chu-Chang & Loritz, 1977; Everson, 1987; Hayes, 1988; Koda, 1987). Conclusions drawn from such a highly limited database must be tentative and applicable only to the situation at hand; still, any work designed to probe the complexities of the human mind as it reads can be eye-opening and productive.

How Do First and Second/Foreign Language Reading Processes Compare?

Although little consensus has been reached among researchers attempting to analyze and compare first and second or foreign language reading processes, their individual and sometimes specialized conclusions provoke examination. The text will first consider experimental results that suggest similarities between reading processes, and then those that indicate differences.

Similarities in the processes. Many researchers concluding that first and second/foreign language reading processes resemble each other do so on the basis of work with advanced second or foreign language learners (cf. Devine, 1981). Ten advanced Hebrew-speaking high school students of English are equally successful in finding main ideas and synthesizing the overall message in both English and Hebrew texts (Sarig, 1987; see Chapter 3 of this text for details about their strategy use). Similarly, native English speakers and advanced ESL students recall a similar number of high-level ideas from English prose texts, although the native speakers recall more propositions in total (Connor, 1984). First and second language readers do, however, use differently what Connor terms perspective. Native English readers consistently use high-level perspective in their recalls, synthesizing rather than restating (e.g., use of the phrase "according to two sociologists"). ESL students use less high-level and more low-level perspective (e.g., naming the sociologists in their recalls). Connor suggests that such differences, perhaps cultural, may contribute to the perceived nonnativeness of writing done by second language students (see in this regard Connor & McCagg, 1983).

Studying students' perceptions of their chief difficulties in reading French texts as opposed to English texts, Kern (1988) concludes that some difficulties are common to both types of reading. Many of the 53 students felt that affective variables, concentration, and background knowledge figure importantly in both first and foreign language reading. The major problems cited in reading French were vocabulary knowledge, synthesis of meaning, and reading speed; these were not problems in reading English for half the subjects.

Differences in the processes. Researchers, who argue that first and second language reading processes differ, commonly declare subjects' language proficiency level to be a determining factor. In general, the reading process of the advanced second or foreign language learner proves analogous to the first language reading process (as studies noted above discover), whereas that of the beginning foreign language learner contrasts with both (Bernhardt, 1987a; Cziko, 1978, 1980; Kozminsky & Graetz, 1986; McLeod & McLaughlin, 1986). Miscue analysis shows that advanced English-speaking and native French students use an interactive strategy to read French, drawing on both graphic and contextual information when reading French (Cziko, 1980). Lower-level students, on the other hand, use contextual information less and rely primarily on graphic information (a bottom-up strategy) (see Hatch, Polin, & Part, 1974, for a different experiment with similar conclusions).

Native German and experienced nonnative readers of German in an eye-movement study tended to fixate on words only briefly and read quickly while still maintaining 80% comprehension, as judged from immediate recall protocols (Bernhardt, 1987a). Inexperienced American readers of German, like inexperienced first language readers, tend to read slowly and fixate on individual words for long periods (thus exhibiting low-level processing strategies), with only 30% comprehension (cf. Oller, 1972 college-level ESL readers require as much fixation time as third-grade native readers). Specific fixation patterns reveal, somewhat surprisingly, that native German readers, on average, pay more attention to function words than to content words in the same phrase. The experienced foreign language readers acted in the same way with the easiest passage. Bernhardt suggests that for German, at least, function words play a larger role in reading comprehension than has been theorized for first language English reading. Languages may well vary in the weight necessarily given to textual elements.

Working from advanced ESL students' summarizing of English texts, Kozminsky and Graetz (1986) modify Rumelhart's interactive model, asserting that it describes a mature reader with good language skills and background knowledge. For them, first language readers with weak knowledge read from the bottom up, relying on language cues. Second language readers with good background knowledge read from the top down, whereas those with poor knowledge read in a fragmented fashion, unable to control either language or topic (see also Perkins, 1983). Although the authors do not cite Stanovich's (1980) work on first language reading, their conclusions fit within his compensatory interactive model, which allows readers to offset weak reading skills with strong ones. Their analysis also supports views of schema theorists and recognizes the impact of readers' strategies.

Similarly, McLeod and McLaughlin (1986) argue that advanced second language readers differ not only from beginning second language readers but also from native readers (cf. Segalowitz, 1986).

Because their advanced ESL readers had noticeable syntactic and semantic competence but were decoding rather than interacting with the text, McLeod and McLaughlin questioned the role of automaticity in reading skill development and suggested that learning sometimes involves a modification of the structure used to store information. With this restructuring comes a *click of understanding*, as when a learner suddenly understands how passive voice is used in English.

Clearly, conclusions about analogies between first and second or foreign language reading processes must take into account experimental disparities between reading proficiency levels, language proficiency levels, the language read as a first and second/foreign language, and individual readers' degree of first language literacy, reading skills, and motivations. Furthermore, since learners who reach an advanced level of second/foreign language proficiency have, to some extent, selected themselves, their reading processes may contrast with those of less proficient first language readers.

Understandably, experienced second and foreign language readers read more like proficient first language readers than do beginning second language readers. We have yet to divine precisely what determines this increased reading proficiency, but it appears that it owes as much to effective management of strategies as to control of language. In addition, although similarities in reading processes in different languages have been noted (e.g., meaningful miscues, phonological encoding, organization of information in memory), different languages may well entail different sorts of processing (e.g., relatively more attention to function words in German than in English [Bernhardt, 1987a]; a culturally determined difference in perspective [Connor, 1984; see also Aron, 1979; Clarke, 1980; and Ulijn, 1984]; first language phonological interference [Hatch, 1974; Muchisky, 1983]). Continued experimentation in a variety of languages should give us more insights.

Do First Language Reading Skills Transfer to Second/Foreign Language Reading?

Many people read efficiently in their first language; can and do they transfer those skills to reading in another language? Naturally, most attention has been focused on good first language readers in the hope that teachers might be able to capitalize on their skills. Unfortunately, an approximately equal number of researchers have found results on both sides of the question: (1) second or foreign language reading ability depends more on general language proficiency than on first language reading skill; (2) first language reading skill does transfer to second and foreign language reading (for another summary of work on these issues, see Alderson, 1984). For teachers, the issue is the relative importance of teaching language and teaching reading strategies.

Language proficiency determines reading skill. For those who maintain the primacy of linguistic knowledge in second or foreign language reading, expertise in sampling graphic, syntactic, and semantic information from the text is essential to efficient top-down or psycholinguistic reading (Cziko, 1978; Devine, 1987). An imperfect knowledge of a language hinders guessing or predicting ability; readers with a poor grasp of language perceive words as the basic elements of reading comprehension and fail to take into account adequately the context and written discourse as a whole (Yorio, 1971). Moreover, their first language interferes with their understanding of the second on syntactic, semantic, and phonological levels. It may also interfere with their ability to construct meaning from a text (Perkins, 1983). Short-term memory is another problem; unfamiliar second language cues take up more of the mind's active processing space and allow less room for cognitive problem-solving processes.

Probably the relevant research most commonly quoted is Clarke's 1980 study which generated the so-called *short circuit hypothesis*: "limited control over the language 'short circuits' the good reader's system, causing him/her to revert to poor reader strategies when confronted with a difficult or confusing task in the second language" (p. 206). Analyzing 21 ESL students' oral miscues and their answers on a rational deletion cloze test, Clarke finds some justification for the view that the reading process is universal but also evidence of a *language competence ceiling* hampering the good first language reader's attempts to use good reading strategies in a second language (See also Laufer & Sim, 1982, 1985, working with EFL readers.)

First language reading skills do transfer. Taking another look at the *short circuit hypothesis*, Hudson (1982) finds that induced schemata (vocabulary or pictures relating to the text topic) can override language proficiency as a factor in comprehension (see, too, Floyd & Carrell, 1987; Goldman & Reyes, 1983; Johnson, 1981; Swaffar, 1988a, 1988b). Thus, good first language readers whose second language skills are relatively weak understand more of what they read if they activate their predictions about text contents (cf. the view of schema theorists); linguistic ceiling is only one determinant of reading comprehension. In accord with the previously cited research relating individual reading process differences to language proficiency levels, Hudson concludes that advanced readers are better able to apply schemata consistently to a text and that the strategies readers choose change across levels of reading and language proficiency (cf. Alderson et al., 1977; Deemer, 1978).

Even advanced foreign and second language readers use first language strategies when reading another language (Benedetto, 1984; Hauptman, 1979; Sarig, 1987). In her case study of five Hispanic advanced ESL learners, Benedetto determines that advanced linguistic development does not necessarily imply parallel development of higher-order reading strategies; in fact, linguistic factors are subordinate to the cognitive domain. Hauptman (1979) concludes that his 47 English-speaking French students use similar strategies in first and second language reading: the ability or inability to use global cues, the willingness or reluctance to take chances, and ease or difficulty in processing semantic information.

Such contradictory research results preclude definitive conclusions. Plainly, unknown or uncontrolled lexical and syntactic aspects of a second language, as well as cultural distance, must impede a reader's attempt to comprehend a writer's message. Therefore, advanced second and foreign language students will normally read more like experienced native readers than do beginning readers; logically, the reading processes of experienced readers in any language are more closely related than the processes of experienced and beginning readers. Yet research results indicate that first language reading skill sometimes transfers for less advanced language users. Individuals with stronger cognitive strategies and logical reasoning skills understand more than do readers tied to the graphic representation of the text. The puzzle of skill transfer may indeed be a question of reading strategy use; the metacognitive data in Chapter

3 of this volume contribute to this issue.

THE ROLE OF THE TEXT

The fact that readers' formal schemata interact with texts substantiates the impact of text type or structure on the ease or difficulty with which readers understand written texts (often called *text readability*). But, emphasis on text variables as separate from reader variables differs among theorists. Some consider text type the determining factor in text readability, although now we seem to pay less attention than previously to readability formulas (cf. Laroche, 1979; Schulz, 1981). Text type is the major component of the reading level definitions in the *ACTFL Proficiency Guidelines* (1986). Researchers also wonder how readers' comprehension is affected by certain textual elements, especially vocabulary, syntax and semantics, and cohesion (logical connectors).

What is the importance of text type or structure?

Considerable work on text typology has been done to generate a standard reading proficiency test (Child, 1986; Dandonoli, 1987; Kaya-Carton & Carton, 1986; Lange & Lowe, 1988). To establish four levels of language texts, Child (1986) analyzes numerous samples of connected English discourse and asserts that the descriptions cover texts in other languages, as well as English. Although syntax is important to his level definitions, Child also notes the importance of subject matter and shared facts and assumptions. Child's levels, from the simplest to the most complex, are *orientation mode, instructive mode, evaluative mode, projective mode.*

Level 1 texts orient the reader (or listener); they include all sorts of signs, and comprehension of them depends largely on external stimuli. Because the grammar and lexicon of these texts are limited, the learner's comprehension may depend much on memorized material. Level 2 texts reflect greater linguistic variety, although they still remain at a factual level, making statements or giving instructions. Level 3 texts require more of the language users, who respond intellectually, intuitively, or even instinctively to the facts given. These evaluative texts, exemplified by editorials, contain more difficult syntax and a more extensive lexicon. Finally, Child cites as the hallmark of Level 4 texts "the relative lack of shared information and assumptions" (p. 102) on the part of author and reader.

Like Child's definitions, the *ACTFL Reading Proficiency Guidelines* (1986) have much to say about text type at each level. Here, for instance, are the Intermediate-Low and Intermediate-Mid definitions.

INTERMEDIATE: The Intermediate level is characterized by an ability to understand main ideas and some facts from simple connected texts.

INTERMEDIATE-LOW: Able to understand main ideas and/ or some facts from the simplest connected texts dealing with basic personal and social needs. Such texts are linguistically noncomplex and have a clear underlying internal structure, for example, chronological sequencing. They impart basic information about which the reader has to make only minimal suppositions or to which the reader brings personal interest and/or knowledge. Examples include messages with social purposes or information for the widest possible audience, such as public announcements and short, straightforward instructions dealing with public life. Some misunderstandings will occur.

INTERMEDIATE-MID: Able to read consistently, with increased understanding, simple connected texts dealing with a variety of basic and social needs. Such texts are still linguistically noncomplex and have a clear underlying internal structure. They impart basic information about which the reader has to make minimal suppositions and to which the reader brings personal interest and/or knowledge. Examples may include short, straightforward descriptions of persons, places, and things written for a wide audience.

Although these descriptions recognize the role of reader interest and background knowledge in text comprehension, they definitely emphasize the linguistic and structural aspects of the text. Moreover, although Kaya-Carton and Carton (1986) posit both a *full* and a *partial* model of reading proficiency, they choose to work with only the partial model in developing a reading proficiency test. The full model includes several reader characteristics (cognitive ability, linguistic knowledge, personal and cultural experience, and general knowledge) together with text characteristics (structure/syntax, semantic and pragmatic content, topical reference, level of formality, literal versus interpretive presentation, and rhetorical organization). The partial model contains only the text characteristics. Of course, text characteristics define how texts can be ranked from novice to superior levels, without considering the reader; workshop participants can learn to rank and rate texts according to the ACTFL reading scales (Lange & Lowe, 1988). Beyond the level definitions themselves, reader strategies enter into the *Proficiency Guidelines* as they have been matched with specific levels (Dandonoli, 1987; Phillips & Dandonoli, 1986). For example, readers at Level 2 decode and classify whereas readers at Level 3 infer, guess, hypothesize, and interpret.

Still, the central role of text in the *Guidelines*, to the semi-exclusion of the reader, has provoked some disagreement from other second language reading specialists. By definition, given the acknowledged role of the individual reader's schemata (Child, 1986), it is questionable whether a particular text would induce the same difficulties for different readers (see Bernhardt, 1986c). Lee (1987a, 1988c) wonders why Kaya-Carton and Carton (1986) choose to work with a partial model when a full model of reading proficiency exists. Some assumptions of readability formulas come into question; simply because *alligator* and *elephant* are long words does not mean they are confusing, and, in fact, beginning first language readers have little difficulty with them (Bernhardt, 1984, Allen et al., 1988). Bernhardt (1986b) also argues persuasively that proficient reading depends on reader skills rather than on text characteristics: topic-dependent, proficient reading demands that readers make appropriate decisions from the beginning of a passage, select the critical features for processing, and process them rapidly.

Lee and Musumeci (1988) designate the ACTFL *Reading Guidelines* as a hierarchy of skills. They test two inherent hypotheses: (1) less proficient readers will not perform well on high-level texts or use high-level skills, and (2) more proficient readers will perform well on both high- and low-level texts and use both high- and low-level skills. Their finding of a lack of significant interaction between text, skill, and level raises questions about the validity of the proficiency model. For example, the American students of Italian in the study were only 47% accurate on questions relating to Skill 1 (recognizing memorized elements) on Text Type 1 (restaurant checks); Lee and Musumeci suggest that the source of the difficulty is unfamiliarity with target culture norms and practices, i.e., where information appears on a restaurant receipt. Yet, cultural implications of texts enter into the *Reading Guidelines* only at the Advanced-Plus level and above.

Similarly, Allen et al. (1988), in a large study of American high school foreign language learners, find a complex interaction between text type analyzed by language but no main effect by text alone, thus finding no support for a hierarchy of text types. They, too, surmise reader background knowledge as a determining factor in text difficulty and suggest that the text typology perspective suits the United States Federal Government because, in that controlled curriculum, students are trained in requisite background information.

Hummel (1985) also notes in the *Reading Proficiency Guidelines* a lack of coherence in defining readers' use of background knowledge and cultural understanding. Moreover, since the ability to draw inferences is a cognitive skill divorced from linguistic ability, it cannot be relegated to only the higher levels of reading proficiency. Finally, he illustrates how grammatical forms tied to certain levels in the language-specific guidelines are not necessary for reading comprehension (cf. Lee, 1987a).

As always, a number of questions remain. The *ACTFL Reading Guidelines* as they stand do recognize reader attributes as essential to reading comprehension, although this aspect has not as yet been fully exploited in test development. Chapter 3 of this volume offers some data about the relative importance of text and reader characteristics to comprehension and their interaction.

What role do textual elements play in reader comprehension?

Some of the earliest work on second and foreign language reading focused on whether certain text elements especially influence comprehension. If poor language proficiency impinges on reading comprehension, can we better define which aspects of language knowledge are crucial? Of course, words make up a text; hence, vocabulary must play a central role. Questions have been raised about when discrete lexical knowledge is necessary, as opposed to the ability to guess word meanings from context. Other researchers have gone beyond the lexicon to wonder about the relative importance of semantics and syntax. Closely associated with syntax and semantics, textual cohesion has given occasion to additional investigation. Relevant research and theory is briefly summarized below.

Vocabulary. Foreign and second language students repeatedly claim that lack of vocabulary knowledge is a major problem when reading (see Kern, 1988; Yorio, 1971); reading specialists also relate lexical knowledge to comprehension and suggest ways of teaching vocabulary to improve reading proficiency (See note for specific references.)[2] Hague (1987) argues that advanced language students need to learn vocabulary as they do in their first language, since they must acquire new concepts along with new labels. Research on the relationship between vocabulary knowledge and reading comprehension, however, is relatively slight and somewhat contradictory.

Hudson (1982), Johnson (1982), and Pak (1986) find that having students study unfamiliar words before reading does not improve their comprehension. Davis (1988) finds the opposite in his study of groups of American students reading French in one of three treatments: (1) with questions and vocabulary definitions before reading; (2) with the same information glossed with the story; and (3) with no help. Students who had background knowledge questions and/or unfamiliar vocabulary glossed had better reading comprehension. Without separate treatments for background knowledge and glossing, however, we cannot be sure whether either variable alone or the interaction of the two is responsible for the higher recall scores. Further research on this question will be helpful to both teachers and textbook authors.

Other vocabulary research treats miscellaneous issues. American students reading simplified German can learn vocabulary from context even when the ratio of new words to familiar words is as high as one to fifteen (Holley, 1973). Extensive reading results in a substantial amount of vocabulary learning even though individuals learn vocabulary in very different ways (Saragi et al., 1978). Word length, frequency, and morphology may affect second and foreign language readers more than first language readers; speakers of different languages may process words differently (Meara, 1984). Obviously, studies on the impact of vocabulary on comprehension diverge, and the database is still relatively limited. As Carrell

(1987b) recommends, we must continue to examine the effect on comprehension of preteaching vocabulary and the role of incidental exposure to vocabulary.

Syntax and semantics. Several researchers have attempted to ascertain the relative importance of text syntax (grammatical structures) and semantics (the meanings, mostly contained in groupings of words, the lexicon or vocabulary) (see Eskey, 1971, Cowan, 1974, Saville-Troike, 1979, for statements on this matter). According to first language psycholinguistic and interactive reading theory, readers use the syntactic, lexical, and semantic levels in a text with varying intensity for text comprehension. (See especially Goodman, 1967; and Rumelhart, 1977a.) For foreign and second language reading, conflicting findings exist. Readers of machine instructions find content words (e.g., technical terms and nominalizations) more difficult than syntactic function words (Ulijn, 1977). Conceptual analysis overrules syntactic analysis, in that syntactic contrasts between the first language (Dutch) and foreign language (French) impede comprehension only if the conceptual content of the text is difficult to understand (Ulijn, 1981; cf. Strother and Ulijn, 1987).

For other researchers, syntax takes the upper hand. Hebrew-speaking college students studying English read a syntactically simplified text significantly more easily than a similar, unsimplified text (Aronson-Berman, 1978; see also Berman, 1984). Students read a syntactically familiar first language (English) passage more quickly than a random passage, but reading times for the differently constructed second language texts showed no variation; knowledge of syntax thus appears to help readers predict and to read more quickly (MacNamara, 1967). Second language readers tend to perceive target language text in terms of native language syntactic structure (Cowan, 1976), thus implying the dominance of syntax in their reading process. ESL students more aware of form class (the morphemes or structure units of a word) comprehend more on a multiple-choice reading comprehension test than those less aware (Guarino & Perkins, 1986).

These complicated results receive implicit confirmation from other studies concluding that reader control of both syntax and semantics affects comprehension. Finding that syntactic, semantic, and discourse constraints serve as important sources of information for fluent first or second language readers, Cziko (1978) hypothesizes a developmental order in the second language reader's ability to use contextual constraints, suggesting that sensitivity to syntactic constraints develops before sensitivity to both semantic and discourse constraints (cf. Clarke, 1980). As ESL students advance in general language and reading proficiency, they show steady improvement in processing both syntactic and semantic cues (Devine, 1987). Conversely, Hauptman (1979) finds that more advanced foreign language students make fewer syntactic errors but more semantic errors than intermediate students; he hypothesizes that this difference springs from increased willingness to guess word meanings. Knowledge of syntax and vocabulary interact to allow American readers to understand French text (Barnett, 1986); only readers with at least average control of both demonstrated good recall. Thus, contrary to some theorists' suggestions, unduly stressing vocabulary-building or inferencing skills may very well not help those students who do not have adequate syntactic knowledge. Language instruction should be integrative and holistic (Devine, 1987). In effect, given these research results, we cannot disregard any aspect of language proficiency in our efforts to develop better second and foreign language readers.

Cohesion. Cohension refers to the way in which ideas and meanings in a text relate to each other. Halliday and Hasan (1976) define first language cohesive ties as follows:

Reference: words referring to others: e.g., pronouns, demonstrative adjectives;

Repetition: the word itself repeated, often with a definite rather than indefinite article ("I just saw a snake!"Where's <u>the snake</u> you saw?);

Substitution: often referred to as repetition without the repeated word ("He wanted to see her but he <u>didn't</u>.";)

Ellipsis: also called *substitution by zero* ("I like Rick's house but I don't like Harry's");

Conjunctions: cohesive because of their meanings rather than through reference to other parts of the text: e.g., *and, but, therefore.*

According to Halliday and Hasan's strong view, cohesion (the semantic functions realized in the surface-level features of the text) creates coherence (the reader's understanding of the text as a coherent entity). Opposing views argue about the impact of reader schemata on the comprehension of second language readers (e.g., Carrell, 1982). Steffensen (1988), comparing the English recall protocols of Americans and East Indians reading about weddings in each of the cultures, does not find evidence to support even the weak view, that cohesion is related to coherence but not the source of it. Instead, she discovers a major problem in attempting to use cohesion as a measure of textual coherence; in subjects' recalls, "cohesive devices may be used at a high frequency, relating items that should not be" (p. 148).

Nevertheless, studying the discourse of a text through cohesion and analyzing foreign or second language readers' ability to follow that discourse are valid fields of investigation. Williams (1983) defines *texture* as the essential characteristics of text, cites studies showing foreign language learners' difficulties in recognizing cohesive ties, and suggests ways to teach cohesive ties (see also Rizzardi, 1980). Students best able to follow reference words have the highest recall protocol scores (Barnett, 1988a). Certainly, more work on the impact on comprehension of reader ability to grasp cohesive ties would help define how this aspect of reading should fit into a pedagogical model.

FUTURE DIRECTIONS

The interactive view of second/foreign language reading appears to be a viable one, recognizing the complexity of the reading process and taking into account both reader and text characteristics and variables. Although far from clearly understanding exactly how people read a foreign language efficiently and comprehend well, we know a great deal. The first and second language reading processes are both similar and different. Comprehension depends in great measure on what readers already know about a topic and on what they expect in terms of text structure. General language proficiency affects how much readers understand. Text factors like vocabulary, syntax, and cohesion have a major impact on comprehension, but much work remains. What precisely is the role of these textual factors in reading, and what are the relative contributions of reader and text characteristics in general?

Equally provocative are other research directions: the role of inference, reader interest and purpose, and difficulties inherent in specific languages. Undoubtedly, readers often must make inferences to construct coherent meaning from a text (Kintsch & van Dijk, 1978; Anderson & Pearson, 1984). Inferences can be correct elaborations or incorrect distortions of a text (cf. Steffensen et al., 1979). A reader may draw faulty inferences because of weak lexical knowledge and/or inappropriate cultural schemata (Bernhardt, 1986a; Parry, 1987). Aside from such general assumptions, few studies have examined how or when second language readers infer (cf. Bialystok & Howard, 1979; Hellgren, 1986; Ozete, 1978). Is the ability to infer information not explicitly stated purely a cognitive skill, or is it related to language proficiency or reading comprehension? If the latter, do good readers infer more or better than poor readers, or vice versa? Language learners sometimes infer incorrectly because they have misunderstood one or more words in a text. How much of a reader's inference depends upon the lexicon or semantics of a text? Does the amount readers infer vary according to text content (e.g., concrete or abstract)?

Reader interest and purpose in reading probably influence what is understood (see Coady, 1979; Moirand, 1979; Royer, Bates, & Konold, 1984). Certainly, these two reader attributes are tied closely together; an interested reader has a defined purpose in reading. A self-imposed purpose usually generates interest. Schematic expectations normally provide purpose, leading a reader to look for confirmation in the text. Kern (1988) theorizes an intermediary level of schemata that metacognitively exerts executive control over the rest of the reading process, setting goals and monitoring comprehension. Working with physicists reading in their first language, Bazerman (1985) finds that purpose and schemata are interrelated; a reader's schemata help define reading objectives, and those objectives may alter the schemata.

Still, many questions remain. How much does reading purpose determine what is comprehended? Do second and foreign language learners approach texts as purposefully as first language readers usually do? If not, can they learn to clarify their purposes? How much do readers' purposes depend on text types (e.g., newspaper articles, guide books, novels), and how much on individual reader interest and initiative? (See Pugh & Ulijn, 1984; Ulijn, 1984; Zuck & Zuck, 1984a). How much does a text influence a reader's interest? Because half her first language subjects modified their level of interest in the topic after reading texts, Olshavsky (1976-77) judges that reading proficiency has much to do with reader interest. Are foreign and second language readers more interested in easily comprehensible texts? Or, on the other hand, is an interested reader a more comprehending reader? Undoubtedly, the intrinsic motivation of a reader's interest is more compelling than any extrinsic motivation a teacher may extend (cf. Fransson, 1984).

Furthermore, although some specialists call reading a universal process, certain difficulties prove inherent to specific languages, cultures, or types of language (e.g., ideographic versus alphabetic). Logical reasoning skills are essential to making inferences and processing text (Perkins, 1983), and different languages contain different patterns of logical reasoning (Kaplan, 1966). Syntactic differences between languages can impede comprehension for second language readers using first language perceptual strategies (Cowan, 1976). Readers of ideographic languages apparently process according to the configuration of characters, whereas English readers apply a rule system (Biederman & Tsao, 1979). Recalls of texts with dissimilar rhetorical organizations vary according to ESL readers' first languages (Carrell, 1984a; cf. Connor, 1984; Connor & McCagg, 1983). Suspecting that French texts might be intrinsically more difficult than Spanish or German texts, for instance, Allen et al. (1988) wonder whether texts can be selected for comparison across languages. They caution against assuming that general principles of reading apply to all learners of any language at any level.

Because the reading process is complex, because readers have varying linguistic proficiency, life experiences, interests and purposes in reading, and because texts differ in structure, audience, author intent, style, and level of language, proficient readers must be able to adapt their approaches. The problem-solving techniques or strategies they use to comprehend are the subject of Chapter 3, which also presents a replicable experiment on one particular reading strategy—guessing word meanings from context.

3

The Impact of Reading Strategy
Use on Comprehension

As research shows, literate adolescent and adult second and foreign language learners bring to their reading a certain level of cognitive skill development, more or less well-formed schemata about the world and about text structure, and some first language reading skill. (As mentioned in the Introduction to this work, second language reading for first language illiterates is a different situation not treated here.) Since first language readers already have useful skills, many specialists have found it logical to suppose that these readers can improve their second or foreign language comprehension by using reading strategies. As used in this book and in most of the work mentioned below, the term *strategy* refers to the mental operations involved when readers purposefully approach a text to make sense of what they read. These may be either conscious techniques controlled by the reader or unconscious processes applied automatically. Both good (successful) and poor (nonsuccessful) strategies exist, yet the term *strategy* as used in pedagogical materials often implies those which are successful.

Toward a Taxonomy of Reading Strategies

The variety of reading strategies and the individual nature of their application have resulted in a lack of consensus about exactly what constitutes these problem-solving strategies promoted by reading specialists. Hosenfeld (1977, 1979, 1984), Block (1986), and Sarig (1987) have offered from their observations of second language readers perhaps the most complete catalogues of types of second/foreign language reading strategies. (The experimental bases for these lists will be described below.) Developed from the self-reports of adolescent foreign language students, the *Interviewer Guide for Reading Strategies* offered by Hosenfeld et al. (1981) (Figure 9) lists a number of effective reading strategies.

INTERVIEWER GUIDE FOR READING STRATEGIES

Name_____

GENERAL READING BEHAVIOR

- •Rarely translates;
  Guesses contextually

- •Translates;
  Guesses noncontextually

- •Translates;
  Guesses contextually

- •Translates;
  Rarely guesses

S U N	OBSERVED STRATEGIES	COMMENTS

1. Keeps meaning in mind _____
2. Skips unknown words (guesses contextually) _____
3. Uses context in preceding and
   succeeding sentences and paragraphs _____
4. Identifies grammatical category of words_____
5. Evaluates guesses_____
6. Reads title (makes inferences) _____
7. Continues if unsuccessful _____
8. Recognizes cognates _____
9. Uses knowledge of the world _____
10. Analyzes unknown words _____
11. Reads as though he or she expects the text
    to make sense _____
12. Reads to identify meaning rather
    than words _____
13. Takes chances in order to
    identify meaning _____
14. Uses illustration _____
15. Uses side-gloss _____
16. Uses glossary as last resort _____
17. Looks up words correctly _____
18. Skips unnecessary words_____
19. Follows through with
    proposed solutions _____
20. Uses a variety of types of context clues _____

Figure 9
From "Second Language Reading: A Curricular Sequence for Teaching
Reading Strategies" in C. Hosenfeld, V. Arnold, J. Kirchofer, J. Laciura
& L. Wilson, (1981). *Foreign Language Annals, 14,* 5. Reprinted by
permission from the American Council on the Teaching of Foreign
Languages, Inc.

Hosenfeld's practical enumeration of observed strategies is frequently cited by foreign/second language reading specialists who suggest ways to develop students' reading strategies and to encourage students to use effective strategies.[1]

Analyzing think-aloud protocols, Block (1986) observes the strategies of six ESL and three native-English-speaking university-level students; she categorizes their strategies as general (comprehension-gathering and comprehension-monitoring) and local (attempts to understand specific linguistic units).

General strategies
- anticipate content
- recognize text structure
- integrate information
- question information in the text
- interpret the text
- use general knowledge and associations
- comment on behavior or processes
- monitor comprehension
- correct behavior
- react to the text

Local strategies
- paraphrase
- reread
- question meaning of a clause or sentence
- question meaning of a word
- solve vocabulary problem

Block also extrapolates from research on writing to define two different modes in readers' strategies: *extensive* (when readers focus on understanding the author's ideas) and *reflexive* (when readers relate ideas in the text to themselves, affectively and personally). This concept of modes is helpful in understanding how individual readers see themselves in relation to a text.

Viewing the second language reading process as the interlingual transfer of reading skills from the readers' metamodel (native) language, Sarig (1987) works from foreign language learners' think-aloud data to classify their reading moves, or strategies, into four types (all containing "comprehension promoting moves" and "comprehension deterring moves"). As Dubin (1987) comments, this first attempt to group learners' strategies into types may be as significant as Sarig's experiment results (summarized below). Here are Sarig's four move types, together with examples of each (for a complete list, see Cohen, 1986):

Technical-aid moves are generally useful for decoding at a local level.

- skimming
- scanning
- skipping
- writing key elements in the text
- marking parts of text for different purposes
- summarizing paragraphs in the margin
- using glossary

Clarification and simplification moves show the reader's intention to clarify and/or simplify text utterances.

- substitutions
- paraphrases
- circumlocutions
- synonyms

Coherence-detecting moves demonstrate the reader's intention to produce coherence from the text.

- effective use of content schemata and formal schemata to predict forthcoming text
- identification of people in the text and their views or actions
- cumulative decoding of text meaning
- relying on summaries given in the text
- identification of text focus

*Monitoring moves are those displaying active monitoring of text
processing, whether metacognitively conscious or not.*

- conscious change of planning and carrying out the tasks
- deserting a hopeless utterance ("I don't understand
    that, so I'll read on")
- flexibility of reading rate
- mistake correction
- ongoing self-evaluation

Undoubtedly, the number and complexity of reading strategies
is just short of overwhelming. Possibilities are numerous, and theorists' viewpoints are close but not identical. In fact, given that
strategies are frequently utilized in combination with each other
(Kern, 1988) and that individual readers use different terminology to
explain the strategies they are using, a conclusive list may not be
possible. Other inventories of strategies have been proposed by
Olshavsky (1977-78) for first language reading and by Groebel
(1981), Knight, Padron, and Waxman (1985), Padron and Waxman
(1988), and Kern (1988) for second language reading. What do we
know about how effective they are?

WHAT DO EXPERIMENTS TELL US ABOUT
READING STRATEGIES?

Aside from Hosenfeld's pioneering studies (1977a/b, 1979, 1984),
only recently have researchers become interested in strategy use in
second and foreign language reading. They are examining different
aspects of reading strategy use: (1) descriptions of strategies naturally used by second or foreign language readers; (2) the transfer of
first language strategies to second or foreign language reading; (3)
the actual effectiveness of strategies generally deemed "successful";
(4) learners' thoughts about what they do when they read (their
metacognitive perception); (5) the relationship between readers'
metacognition and their comprehension and actual strategy use;
and (6) the usefulness of training students to use productive strategies. These different facets of reading strategies intermingle in the
following review of work on strategy use in second and foreign

language reading. Because we need to see the reading process at work in order to define and analyze strategy use, much of this research depends on mentalistic data, i.e, the information obtained by having learners verbalize or analyze their thought processes as they perform various tasks. [2]

Describing Reading Strategies

Foreign and second language students can observe and verbalize their learning strategies, and their strategies are often quite different from the strategies their teachers assume they are using (Hosenfeld, 1977a). [3] In her original study on reading, Hosenfeld (1977b) asked forty adolescent foreign language students (half tested as proficient and half as nonproficient readers) to think aloud as they read silently. From the self-reported data, Hosenfeld constructed *reading maps* providing graphic, visual portrayals of individual students' reading strategies. She discovered distinct differences between the strategies used by successful and unsuccessful readers. For instance, successful readers kept the meaning of the passage in mind while reading, read (translated) in broad phrases, skipped words they saw as unimportant to total phrase meaning, and had a positive self-concept as readers. Unsuccessful readers lost the meaning of sentences as soon as they decoded them, read (translated) in short phrases, seldom skipped any words as unimportant but rather viewed them all as "equal," and had a negative self-concept as readers.

Case studies of two ninth-grade foreign language readers who use think-aloud and introspective/retrospective procedures to uncover their problem-solving strategies reveal precisely how these individuals read before and after receiving training in particular reading strategies (Hosenfeld, 1979, 1984). Readers who use inefficient techniques can acquire efficient strategies from either inductive or deductive training methods, but Hosenfeld hesitates to dictate any particular pedagogical method based on her exploratory studies.

Transfer of First Language Strategies

In four studies of the transfer of first language reading strategies to second language reading, researchers present conflicting findings. Laufer and Sim (1982) compare the reading performance and strategy use of a test group of six Hebrew-speaking EFL learners (who are at an intermediate-level in English) with the performance and strategy use of a control group of six nonnative speakers of English (who have near-native proficiency). Whereas the test group had been explicitly taught reading comprehension strategies (the nature of this training is not specified), the control group had no such instruction. Using three relatively difficult English reading passages, Laufer and Sim tested five strategies by asking questions related to them and by interviewing the subjects about how they had arrived at their answers. The strategies tested were skimming for key words and phrases, finding the implication, distinguishing between main and peripheral matter, recognizing the author's intent, and contextual guessing. Test group subjects who had difficulty with an English passage read a Hebrew translation of that passage and answered the same questions that tested the same reading strategies. The members of the control group showed no such difficulties with first language passages.

Results show that although members of the test group applied the selected strategies in their first language, none of them used the same strategies as effectively in the foreign language. Because the students with fewer language difficulties answered "better" and since the control group subjects had no problems applying the strategies, Laufer and Sim conclude that foreign language reading is a function of foreign language competence. Unfortunately, however, they give no examples of the type of questions asked and no clear indication of what constituted a "better" answer. Their analysis of student interpretations of certain text sentences, on the other hand, provides insights into the reading process of second/foreign language learners. Intermediate students depend more on lexical items than on syntax to understand and when their linguistic knowledge fails them, they may rely on their own knowledge of the world to the point of misreading the text (cf. Bernhardt, 1986a). For Laufer and Sim, "higher order reading strategies appear to be ineffectual if the lower order language base is too insecure" (p. 17).

Working with elementary school children (23 Spanish-speaking ESL students and 15 English monolingual students), Knight, Padron, and Waxman (1985) study whether these two groups of students report any differences in either the type or frequency of cognitive reading strategies used. Rated according to their individual English reading levels, the students read an English passage appropriate to their level, stopping at pre-marked intervals to talk (in their native language) about their reading strategies. Analyses of the transcribed interviews indicate that the monolingual English students used about twice as many strategies as the Spanish-speaking ESL students. In addition, three strategies (concentrating, noting details, and generating questions) were reported significantly more often by the monolinguals than by the ESL students (who, moreover, did not report using at all the three strategies of imaging, noting details, and predicting outcomes). The researchers suggest that perhaps the Spanish-speaking students were transferred to ESL courses before they had a chance to develop their first language reading strategies. The researchers thus echo the opinion of Laufer and Sim (1982), although they do not cite them.

Benedetto (1984, 1985) compares the first and second language reading behaviors of five Hispanic advanced ESL learners and studies issues similar to those of Laufer and Sim: (1) the relationship between language ability and the use of top-level organizational strategies in first and second language reading and (2) the comparative use of these strategies when reading first and second language expository texts. Subjects' oral and written recall protocols were scored for their adherence to the writer's top-level structure and for the presence or absence of rhetorical content and relationships. Whereas Laufer and Sim decide that language ability dominates cognitive strategy use, Benedetto concludes that the development of advanced linguistic ability does not necessarily imply parallel development of the high-order strategies necessary for effective reading. Moreover, she terms the relationship between the two skills hierarchical, with the linguistic subordinate to the cognitive domain. She finds that her subjects continue to rely on whatever first language strategies they have, even if their knowledge of the second language makes that reliance inappropriate. Of course, Benedetto worked with "advanced" ESL learners, Laufer and Sim with "intermediate" students.

Sarig (1987) also studies "advanced" learners: ten Hebrew-speaking high school seniors who had formally studied English for an average of eight years. Included in this (relatively small) sample were subjects with low, intermediate, and high English proficiency levels, as established by teacher evaluations and an English test. Viewing reading as a problem-solving process, Sarig assigned two problem-solving tasks: main idea analysis and synthesis of overall message. After being trained to understand the tasks and to provide think-aloud and introspection data, the subjects read and reacted to texts in Hebrew and English.

Analyzing the data for the reading strategies or moves listed above, Sarig discovers great similarity between first and second/foreign language reading. The different move types produced almost identical success or failure rates in both languages. A high correlation also exists between the type of move used in each language to perform each of the three stages in the tasks: (1) identification of main propositions; (2) identification of the one main proposition underlying the entire text; and (3) synthesis of overall message. Thus, she finds, like Benedetto (1985), that first language reading strategies do appear to transfer to second/foreign language reading. Finally, Sarig's categorization of moves according to how many readers used them and how frequently they were used clearly demonstrates the highly individual nature of reading; most readers use a unique combination of moves. Sarig questions the traditional good reader/poor reader dichotomy: readers may use many good strategies but fail to comprehend something because of only a few wrong moves.

In a descriptive study, Block (1986) had six ESL students (with Chinese or Spanish as native language) and three native English speakers think aloud about what they understood and thought about while reading two English passages from a college textbook. From their results on cloze tests in English and in their first language, the ESL students proved to have a level of reading proficiency similar to that of the American students. Thus, Block came to conclusions similar to those of Sarig, even though Block worked with college ESL and native English speakers designated as non-proficient readers and enrolled in remedial reading classes. She suggests, as do Lee and Musumeci (1988), that "strategy use is a stable phenomenon which is not tied to specific language features" (p. 485) and that readers should be able to transfer their successful first language reading strategies.

As with the more general question of transferability of first language reading skill to second/foreign language reading, the data on reading strategy transfer to a second or foreign language are inconclusive. The ability to use reading strategies in another language may depend to some extent on first language literacy, second/foreign language proficiency, and level of study in the second/foreign language. Probably the ability to utilize effective strategies varies from reader to reader, as cognitive skill development differs. One unanswered (and perhaps unasked) question can be extrapolated from work on writing: can students who have been trained to use second or foreign language reading strategies transfer what they have learned to first language reading?

Metacognitive Awareness and Effectiveness of Strategy Use

Despite the unresolved question of whether reading strategies transfer, many reading specialists have called for pedagogical methods to develop students' strategies (see note 1 for references). In part because of this relatively new emphasis, researchers have recently begun examining the effectiveness of reading strategies in a second or foreign language without reference to readers' first language reading proficiency. Barnett (1988c) and Kern (1988) investigated whether experimental groups of French students, who have been taught reading strategies, would comprehend more than control groups who have not been taught specific reading strategies. Barnett (1988a,b), Kern (1988), and Padron and Waxman (1988) studied the relationship between comprehension and readers' perceptions about the strategies they use (their metacognitive awareness of their reading process). Devine (1984) considers how readers' views of the reading process determine how they approach a text. Barnett (1988a,b) explains a series of studies to determine whether students who naturally use strategies or think they use strategies better than their peers comprehend better. Casanave (1988) suggests the possibility of adding to our concept of schema theory a third type of schema, *strategy schema*, "the generic knowledge we have of the routine monitoring and repair strategies available to us as we read" (297). (For studies of learner strategies in general, see Bialystok, 1979, and Wenden and Rubin, 1987; for results showing that first language reading strategies can be taught, see Bereiter and Bird, 1985.)

Kern (1988) undertook a project to train American students of intermediate French to use specific strategies designed to help them

(1) infer the meaning of unknown words and (2) synthesize meaning in large segments of text. The specific strategies taught were (1) recognizing cognates, prefixes, suffixes, and orthographic cues; (2) recognizing and utilizing sentence and discourse level signalling cues (e.g., *if ... then*, relative clauses); (3) recognizing cohesion markers (e.g., *therefore)*,; (4) inferring the meanings of unfamiliar words; and (5) finding main ideas. Course content was the same for experimental and control groups; manner and focus of instruction varied. Kern hypothesized that foreign language readers provided with reading strategies would be able to automatize their lower-level processing skills to a greater degree than their untrained peers and therefore would use their cognitive resources more efficiently, comprehending more as a result.

After randomly assigning 53 students to experimental (strategy instruction) or control (normal instruction) conditions, Kern obtained three types of data: (1) self-report data from an interview designed to assess reading strategy use and comprehension; (2) subjects' scores on comprehension and word inference measures; and (3) subjects' responses to a questionnaire about their language background and their general perceptions about how they read French. The analysis of the quantitative data reveals significantly better scores on both the comprehension and word inference measures for the experimental group than for the control group (cf. Bialystok's [1983] finding that trained students were more willing to guess word meanings). Kern also finds that low ability readers benefit from strategy instruction more than either middle or high ability readers, although middle ability readers made strong gains. Determining categories of strategy use from subjects' interview protocols, Kern discovers that frequency of strategy use does not affect comprehension significantly but that combinations of strategies are more effective than strategies used in isolation.

Barnett's (1988c) results from a similar study are less conclusive. After a semester of instruction, intermediate foreign language students trained in reading strategies did outperform a control group on a standardized reading comprehension test, but the difference in scores was not quite statistically significant. This lack of significant effects may derive from the relatively weak control the researcher exerted over the six instructors of the experimental sections. (Kern, on the other hand, taught one of his two experimental sections himself.) After Barnett's experiment, one instructor admitted having been somewhat confused about the point of the experimental readings and activities; student remarks indicated that another instructor had not incorporated all aspects of the experimental procedures. Clearly, a certain amount of teacher dedication to an experimental methodology is necessary for complete effectiveness; conversely, the experimenter needs to avoid introducing an enthusiastic bias for a new methodology. In response to a questionnaire, experimental group students did, however, react positively to pre-reading activities and to guessing word meanings from context; like Kern (1988), Barnett finds strategy instruction to be beneficial to reader morale and confidence.

Working as before, with elementary school children (82 Hispanic ESL students), Padron and Waxman (1988) investigated the relationship between students' reported use of cognitive reading strategies (i.e., their metacognitive awareness about how they read) and their performance on measures of reading comprehension. A standardized reading comprehension exam was given twice, at a four-month interval, to determine the relationship between gains in reading ability and strategies noted on a self-report instrument. This Reading Strategy Questionnaire (RSQ) contains fourteen strategies, half negatively related to students' reading achievement (e.g., writing down every word, skipping the parts you don't understand in the story) and half positively related to achievement (e.g., summarizing in writing, underlining important parts of the story). Students indicated how much they used each described strategy (always, sometimes, or never).

Pretest achievement had the greatest effect on posttest achievement, as would be expected. In addition, students had lower achievement gain when they reported using either of two strategies: thinking about something else while reading and saying the main idea over and over. Therefore, Padron and Waxman conclude that students' perceptions of their cognitive strategies have predictive validity for their comprehension. However, it is curious that only two of the fourteen strategies examined significantly predicted posttest achievement. Replications of this experiment—including a comparison with readers' first language strategies—should tell us more.

Similarly, in her study of twenty adult beginning/low-intermediate second language readers, Devine (1984) finds that nineteen of them can articulate their theoretical orientations to reading clearly; she classifies these readers as sound-, word-, or meaning-centered. Then, analyzing their miscues during their oral reading of English texts and their unaided retellings of the selections, she concludes that their theoretical orientations influence their reading performance and comprehension. For instance, meaning-centered readers made a relatively high proportion of semantically acceptable miscues and demonstrated good to excellent comprehension. Sound-centered readers produced the most non-words, had high mean scores for miscues with high graphic or phonemic similarity, and had either poor or very poor comprehension. Although the reading comprehension of the word-centered readers varied considerably, the study still reveals a relationship between how readers view second language reading and how they go about reading.

These research initiatives support the pedagogical calls for teaching students to use reading strategies; but so far they are few in number; their results must be strengthened by replication and by research with language learners at different levels reading other languages. As we see from the research surveys in this chapter and in Chapter 2, experimentation on second language reading differs in format and objective; much of it originates from ideas teachers derive inductively from working with their students. Common sense plays a surprisingly large role in experimental design. By combining objective observation of students and an effort to eliminate bias as much as possible, a motivated classroom teacher can become a researcher (cf. Seliger & Long, 1983). The following section is intended, in part, to illustrate how an experiment can be devised to investigate the effectiveness of a particular reading strategy and to provide information necessary for replication or adaptation. It also provides a sample experimental design, incorporating a variety of research methodologies: recall protocols, multiple-choice items, a questionnaire on student perceptions, and think-aloud protocols. All texts and items appear in the Appendices.

An Experiment: Guessing Word Meaning From Context

To expand the relatively small pool of data on reading strategy use and on learner perceptions of strategy use, Barnett designed a study to analyze the impact on foreign language reading comprehension of three strategies generally considered effective. Two general hypotheses were formulated: (1) readers who use certain problem-solving strategies will understand more of what they read than those who do not use these reading strategies; and (2) readers who perceive that they use strategies generally considered effective will understand more of what they read than those who do not think they use such strategies. (For an overview of the entire experimental design, see Barnett, 1988b.) Separate experiments conforming to the same format have so far shown two strategies to be effective: reading at the level of discourse rather than at the level of words and sentences, (Barnett, 1988b) and following key words such as nouns, subject pronouns, and adjectives (Barnett, 1988a). The strategy studied in the replicable experiment discussed here is the ability to use context and morphology to guess the meaning of unfamiliar or unknown words.

Previous Research on Word Meanings in Context

For the purposes of this experiment, context is considered to be the inherent relationship of surrounding words, phrases, and sentences to any particular word or expression within them (for more elaborate definitions, see note).[4] The mental activity involved when readers assign meaning to unfamiliar words or phrases is termed "to guess" throughout this work; the verb "to infer" may then be used exclusively to mean "to draw inferences beyond the actual words of a text," thus adding to the writer's stated meaning. Furthermore, as the literature review and experiment results show, *guess* probably more accurately describes what many students do with unknown words.

Possibly more has been written on the strategy of guessing word meanings from context than on any other foreign or second language reading strategy, and research and pedagogical suggestions follow separate trends.[5] Some theorists focus on receptive acquisition of vocabulary and recommend that students learn word-guessing techniques in order to enlarge their vocabularies (Bramski & Williams, 1984; Crow, 1986; Twaddell, 1973). For researchers investigating the relationship between language learners' word-guessing strategies and reading comprehension, results tend in two directions: (1) toward a categorization of contextual clues students use or might use (Bramski & Williams, 1984; Hosenfeld et al., 1981; Siebert, 1945), and (2) toward an explanation of precisely how students discover the meanings of unfamiliar words. Here is a summary of research results:

(a) All researchers find that second or foreign language readers (of different linguistic levels and first language backgrounds) can guess word meanings to some extent. Bensoussan and Laufer (1984) differ from the majority, however; although advocating that students be taught word-guessing strategies, they find that most students do not effectively use context to guess word meanings when left to themselves (cf. Schatz and Baldwin's [1986] finding that first language readers frequently cannot use context clues in naturally occurring first language texts).

(b) To guess word meanings, most readers greatly depend on the form of the unknown word, the "lexical level," as van Parreren and Schouten-van Parreren (1981) term it. That is, readers usually attribute meaning to a word based on its apparent graphophonemic similarity to familiar first language words rather than consider the greater context (Bensoussan & Laufer, 1984; Clarke & Nation, 1980; Haynes, 1984q; Palmberg, 1987; van Parreren & Schouten-van Parreren). Kern (1988), however, finds that his subjects who have been trained in strategy use guessed words from context more often than they resorted to English.

(c) Readers' guesses are frequently defined by the schemata directing their reading when they encounter the unfamiliar word (Adams, 1982; Bernhardt, 1986a, in press; Parry, 1987).

(d) Readers familiar with text content guess word meanings better than peers unfamiliar with the text topic (Adams, 1982; Palmberg, 1987).

(e) The amount of usable context varies for each unknown word; sometimes the meaning of a target word is clear, whereas another context may give no clue (Bensoussan & Laufer, 1984; Bialystok,

1983; Haynes, 1984). Of course, usefulness of context depends in part on the proportion of known words to unknown words.

(f) Learners vary in their willingness to guess and take risks; some have an affective need for more context than others (Hosenfeld et al., 1981; Perkins & Brutten, 1983).

(g) Readers with larger active vocabularies are better able to utilize available context and are better guessers than readers with smaller vocabularies (Haynes, 1984; van Parreren & Schouten-van Parreren, 1981). Bensoussan and Laufer (1984) find, on the contrary, that vocabulary size is not significant.

(h) Not yet answered is the question of whether second/foreign language reading proficiency and the ability to guess from context are related. Walker (1983) finds that they are related; Bensoussan and Laufer (1984) and Palmberg (1987) find that they are not.

Research Questions

Given the popular support for teaching students to guess word meanings from context, the experiment described below was undertaken in an effort to increase our knowledge of how language learners' reading comprehension is affected by: (1) their ability to guess or infer word meanings in context; and (2) their metacognitive awareness of the strategies they use while reading. Five research questions were asked:

(1) Does comprehension differ according to readers' ability to guess word meanings from context in authentic text? (2) Does comprehension differ according to readers' perceived use of general reading strategies? (3) Do readers provided with morphological clues in the form of original words in a text perform better on guessing word meanings than do those who have only context with which to work? (4) Do readers actually use reading strategies as they perceive they do? (5) Does the particular text influence any of these results?

Methodology

Subjects. The subjects were all University of Virginia students enrolled in French 202, the fourth semester and last course within the foreign language requirement. After eliminating the scores of subjects who had arrived late to class or who had otherwise not completed one or more sections of the experiment, we retained 216 scores. Eleven graduate teaching assistants (TAs) taught the 22 sections involved. Three other TAs and thirty students from four different sections took part in the pilot phase described below. The students received instruction following a standard four-skills approach; reading was practiced, discussed, and tested, but reading strategies were not generally stressed. These TAs received no special training in teaching second language reading.

Instruments. The instruments were administered during the tenth week of the semester. The experiment included questions designed to elicit background knowledge relevant to the texts, a text to gauge reading comprehension, one of two different texts to gauge reading strategy use (randomly distributed), and a questionnaire to discover which strategies subjects thought they used when reading French. The format of the experiment and a detailed description of the instruments appear below.

(1) Subjects answered eight multiple-choice background knowledge questions in English: six of these questions concerned World War II (the setting of the comprehension text); two other questions about World War I were included as distractors and are not included in the analysis (see Appendix A).

(2) Subjects read an unfamiliar passage (the first 615 words of Joseph Kessel's story L'Evasion, reentitled "Prisonnier de guerre" to reflect better the text content); they then returned their copies of the text and wrote in English what they remembered of it (a recall protocol). Although only the beginning of Kessel's novelette, this section of the story comes to a satisfactory conclusion. This authentic modern text was unedited except that verbs in the *passé simple* literary tense were rewritten in the more familiar *passé composé*. (see Appendix B).

(3) Before the subjects read one of two texts designed to elicit their ability to use a word-guessing strategy, they answered six multiple-choice English questions designed to gauge their background knowledge relative to the text they would read (see Appen-

dix D).

(4) The ability to guess word meanings from context depends to a certain extent on the context available (cf. Bensoussan & Laufer, 1984; Haynes, 1984; Schatz & Baldwin in first language, 1986; Walker, 1983). Thus, two different authentic articles from French magazines were distributed randomly to study how well the subjects were able to guess word meanings from unaltered context and word morphology. If the experiment results were to vary according to which text subjects read, then it would be likely that different texts and contexts affected the way the reader uses word-guessing strategies (research question #5). The two articles differed in topic, author style, and structure. Because we now know that readers find culturally distant texts difficult, it was deemed unnecessary to retest this point by including a text on an unfamiliar topic.

The two experimental texts were chosen, then, with an eye to offering familiar content in a culturally familiar or neutral setting. "Clint Eastwood sur les traces de Reagan" (from *France-Soir Magazine*, 566 words) describes Eastwood's successful campaign for the mayoralty of Carmel, California. "J'ai vécu dans la maison de l'An 2000" (from *Le Figaro Magazine*, 572 words) describes a house in Belgium run by a computer. Since our American student body contains few international students, the "Eastwood" topic was assumed to be culturally familiar. Since our students are generally computer literate, the "An 2000" topic was assumed to be accessible to our students and culturally neutral since the activities described would normally be found in any modern Western state. Neither text was edited for difficult passages, although "Eastwood" was edited for length (see Appendix E).

The rhetorical structures of the two texts are different. The author of the "Eastwood" article describes familiar subject matter in a relatively informal and disjointed style, with frequent incomplete sentences. For instance, he first remarks, "So, this is the first step toward the White House," and then presents the results of a *National Enquirer* survey demonstrating Eastwood's popularity before reaching the main point of the essay: the Carmel campaign and election. The author of "An 2000," on the other hand, describes in highly organized fashion a phenomenon usually relegated to science fiction. Introducing his topic in the first paragraph, he gives four distinct, detailed examples of what the computer can do before concluding with a summarizing quotation from the designer of the house. (For information on the pilot phase of text development, see note.)[6]

(5) In each text, twenty words that proved in the pilot phase to be unfamiliar to French 202 students were underlined and five English choices for each were offered.[7] In the *real words* treatment, original words were left in the text. Readers thus had many morphological clues available in the original text (e.g., cognates, false cognates, root words, suffixes, prefixes, words related to familiar French words, part of speech, inflections). In the *nonsense words* treatment, the original words were all replaced by the same nonsense word, *clousel*. As a result, readers of this version had only context from which to infer word meanings. The same choices were offered in the same order for each treatment (see Appendix F). To summarize, each subject read a text in one of four treatment conditions: "Eastwood" with real words; "Eastwood" with nonsense words; "An 2000" with real words; or "An 2000" with nonsense words. Results from these data provide the answer to research question #3.

(6) Subjects then answered a seventeen-item questionnaire in English about the types of reading strategies they thought best described the way they read (*perceived-strategy questionnaire*). This section provided part of the data to answer research question #2 (see Appendix H). (For details of how this instrument was generated, see note.)[8]

(7) To answer the fourth research question, *think-aloud data* about their strategy use were elicited from eight subjects randomly selected on the basis of their performance on the perceived-strategy questionnaire. Four of them had scored in the top ten percent on the questionnaire; four had scored in the bottom ten percent (for sample results, see Appendix I.)

Procedures. To administer the experiment, the eleven TAs received detailed instructions on methodology and timing and attended an orientation meeting explaining the experiment. The TAs also helped to eliminate ambiguities in the multiple-choice possibilities for unknown words in "Eastwood" and "An 2000".[9]

The think-aloud procedure with four high and four low perceived-strategy-use subjects took place a month after the experiment. These subjects were asked to read silently the article they had not already read, to talk about what they understood from the text, to explain how they understood, and to tell how they guessed meanings of unknown words. Asked to verbalize their thoughts each time they found themselves pausing in their reading, subjects first practiced with a separate text and asked any questions they had. The researcher did not interfere in the think-aloud process; after fewer verbal subjects had completed the text, however, the researcher asked them to explain in more detail how they understood certain underlined words. The tape-recorded interviews took place in the researcher's office, after classes had ended for the semester.

Data Analysis

Because of the relatively large size of the experimental group and the time necessary to score each recall protocol individually, a random sample was selected by computer (total N = 120). Thirty subjects were chosen from each of the treatment groups, text by real words and text by nonsense words.

Quantitative data. To analyze the quantitative data, *background-knowledge scores, recall scores, strategy-use scores* and *perceived-use scores* were obtained. *Background-knowledge scores* are individual subjects' correct answers to the questions about World War II (possible range 0-6) and about either Clint Eastwood or computers (possible range 0-6) (Appendices A and D). Because, as we have seen, reader schemata have a strong impact on second language reading comprehension, it was hoped that the chosen texts would be familiar to the subjects. In fact, the subjects did score well on these sections of the experiment (see Table I).

Recall scores, indicating the general reading ability of each subject, came from the English recall protocols done on the first passage, "Prisonnier de guerre." To establish these scores, the researcher reduced the passage to its basic propositions, i.e., its simplest points and ideas, and performed a propositional analysis (sample, Appendix C).[10] Each subject's recall score is his or her correct recapitulation

TABLE I

Performance on Background Knowledge Questions			
Text	Mean score (range 0-6)	Percentage	Percentage of students scoring 4, 5, or 6
World War II (N = 120)	4.217	70.3%	77.4%
"Eastwood" (N = 60)	5.167	86.1%	95%
"An 2000" (N = 60)	4.45	74.2%	86.7%

TABLE II
Ranges and Means of Strategy-Use Scores, Perceived-Use Scores, Recall Scores

	Range	Mean
Strategy-use scores	(0-20)	
Eastwood--NW (N = 30)	5-17	9.4667
Eastwood--RW (N = 30)	5-17	11.3667
An 2000--NW (N = 30)	2-17	11.50
An 2000--RW (N = 30)	3-16	11.4333
Perceived-use scores	(0-17)	
Eastwood--NW (N = 30)	7-16	11.267
Eastwood--RW (N = 30)	6-17	11.133
An 2000--NW (N = 30)	4-15	10.0
An 2000--RW (N = 30)	5-17	11.20
Total Group (N = 120)	4-17	10.90
Recall scores	(0-143)	
Eastwood--NW (N = 30)	6-42	19.30
Eastwood--RW (N = 30)	3-37	19.333
An 2000--NW (N = 30)	7-52	20.633
An 2000--RW (N = 30)	6-33	18.033
Total Group (N = 120)	3-52	19.325

(NOTE: NW = nonsense words; RW = real words)

of these propositions. Although the possible range is 0-143, it is not expected that readers will score near the top of the range because of the number of details in the text and because of the time limit on writing.

Strategy-use scores are individual subjects' correct answers to the multiple-choice questions on guessing word meanings in "Eastwood" or "An 2000" (possible range 0-20) (Appendix F).

Finally, each subject's *perceived-use score* is the total number of generally accepted strategies he or she claims to use when reading (possible range 0-17) (Appendix H).

To answer the research questions about the impact of strategy use and perceived strategy use on reading comprehension (#1 and #2), the data were analyzed using the Analysis of Variance procedure (ANOVA). This test indicates how much of the variance in scores is not due to chance. In the three-factor analysis of variance, the dependent variable was recall scores and the independent variables were: (1) strategy use by both the treatments of nonsense and real words; and (2) perceived use. Results from subjects reading each text ("Eastwood" or "An 2000") were analyzed separately. To answer the research question about the relative ease of guessing word meanings with or without morphological cues (#3), a t-test was used to compare the means of subjects working with the two treatments of each text. The probability acceptance level for both procedures was set at .05.

Qualitative data. Qualitative data analysis proved enlightening for both the question of actual reading strategy use and that of perceived strategy use (research questions #3 and #4). On the one hand, particular items from the strategy-use section of the experiment were examined to investigate why subjects sometimes performed better with the real word treatment and sometimes better with the nonsense words. The items chosen for closer scrutiny were those on which the percentage of correct answers for each treatment group differed by at least twenty percent.

To study perceived strategy use, the eight students' think-aloud protocols were transcribed; the strategies they acknowledged using were categorized according to the questionnaire used in the experiment (Appendix H). This actual strategy use was compared across the two groups of high and low perceived-strategy users, and individual students' think-aloud data were compared to their responses on the perceived-strategy questionnaire.

Results

Strategy-use effectiveness and perceived-strategy use: quantitative results. Since the range and distribution of strategy-use scores (Table II on p. 86, Table IV) and the t-test results (Table III) clearly indicate that how the subjects guessed word meanings from context did depend on which text they read, ("Eastwood" or "An 2000") or on the text treatment (real words [RW] or nonsense words [NW]), the analysis of variance was performed separately for each text group (N = 60), and text treatment was entered as a factor. Table II gives the ranges and means of strategy-use scores, perceived-use scores, and recall scores for each group as well as the ranges and means of perceived-use scores and recall scores for the entire group.

In answer to the research question about the impact of real words versus nonsense words in context, the t-test results (Table III) show a significant difference in the means of the two groups of subjects working with nonsense or real words in the "Eastwood" text but no significant difference for those reading the "An 2000" text. In some way, then, the text read made a difference in how the subjects used morphological clues and context to guess word meanings. The fact that there are no significant differences in the means on the background knowledge questions for each text or on the perceived-strategy questionnaire indicates that the groups performed comparably in these areas.

For the analysis of variance, the subjects were divided as equally as possible into low, medium, and high skill groups by means of their strategy-use and perceived-use scores (see Table IV). These level divisions were made upon consideration of two criteria: (1) decisions about what logically constituted a "high" level of strategy use (set at 65% correct) and perceived-strategy use (set at 71% correct); and (2) a need to make the high and low groups as nearly equal in size as possible, given the score distributions. Recall scores, as the dependent variable, were then categorized according to subjects' performance on the strategy-use section and on the perceived-strategy questionnaire (see Table V). The mean recall scores of all groups increase (though not in even increments) from low through medium to high levels of strategy use and perceived-

TABLE III
Differences Between the Means of Groups Working with
Nonsense Words (NW) and Real Words (RW)
(T-test, pooled variance estimate)
N = 30 for all groups

EASTWOOD

Treatment Group	Mean	S.D.	T	DF	P
Background NW	5.133	.973			
			-.32	58	.752
Background RW	5.200	.610			
Strategy-use NW	9.467	3.014			
			-2.41	58	.019*
Strategy-use RW	11.367	3.090			
Perceived-use NW	11.267	2.420			
			.19	58	.849
Perceived-use RW	11.133	2.945			

AN 2000

Treatment Group	Mean	S.D.	T	DF	P
Background NW	4.467	.973			
			.14	58	.893
Background RW	4.433	.935			
Strategy-use NW	11.50	3.785			
			.07	58	.941
Strategy-use RW	11.433	3.070			
Perceived-use NW	10.00	2.959			
			-1.58	58	.121
Perceived-use RW	11.20	2.941			

*p is significant at p < .05.

TABLE IV
Strategy-Use and Perceived-Use Scores Grouped as High, Medium, or Low

	·Score range	Percentage correct	Number of students	Percentage of students
Strategy-Use Scores (possible score: 20)				
Eastwood (N = 60)				
Low	5-8	0-40%	16	26.7%
Medium	9-12	45-60%	27	45%
High	13-17	65-85%	17	28.3%
An 2000 (N = 60)				
Low	2-8	0-40%	11	18.3%
Medium	9-12	45-65%	26	43.3%
High	13-17	65-85%	23	38.3%
Perceived-Use Scores (Total Group; N = 120) (possible score: 17)				
Low	4-9	24-53%	44	36.7%
Medium	10-11	59-65%	31	25.8%
High	12-17	71-100%	45	37.5%

(NOTE: NW = nonsense words; RW = real words)

TABLE V
Mean Recall Scores of Students in Each Group

Grouped by Text and Treatment (N = 30)

	Eastwood NW	Eastwood RW	An 2000 NW	An 2000 RW
Mean recall	19.30	19.33	20.63	18.03

Grouped by Strategy Use	Low	Medium	High
Eastwood (N = 60)			
Mean recall	16.19	16.37	26.94
Number of students	(16)	(27)	(17)
An 2000 (N = 60)			
Mean recall	16.45	18.27	21.91
Number of students	(11)	(26)	(23)

Grouped by Perceived Strategy Use			
Eastwood (N = 60)			
Mean recall	15.55	18.95	23.24
Number of students	(20)	(19)	(21)
An 2000 (N = 60)			
Mean recall	15.88	21.75	21.58
Number of students	(24)	(12)	(24)

(NOTE: NW = nonsense words; RW = real words)

strategy use, except for the "An 2000" subjects with the highest perceived-use scores; their mean recall score is slightly lower (21.58) than that of the medium perceived-use group (21.75).

The results of the three-factor analysis of variance appear in Tables VI and VII; for this ANOVA, text treatment ("real word" or "nonsense word"), strategy-use scores, and perceived-use scores acted as independent variables, and recall was the dependent variable. Since no two-way interactions were significant, they are not included on the tables. The results clearly depend on which text subjects read. That is, for the subjects who read "Eastwood," the statistics show that the variation is more than random; a significant interaction ($p < .05$) is found for recall and strategy-use and for recall and perceived-use scores. Moreover, the three-way interaction of all factors is significant at $p = .049$, implying a complex interrelationship between the text treatment that subjects received, the subjects' use of strategies, their perceived strategy use, and how much they recalled. For "An 2000," however, no interactions are statistically significant. Thus, we cannot confidently answer the first research question, Does comprehension differ according to readers' ability to guess word meanings from context? It did so for one text. The second research question, of whether comprehension differs according to readers' perceived use of general reading strategies, is answered in the affirmative for the "Eastwood" text and in the negative for the "An 2000" text.

The Pearson's correlation coefficients (Table VIII) support, for the most part, the ANOVA results. The strategy-use scores of each text read correlate differently with subjects' recall and perceived-use scores. Whereas "Eastwood" strategy-use scores correlate significantly with the subjects' recall scores but not with their perceived-use scores, the strategy-use scores of the subjects who read "An 2000" do not correlate significantly with their recall scores but do correlate with their perceived-use scores. Although this experiment was not designed to explain how text type or content affects reading comprehension, it is clear that the text does matter. The perceived-use scores and recall scores of all subjects correlate significantly, independent of the text they read; therefore, these data tend to support the hypothesis that readers who perceive that they use strategies generally considered effective actually do comprehend

TABLE VI
Three-Factor Analysis of Variance: Interactions of Strategy-Use and Perceived-Use Scores for Students who Read "Eastwood" (N = 60)

	Low Perceived-Use	Medium Perceived-Use	High Perceived-Use
Low Strategy-Use	10.50	12.87	22.50
	(2)	(8)	(6)
Medium Strategy-Use	13.54	22.50	16.38
	(13)	(6)	(8)
High Strategy-Use	22.80	24.40	31.71
	(5)	(5)	(7)

Source of variation in recall	Sum of squares	df	Mean Square	F	Signif. of F (p < .05)
Main Effects	1963.645	5	392.729	6.450	.001*
Text Treatment	77.408	1	77.408	1.271	.266
Strategy-Use	1351.911	2	675.961	11.102	.001*
Perceived-Use	484.215	2	242.107	3.976	.026*
3-way Interactions	520.281	3	173.427	2.848	.049*
(text treatment by strategy-use by perceived-use)					
Residual	2618.095	43	60.886		
Total	5774.983	59	97.881		

TABLE VII

Three-Factor Analysis of Variance: Interactions of Strategy-Use and Perceived-Use Scores for Students who Read "An 2000" (N = 60)

	Low Perceived-Use	Medium Perceived-Use	High Perceived-Use
Low Strategy-Use	14.87 (8)	15.00 (1)	23.50 (2)
Medium Strategy-Use	16.50 (10)	20.29 (7)	18.67 (9)
High Strategy-Use	16.17 (6)	26.00 (4)	23.31 (13)

Source of variation in recall	Sum of squares	df	Mean Square	F	Signif. of F (p < .05)
Main Effects	784.428	5	156.886	1.922	.110
Text Treatment	176.678	1	176.678	2.164	.149
Strategy-Use	131.842	2	65.921	.808	.453
Perceived-Use	394.414	2	197.207	2.416	.101
3-way Interactions	370.940	3	123.647	1.515	.224
(text treatment by strategy-use by perceived-use)					
Residual	3510.050	43	81.629		
Total	5235.333	59	88.734		

Refining the task. *Die Unterrichtspraxis, 19,* 178-84.

Wenden, A., & Rubin, J. (1987). *Learner strategies in language learning.* Englewood Cliffs, NJ: Prentice-Hall International.

Westphal, P. B. (1979). Coping with "la lecture." *French Review, 52* (4), 618-19.

Williams, R. (1983). Teaching the recognition of cohesive ties in reading a foreign language. *Reading in a Foreign Language, 1* (1), 35-53.

Williams, R., & Dallas, D. (1984). Aspects of vocabulary in the readability of content area L2 educational textbooks: A case study. In J. C. Alderson & A. H. Urquhart (Eds.), *Reading in a Foreign Language* (pp.199-210). New York: Longman.

Woytak, L. (1984). Reading proficiency and a psycholinguistic approach to second language reading. *Foreign Language Annals, 17,* 509-17.

Wyatt, D. H. (1984). Computer-assisted teaching and testing of reading and listening. *Foreign Language Annals, 17* (4), 393- 407.

Yorio, C. A. (1971). Some sources of reading problems for foreign language learners. *Language Learning, 21,* 107-15.

Zuck, L. V., & Zuck, J. G. (1984a). The main idea: Specialist and non-specialist judgments. In A. K. Pugh & J. M. Ulijn (Eds.), *Reading for professional purposes: Studies and practices in native and foreign languages* (pp.130-135). London: Heinemann.

Zuck, J. G., & Zuck, L. V. (1984b). Scripts: An example from newspaper texts. *Reading in a Foreign Language, 2* (1), 147- 55.

Zvetina, M. (1987). From research to pedagogy: What do L2 reading studies suggest? *Foreign Language Annals, 20,* 233-38.

TABLE VIII

Pearson's Correlation Coefficients for Recall, Background-Knowledge (for "Eastwood" or "An 2000"), Strategy-Use, and Perceived-Strategy Scores (N = 60)

	Recall	Background Knowledge	Strategy-Use	Perceived-Use
		EASTWOOD		
Recall	1.00	.1017	.4318**	.2994*
Background Knowledge	.1017	1.00	.0519	-.1336
Strategy-Use	.4318**	.0519	1.00	.1138
Perceived-Use	.2994*	-.1337	.1138	1.00
		AN 2000		
Recall	1.00	.0684	.1994	.2771*
Background Knowledge	.0684	1.00	.1698	.0827
Strategy-Use	.1994	.1698	1.00	.3341**
Perceived-Use	.2771*	0827	.3341**	1.00

(NOTE: * indicates correlations significant at p < .05;
** indicates correlations significant at p < .01.)

better than their peers who use less productive strategies (research question #2).

Strategy-use effectiveness: qualitative results. A detailed comparison of subject responses on the strategy-use section within different treatment groups certainly provokes speculation about when and how morphological clues help readers guess word meanings, although, like most qualitative data, it yields no definite answers. Whether the subjects with the original words or the subjects with the *clousel* text performed better on individual items (research question #3) seemed to depend on the text and on the specific underlined words and surrounding context. That is, the subjects reading "Eastwood" with real words had higher percentages of correct responses than their nonsense word peers on fifteen of the twenty items; for three items (#18, 22, 28), the nonsense word group did better; for two items (#15, 16), the percentages were the same. The "An 2000" subjects with real words, however, outperformed their peers on only eight items; on nine items, the nonsense word group had higher percentages (#15, 16, 17, 18, 19, 20, 22, 28, 33); on three items (#24, 31, 32), the percentages were the same.

The percentage of correct subject responses varied greatly from item to item. (See Appendix E for the texts; see Appendix F for the items.) On "Eastwood," Item #25 was answered correctly by 90% of the real word subjects and by 86.7% of the nonsense word subjects. Item #34, on the other hand, was one of the most difficult, producing scores of 33.3% for the real word subjects and only 16.7% for the nonsense word subjects. For "An 2000," the scores also ranged broadly: 16.7% for both groups for Item #32; 96.7% for the nonsense word subjects and 86.7% for the real word subjects on Item #20. A look at a few of these items gives some indication of the source of this variance. The items most successfully answered from both texts appear in an undoubtedly clear context based on schemata familiar to most American readers: Reagan's failure to capture the presidency in 1976 (#25 in "Eastwood") and the need to call the police if someone breaks into the house (#20 for "An 2000").

The poor performance on Item #34 of "Eastwood" may also be attributed to context, this time to the fact that most of the context depends, in fact, on the target word *jumeler* (literally, "to twin" or "to join"), which means here "to link two cities together as sister cities."

The previous sentences, in which the author discusses Eastwood's lack of knowledge of French and his success in the French film world, do little to enhance a reader's ability to predict Eastwood's stated desire to join Carmel to a sister city in France. The poor performance on Item #32 of "An 2000" is somewhat more difficult to explain. Subjects in both treatment conditions performed comparably on the items surrounding it: 63.3%-70% correct on Items #31 and 33 but only 16.7%-23.3% correct on Item #34. Subjects seemed to understand only vaguely this final paragraph (which tells how the computer can have the car washed or the ice melted off the slope leading to the garage). For instance, the most popular responses to Item #34 were "sprinkler" and "garage." Subjects in both groups seem to have perceived the gist without grasping the scene precisely. Clearly, type and amount of context vary greatly, even within a single text. For examples of relatively clear context, see "Eastwood" Items #15, 25, 30, and "An 2000" Items #16, 18, 19, 20, 24. Ambiguous context includes "Eastwood" Items #23, 24, 34, and "An 2000" Items #22, 28, 32, 34.

On certain items, subjects in one treatment group or the other radically outperformed their peers. Those items on which the percentage of correct responses from each group differed by at least 20% appear in Table IX. For six of these eleven items, the real word group performed better; for five of them, the nonsense word group did better.

Looking at individual items, we can see some specific reasons for score differences. Most striking, perhaps, are the occasions on which subjects, who were provided with real words, were misled by false cognates or by words that looked like other French words, and who chose a meaning that makes no sense in context. For instance, with Items #15, #18, and #22 of "An 2000," subjects who had the original word were much more likely than their nonsense word peers to choose "would charge" for *se chargerait*, "grows older" for *veille* (which resembles *vieille* ["old"]), and "prevent" for *prévenir*. True meanings are "would take care of," "watches over," and "inform."

Of course, this type of word-guessing strategy is productive for true cognates and for French words that are actually related to each other. With Item #33 of "Eastwood," for example, subjects provided with *guirlandes* chose "garlands," whereas those with *clousel*, misled

TABLE IX
Items on Which Strategy-Use Responses Differ by 20% or More
(Better performance marked with *)
EASTWOOD
Percentage of correct responses

	Real word group	Nonsense word group
Item #18	43.3%	63.3% *
Item #24	40% *	16.7%
Item #27	60% *	20%
Item #28	36.7%	66.7% *
Item #32	53.3% *	26.7%
Item #33	46.7% *	6.7%

AN 2000
Percentage of correct responses

	Real word group	Nonsense word group
Item #15	46.7%	66.7% *
Item #18	56.7%	83.3% *
Item #22	6.7%	30% *
Item #23	73.3% *	46.7%
Item #26	70% *	30%

by "red, white, and blue," ignored syntax and chose "flags" (see also the choice of "presidency" instead of "mayoralty" in "Eastwood" Item #27). In a similar situation (Item #32) *visière* ("visor") was logically misperceived as "sign" when the original word was not available. *Auprès de* (Item #18) looks enough like a preposition of location to have deceived a number of real word subjects. Subjects who had *sécheresse* (clearly related to the familiar *sec* ["dry"])in Item #26 of "An 2000" impressively outperformed the nonsense word group who were otherwise dependent on a rather complex context.

Perhaps the most obvious point of these results is that some readers are exceedingly dependent on individual words, that is, on cognates and on what they perceive as recognizable words. Misperception of words can dominate awareness of context, thus leading subjects to choose translations that are absurd when put back into context (e.g., "Eastwood" Items #18, 28, and "An 2000" Items #15, 17, 18, 22) (cf. Bernhardt, 1986a, in press, who finds that reader schemata can be more important than the actual text). Moreover, many errors indicated a certain lack of attention to syntax. Given the already complex nature of the experimental design, it was decided not to isolate subjects' ability to guess word meanings by using inflections or parts of speech. Yet, because some subjects chose syntactically wrong distractors (e.g., "Eastwood" Items #18, 28), an experiment comparing learners' performance with and without inflected target words should prove interesting. Moreover, increased research attention to detailed analysis of exactly how different aspects of reading work can only help us understand better how the reading process works and how best to develop it in our language learners.

Perceived use of strategies: qualitative results. As explained earlier, eight subjects agreed to take part in a second phase of the experiment, thinking aloud as they read. An analysis of their strategies as observed by the researcher reveals some discrepancies between what these subjects believe they do when they read and what they actually do. Table X summarizes the comparison of their self-perceived and actual strategy use, including strategies explicitly mentioned by the subjects during their think-alouds and strategies extrapolated by the researcher from subject protocols, with an emphasis on strategies related to guessing the meaning of unknown words. These strategies come from the perceived-strategy question-naire, (Appendix H). The asterisk marks effective strategies.

2. When I read French, I
   b. read part of the passage, then reread that part before going on.*
   e. read straight through the passage and do not reread.
4. When I begin reading a French passage, I
   a. don't usually consider how it relates to what I already know.
   b. think about what I know about the topic or source of the passage.*
7. When I read in French, I
   e. try to relate the points of ideas mentioned together.
8. When a French reading passage has a title, I
   a. read the title but don't consider it as I read the passage.
   b. read it first and imagine what the passage might be about.*
   [e. don't read the title. (not on the original questionnaire)]
12. If I come to a word I don't know, I
   a. skip the word and come back to it later [or do not come back to it].
   b. guess what the word might mean and go on.*
   c. guess what the word might mean and reread the sentence.*
14. To figure out what an unfamiliar word might mean, I
   a. consider what the rest of the sentence or paragraph says.*
   b. note whether the word looks like an English or other French word I know.*
   c. analyze the grammatical form of the word.*
16. When an unfamiliar word looks like an English word or other French word, I
   a. assume the unfamiliar word means the same thing as the similar word.
   b. consider whether the unfamiliar word may mean the same thing as the similar word.*
17. When I read in French, I
   a. am often confused by what I read.
   b. don't often make much sense of what I read.
   c. expect what I read to make sense.*

d. find that what I'm reading makes sense.*

A glance at Table X shows wide variation in the number and types of strategies used by subjects in both the high and low perceived-strategy-use groups. Subjects frequently used strategies different from those they had perceived as the strategies they most commonly use; AP, for example, skipped unknown words 18 times (#12a) whereas she reread sentences after guessing meanings only three times (#12c) (her perceived strategy). A comparison of the answers for Item 16a,b similarly shows that although seven of these eight subjects claim to consider context when recognizing cognates, they just as regularly assumed the English meaning immediately.

The qualitative nature of these data and the low population sample cannot yield definitive results. Yet certain tendencies provoke comment. All four high perceived-strategy users believe they expect to find or do find sense when reading French (#17d,e), whereas all the low perceived-strategy users expect to be or are confused by what they read (#17a,c). Subjects' verbalized reactions to the texts they read generally support these perceptions, except that both JS and RW looked for sense from their texts during their think-alouds. The recall scores of high perceived-strategy users are also noticeably higher than those of the low perceived-strategy users (except for that of GG). A relationship seems to exist between reading proficiency and the self-image of second language readers (cf. Hosenfeld, 1977; Kern, 1988 in second language; Peters, 1978, in first language).

A comparison of the total number of observed strategies for each subject, while again not statistically verifiable, shows the variation in strategy use from reader to reader and, perhaps, the impact of learner styles and personality on reading skill development. Both JS and RW used more observable effective reading strategies than ineffective ones, but they both described themselves as poor strategy users. The transcriptions of JS's and RW's think-alouds (Appendix I) also show that although they constantly stated that they were uncertain about the meaning of what they were reading, they did, in fact, get the gist of the articles (cf. Sarig, 1987, on the good reader/ poor reader dichotomy). TH, on the contrary, during the think-aloud procedure voiced his opinion that he checks apparent cog-

TABLE X

TABLE X: A Comparison of Students' Questionnaire Responses and Actual Strategy Use

Student (M=Male) (F=Female)	Think-Aloud Text	Recall Score	Strategy-Use Score (0-20)	Perceived-Use Score (0-17)	Total Observed Strategies (Good/Poor)
High Perceived-Strategy Users:					
EB (F)	Eastwood	25	13 (An 2000, RW)	17	17/12
AP (F)	An 2000	10	10 (Eastwood, NW)	16	60/43
DR (F)	An 2000	42	17 (Eastwood, RW)	15	25/16
TH (M)	Eastwood	24	10 (An 2000, NW)	15	9/16
Low Perceived-Strategy Users:					
RW (M)	An 2000	7	13 (Eastwood, NW)	7	29/24
JG (M)	Eastwood	7	8 (An 2000, RW)	7	0/6
JS (F)	Eastwood	8	11 (An 2000, NW)	6	41/36
GG (M)	An 2000	32	14 (Eastwood, RW)	6	2/9

TABLE X continued

TABLE X continued
Number of Times Strategies Actually Used
(+ indicates student marked this strategy on the Perceived-strategy questionnaire)
(* indicates a strategy considered effective)

High Perceived-Strategy Users:

	2b	2e	4a	4b	7e*	8a	8b*	12a	12b*	12c*	14a*	14b*	14c*	16a	16b*	17ac	17de*
EB	2		9	1		1		1	1	3	5		2		2		3
			+	+				+		+	+				+		+
AP	10		2	5	7	1		18	4	3	13	11		8	8		13
			+	+		+				+	+				+		+
DR	3		2	1	1	1		5		2	8	7	1	4	2		4
			+	+						+	+				+		+
TH	1			1	1			7			1		2	6	4	1	1
			+	+						+		+			+		+

Low Perceived-Strategy Users:

	2b	2e	4a	4b	7e*	8a	8b*	12a	12b	12c*	14a*	14b*	14c*	16a	16b*	17ac	17de*
RW	9		1		7			12		4	14	1	1		3		1
	+						+				+				+	+	
JG		1		2				2									1
				+			+								+		1
JS	5			7	3			6		8	8	6	16	2	8	7	2
				+		+						+			+	+	
CG								1			1	1		7		1	
				+								+			+	+	

nates in context; the analysis of his recall shows a clearly word-by-word translation approach to reading in which he accepts absurd interpretations of individual French words (see Appendix I). Certainly, these three subjects are misperceiving their own reading styles.

These eight subjects verbalized their strategies to very different degrees (see Appendix I). In addition, some (AP and JS, in particular) recurrently paused in their reading to detail their strategies. Others (EB and GG) commented little on their strategies, preferring to render the text into English, EB with great success, GG with very little. The difference in subject ability to verbalize thoughts must color think-aloud data results; yet if subjects are trained to verbalize strategies in order to provide more detailed data, the researcher risks altering their personal strategies through the training. For this reason, among others, it is sensible to consider think-aloud in conjunction with other research methods.

The think-aloud transcriptions also show that some of these readers repeatedly resorted to one predominant strategy, though not the same strategy for all readers. RW "read ahead" when he did not understand a word, avowedly expecting to find clues in the context to come. TH and JS depended on their memories; if they could not remember what a word meant or simply did not know it, they usually skipped it. GG skipped unfamiliar words after reading them aloud in French. These subjects showed themselves to be single-strategy users. EB and AP, conversely, are multiple-strategy users; they employed a variety of techniques to decode unfamiliar words (see their results on Items #12, 14, 16), put the meaning back into context, and then summarized the phrase or sentence in their own words before going on. They both volunteered to give the gist of the texts they had just read and showed that they understood well; yet neither their original strategy-use scores nor their original recall scores are the highest for subjects in this group.

Finally, a few generalizations about how these eight subjects read French are possible:

(1) They are more likely to look ahead at context than to review what they have already read to establish meaning (EB and AP are exceptions).

(2) They more often notice cognates and familiar-looking French

words than syntax and morphology (JS is a notable exception) (cf. Kern, 1988). Some subjects, in fact, imagine unlikely similarities: RW explained that "avertit" looked like "alert" because of the "a" and "r"; TH translated "paisibles" as "plausible" and "déplacent" as "deplace" without mentioning the senselessness of these words in context (see Appendix I). Bialystok (1983) submits that students realize the tenuousness of some hypotheses and would check their guesses in a dictionary, were one available.

(3) Their schema clearly comes into play: these subjects knew about Clint Eastwood and were able to imagine how a computer can run a household (see, especially, the transcription of AP's think-aloud protocol, Appendix I).

(4) The subjects almost never verbally predict or hypothesize about what might come next in the article.

(5) Although the subjects were asked to read silently, all of them read aloud at least some of the underlined words and other words and phrases that they found difficult. JS and RW also mentioned that they did not know how to pronounce unfamiliar words. RW, AP, and DR compared the sound of an unknown word to English in an effort to figure out its meaning (cf. Haynes' finding [1984] that the graphophonemic form of a word may have a strong impact on learners' guesses).

Discussion and Implications

This experiment, undertaken to provide more information on how students' ability to guess word meanings affects reading comprehension, offers few crystal clear results. Consequently, it generates productive questions about the role of reading strategy use in the second/foreign language reading process. Perhaps the most thought-provoking result is the surprising difference in the amount of significant interaction among the variables of text, treatment, strategy use, perceived use, and recall. The t-test, Pearson's correlation coefficients, and ANOVA, as well as the qualitative review of the strategy-use scores, show varying subject success and score interaction depending on the text read, "Eastwood" or "An 2000." Although these results do not clarify how or why, they clearly indicate that text matters in readers' comprehension. Experiments sometimes initiate more questions than they answer and provoke deeper consideration of the issues. In this case, the dissimilarities between the two texts read (different rhetorical structures, vocabulary, and contexts) clearly influence the interaction of particular reader abilities with particular textual situations (cf. Allen et al., 1988). Thus, the question of how text affects comprehension and strategy use becomes the subject of a future investigation. Furthermore, as always, this study should be replicated, with literary texts, with language learners at different levels of expertise, and in different languages.

Viewing the reading process as at least partially dependent on specific situations also implies difficulty in establishing reading proficiency norms. As we determine that neither text nor reader characteristics completely defines text readability or reader proficiency, establishing universal standards becomes problematic. More coherent research on how readers, text type, and text structure interact to bring readers to comprehension should prove valuable. Certainly, readers' success in guessing word meanings depends on text criteria as well as on reader criteria. The former include language elements affecting clarity of context, textual cohesion, and the role of the target word in establishing context; these experiment results confirm that the difficulty level of context varies a great deal, even within a single text. Reader criteria include knowledge of the words surrounding the target word, cognitive skill and willingness to take risks, appropriate schemata for the text topic and for the situation at hand, and parallels between reader and author schemata.

The think-aloud data reveal that some readers misperceive how they use reading strategies, holding false global images of themselves as readers; they voice misunderstanding while actually getting the gist of the text. These qualitative results thus support calls for paying more attention to what our students really do while reading (cf. Bernhardt, 1987b, Carrell & Eisterhold, 1983, Parry, 1987). Furthermore, one unanswered question is whether analyzing one's own reading process affects reading proficiency. Students may learn much by going beyond the think-aloud stage to analyze and evaluate their actual strategy use. (See Casanave, 1988, for an analysis of comprehension-monitoring; see Harri-Augstein and Thomas, 1984, for a "conversational approach" to analyzing learners' reading.)

Reading strategy use undoubtedly varies from reader to reader and within a single reader depending on the text and on reader purpose, enthusiasm, language proficiency, schemata, time available, and willingness to guess. Individuals often have distinctive approaches to the same text; subjects comment that they read differently when they are tired or when they know a great deal about the text topic (cf. Alderson & Urquhart, 1984; Kern, 1988; Sarig, 1987). Recognizing this variation, teachers can help students learn from each other, expand their ability to use strategies, and cultivate effective reader skills. Students need to learn how to adapt strategy use to each text at hand. They must analyze cognates as true or false; consider knowledge about setting, event, character type, text organization; predict possible text content; check interpretations of word meanings against the context; and take intelligent risks. Part II discusses these and other ideas for teaching foreign language students to understand better when they read; it offers pedagogical applications derived from the now extensive research on second and foreign language reading.

Part II

Applications and Practice

4

Helping Students Interact with Texts

Provocative second/foreign language reading theories and research are exciting to specialists and do enhance our awareness of the reading process, but they serve little practical purpose until they have a positive impact on how we teach language learners to read better. Part II of this volume, then, is intended to apply the theoretical principles and research results explained and summarized in Part I to classroom teaching. These pedagogical suggestions are designed for foreign language teachers at all levels; targeted students are first language literate, with reasonably well developed cognitive skills (see note for ESL applications).[1] Texts are assumed to be authentic, that is, written originally for native speakers of the target language.[2]

After linking established second language reading theory to practice, this chapter delineates a basic lesson plan for teaching foreign language students to use a variety of reading techniques; these derive from reading specialists' recommendations and from this author's classroom experiences with American university students reading French. High school teachers, who have been trained to use these techniques with English-speaking students of foreign languages, find the techniques to be effective. Some ideas need modification, however, for use with students of different first language backgrounds, and with those learning a non-Romance language. A practical guide is nothing more than a guide; the teacher can best adapt procedures and implement suggestions to suit teaching style and students' needs. For this reason, too, relatively few specific applications are offered.

Chapter 5 goes beyond the reading lesson to consider such related issues as choosing appropriate foreign language reading texts, (including students' self-selected reading and adaptations of textbook passages), moving from reading comprehension to literary analysis, and testing reading skill development. Again, learners are assumed to be adolescents or adults literate in their first language.

GENERAL PEDAGOGICAL PRINCIPLES

Our understanding of the second language reading process has been revolutionized in the past decade. We recognize the primary role of the reader. Foreign language reading can no longer be seen as simply the decoding of more or less unknown vocabulary and grammar. The text, of course, is still essential. Comprehension, however, truly depends on the reader's expectations as defined by his or her content and formal schemata, linguistic proficiency, first language reading skill, reading strategies, and interest and purpose in reading the text. Unique reader characteristics determine the meaning that an individual reader will create for any particular text. Unfortunately, but naturally, some foreign language learners have developed these skills less well than have their peers. Thus, teachers face the challenge of cultivating in all students the appropriate knowledge and techniques to read with as much efficiency and understanding as possible. This section touches on how each reader characteristic can be strengthened for better comprehension. The following sections describe specific classroom approaches.

Reader schemata are vital to understanding foreign language texts, but this relationship is highly problematic: i.e., authentic texts are culturally (and sometimes rhetorically) distant from learners' personal experiences. They are, at the same time, essential vehicles for introducing students to that target culture. For instance, asking an average American to read a Russian text describing the Russian Revolution from the Communist position is analogous to throwing a nonswimmer into the sea with no life preserver; yet the information in that text is fundamental to understanding Russian history. Readers need to obtain or learn how to activate pertinent background knowledge about text topic, author point of view, and, sometimes, text structure. Furnishing such an orientation before reading puts students on the right track from the beginning. With training, they can eventually utilize background knowledge on their own and learn to discover new information from the text as they read.

Although expectations and logical reasoning can help an intelligent reader to understand more of a written text than might be expected given his or her knowledge of the language, a certain level of linguistic proficiency is undoubtedly necessary to comprehension. In fact, a reader cannot activate appropriate schemata unless he or she understands enough of the text to decide which schema is needed (Carrell & Eisterhold, 1983; Hudson, 1982). The development of students' control of language is usually a primary concern of foreign language teachers and, in fact, occupies more class time than does reading. Relating language development to reading skills development is also beneficial. Work on intensive reading of short passages and an emphasis on decoding of intricate or perplexing syntax can teach students how to handle similar situations without help. General vocabulary development still assists in reading comprehension (Haynes, 1984; van Parreren & Schouten-van Parreren, 1981), whereas providing students with specific words just before they read a text seems to be of no more help than glossing these words (Davis, 1988). Below, we consider ways to help readers recognize vocabulary passively as they read.

Conflicting research results show that the relationship between first and second/foreign language reading skill is not yet clear. Certainly, individual cognitive skill development varies, and reading skill interacts intricately with language proficiency. As a result, teachers must remember that each student probably reads first language texts somewhat differently from any other student and will, therefore, take diverse approaches to foreign language texts. Although initial reading strategies normally develop in first language reading, experience has shown that they can develop equally well in foreign language reading (Hosenfeld, 1979, 1984; Kern, 1988). The "While Reading" section that follows includes ideas about reviewing students' first language reading skills with an eye to applying them to foreign language reading. Poor readers may find improvement in their first language reading after instruction in the foreign language.

Finally, learners' interest in a text and their purposes for reading it form most of the motivation they have for reading that text. Unfortunately, most foreign language reading is determined by teachers and/or by textbook authors. Their choices are based on legitimate needs: teaching target language culture, furnishing students with authentic texts suitable to their knowledge of grammar and vocabulary, or relating topics to vocabulary studied. Still, learners may have no natural interest in selected texts; and the teacher needs to kindle interest in, or at least purpose for, assigned readings by a propitious use of prereading and/or postreading. On the other hand, it may be feasible to allow students to select some of their own reading materials (see Chapter 5).

Ultimately, reading-strategy training aims not to continue helping students interpret texts acceptably, but rather to prepare them to activate relevant knowledge and productive strategies when necessary—to be independent foreign language readers. All the techniques offered here as a fundamental approach do not work for every teacher nor for every reader. The reading skill is highly individual; at different times, readers reach varied levels of development in cognitive and metacognitive skills, first language reading competence and strategy use, language knowledge, and motivation. Students react differently to teacher intervention in their reading process; they have different purposes and motivations for language study in general and for reading within it. We need to listen to our students and watch their reading process from the inside as we help them develop their skills.

A Basic Lesson Plan

So far, few textbooks treat foreign language reading as the complex activity that it is. To teach reading well, teachers must often design lesson plans for chosen texts. Although reading specialists have their own emphases, many specialists recommend reading lesson plans similar to the one outlined below.[3] To help students learn and practice skills necessary for proficient reading, this plan contains four phases: *prereading, while reading, postreading, follow-up*. The objectives of each phase are delineated in the following section and a summary is given of how the teacher can develop suitable materials for this new approach to reading. To design a useful, appropriate lesson plan, choose a reading text and ask yourself these questions:

- What is the major thrust of the text? This might be a theme, a description, a philosophical argument, a pun. What would a native reader find most important in this text? Why would a person normally read it? Such questions and answers make the text real for learners.

- What are the best strategies for understanding the main point of the text? Would it help readers most to recognize the text structure, or author point of view, or setting, or certain vocabulary items? Knowing what you did to comprehend a text prepares you to help your students.

- How can the students be brought to use the necessary strategies? Do you need to tell them which strategies to use, or can you simply point them in the right direction? Do they first need to practice any strategy in their first language? Focusing on only one or two strategies per text can be very beneficial to students who are not first language strategy users.

- Do your foreign language learners need special information to understand this text? How can you best determine what students know or best provide new information to them?

- What is the most effective way of checking on student comprehension of the main point of the text? Below (and in the references) are a number of different approaches to checking reading comprehension.

Answers to these questions guide the approach to each text. Sample ideas appear in the various sections of the reading lesson below.

Each lesson plan phase is detailed below. Although procedures are at first quite directive, they are designed to teach students how eventually to accomplish the same purpose with no teacher direction. In practice, specific elements of each phase depend on the text and on the students who read it.

PREREADING activities involve students in reading a particular text, elicit or provide appropriate background knowledge, and activate necessary schemata. The activities should provoke reader interest, create or determine reader purpose if none exists naturally, and guarantee that students begin a text "on the right foot."

WHILE READING exercises help students develop reading strategies, improve control of the foreign language, and decode problematic text passages. They may be done in class or independently.

POSTREADING exercises check students' comprehension and then lead students to a deeper analysis of the text when warranted. These exercises may take a variety of forms, as detailed below.

FOLLOW-UP activities take students beyond the particular reading text in one of two ways: by transferring skills, and by integrating reading with other language skills (Phillips, 1985). Transferable reading strategies are those that learners can assimilate and use with other texts. Integrative activities use text language and ideas in foreign language listening, speaking, and/or writing. Thus, the information and techniques learned from each reading help students in both their language skill and cognitive skill development. (See note for references to other classroom activities for each phase.[4])

Prereading

People usually have some idea about what they are about to read before they begin: *The Wall Street Journal* does not contain the same information as *The Washington Post* or *Consumer Reports*. Similarly, an experienced reader does not approach Jane Austen and Kurt Vonnegut novels in quite the same fashion. Depending on what the reader knows about the source, title, or subject matter of a text, he or she expects to find a certain content. In the real world, people read to discover what that content means: information they need, what the author has to say, how it applies to them. Too often, foreign language learners do not naturally bring such interest and intent to their reading, nor do they always expect to find meaning there, because the reading is forced upon them or because the foreign language code is unfamiliar. Working with students before and just as they begin reading a text helps them get more involved. Most prereading techniques explored below can be adapted for the class as a whole, for pairs or small groups, or as homework, depending on the text and students.

Text topic, source, author. With any text either most of the students are familiar with the text topic, source, and/or author, or they are not. In the first case, it is necessary only to elicit relevant information from the students and make certain they understand how it applies to the text at hand. For example, a selection from *Les Vacances du petit Nicolas* by Sempé and Goscinny recounts a family's summer vacation at the beach. Students who already know Sempé as a French cartoonist who pokes fun at the foibles of human nature, and Goscinny as the author of the famous *Asterix* comic books, will expect to find something funny, silly, or ridiculous in what they read, just as if they were about to read the familiar *Doonesbury* or *The Far Side*. To introduce the idea of story content, a class or small group discussion of students' vacations, holiday break plans, and/or vacation spots may serve several purposes: changing from previous activities, introducing text vocabulary for active use, generating interest in the topic, and orienting students to the reading.

To present non-fiction topics, the teacher may elicit all the related *debatable issues* that students can imagine: for example, nuclear energy, U.S. intervention, water pollution. Originally used for pre-writing, *brainstorming* and *freewriting* (in which students briefly write whatever comes to mind about a given subject) effectively apprise students of how much they know about a topic; by comparing their ideas, students broaden the scope of their thoughts. Another activity that elicits similar knowledge and reviews vocabulary directly is *semantic mapping*. It encourages students to enumerate all the words they know relating to a certain topic and then group them logically (Johnson & Pearson, 1984; applied to second language vocabulary teaching in Hague, 1987). The *source of a text* can be particularly telling, especially in the case of nonfiction: Does an article come from a left- or right-wing newspaper? In which South American country does a magazine originate?

If the text situation is familiar but somewhat unusual, the discussion might center on what normally happens in that situation: What might a person who had received a poison pen letter do? (Call the police, throw it away, tell friends, laugh about it, suspect friends.) How do theater audiences typically act? (Wait for the usher, read the program, talk quietly, watch the play.) Unusual, absurd, or ironic events in a passage thus fall immediately into perspective. In fact, less proficient students may copy the list of normal reactions or experiences and then change it, as a postreading exercise, to reflect what happens in the text.

Reviewing familiar stories can also provide context for students approaching an unknown author or text. For instance, elementary French students can easily read a version of Perrault's "Cendrillon" if they recognize it as "Cinderella." Before reading, they can recount the Cinderella story in the foreign language, decide which listed events or characters belong in the story, or identify pictured characters. Previewing with a familiar story is particularly advantageous for culturally distant texts. Bernard Dadié's "Le Pagne noir," from the Ivory Coast, is about a wicked stepmother who gives her stepdaughter an impossible task; the daughter is helped by her mother's spirit. Since this story has a Cinderella theme but differs from the fairy tale in details, students may well compare the African story to the one they know. When reading authors who flavor their writing with local color and dialect, alerting students to the framework of familiar plot and themes helps them approach an apparently foreign story more positively and more meaningfully.

Still, the teacher must *provide necessary background information* for texts from unfamiliar cultural backgrounds: folklore, historical settings, essays about social and political systems, even advertisements (see note for references to other schemata-activating exercises[5]). If the textbook introduces the reading informatively (without divulging the ending or main point and thus nullifying any need to read the text), students may gain requisite facts from it. If not, the teacher can give basic essential information by means of *lecture, maps, charts, timetables,* and, for major reading projects, *student reports.* To monitor student comprehension and to encourage participation, teachers should use lectures and reports that are short and that offer opportunities for student-teacher interaction. Students learn better when they contribute whatever information they can.

Illustrations and titles. Drawings, *photographs, figures, tables, charts, graphs, statistics* are eminently valuable for prereading. Some titles are equally useful, but others are less intuitively appealing. Suggestions given here apply to both titles and illustrations. Although the title of a well written text is normally descriptive, informative, or provocative, and illustrations exist to clarify the text content, some foreign language learners skip the title and ignore illustrations (Hosenfeld *et al.,* 1981). Readers who do look at illustrations generally find them interesting. Teachers can catch students' attention, capitalize on natural curiosity, and encourage prediction by asking how the illustrations and/or title might relate to the text. With a carefully illustrated story, they can ascertain the characters, the period, and major events (cf. Omaggio, 1979). When they realize

117

that titles and illustrations can indicate text direction and define a context in which to search for meaning, students see the value of considering illustration and title as part of the text.

Text structure. As research on formal schemata shows, readers' familiarity with standard text structures and their ability to recognize and follow structure help them comprehend. Teachers may need at first to identify text structure for beginning or weaker readers; later, students should learn to recognize it on their own. The teacher will not always be there to lead them; moreover, too much direction can destroy reader interest. To review or introduce text structures, the teacher can furnish a *summary of structure types* to which students may refer (in their first or foreign language, as necessary). Such a summary, drawn from the author's experience and written to the student, appears in Appendix J and introduces these logical organizations: chronological sequence, general statements supported by examples, main ideas and supporting details, descriptions, comparisons and/or contrasts, cause and effect relationships, arguments and counter-arguments. Meyer, 1975, 1979, cites five basic types of organization for expository prose: collection, description, causation, problem/solution, comparison. (See Mackay & Mountford, 1979, on scientific and technological English text structure.) Sample function words alerting readers to a particular structure should be added or elicited from the students in the foreign language.

To apply the information reviewed in Appendix J, students read a text ordered by a recognizable structure and underline or list key function words in order to discover the text structure. Postreading work might, if relevant, have them analyze why the author chose that particular structure. Students can then transfer what they have practiced to another text with the same structure or to one with the same structure together with a new structure.

Simple text patterns, like chronology or flashbacks, can also link prereading to the *while reading* phase. After reading a list of story events in mixed order, students know basic facts and probably the major characters. After making certain that students understand this list, the teacher asks them to read the story with an eye toward numbering (or relisting) the events in the correct order. This first step is especially helpful for relatively inexperienced readers because the list of episodes introduces the plot in simple sentences. Learners know what to look for and what to expect. When they find a fact listed, they know they are understanding correctly. Asking students to reorder the happenings forces them to review what they have read and leads them to summarize the plot. As a variation, the teacher furnishes questions about story incidents rather than statements, for example asking, "Who partied late the night before?" Because the questions monitor comprehension within a coherent context, even the least adept students have something to discuss. If the story contains flashbacks, the teacher may tell students about the flashback(s) and ask that the story be retold with the actual sequence of actions, that the students reestablish the true chronology. In class, students compare the order of the events as they are written in the text and the order in which they really happened.

Text genre. Many text genres are well-established forms with predictable structures and, sometimes, predictable content. Literary genres include, for example, detective stories, epistolary novels, elegiac poetry, suspense stories, science fiction, dialogues, fables. Some nonfiction genres are especially well-defined: newspaper articles, editorials, research reports, *Reader's Digest* articles, philo-sophical treatises, biographies. Once students perceive that a text belongs to a certain familiar genre, many unfamiliar words and even sentence structures may become less difficult. Since first language readers generally know (from source, title, or illustrations) the genre of a text they are about to read, it is fair to enlighten foreign language students before they begin reading and to ask what they know about that genre.

The *fairy tale genre,* popular and easy to use, exemplifies the approach (see also Byrnes & Fink, 1985). Before reading, students identify and define the characteristics of a fairy tale. By discussing the following questions, students enter into dialogue that helps to define these literary characteristics.

**What sort of characters typically appear in fairy tales? (good guys, bad guys, animals, incarnations of character traits [laziness, cleverness, meanness])

**What is the hero or heroine usually like? (honest, pure, strong,

119

handsome/beautiful)

**How are the events ordered? (chronologically)

**Are the events closely tied to reality? (no, magic and the super-natural)

**How does a fairy tale end? (happily)

After reading, students may cite characteristics from the story, summarize story chronology, or draw parallels with known fairy tales.

Of course, some students may not be familiar with even a common genre, and many students may never have encountered those more esoteric or those not extant in their native culture. They can certainly learn about them in the foreign language, however, if the teacher provides several texts of one genre and asks questions like those listed above.

Skimming and scanning. During the prereading phase, students may begin reading the text to discover the structure, pinpoint main characters, define the setting or period, determine the author's tone or point of view, predict future directions, and so on. The teacher decides what will most help students get a strong grasp on the text. Skimming and scanning require students to interact with the text that they are to read (see Phillips, 1984, 1985); teacher questions and student answers establish basic facts about the text.

Reassured by support from the teacher--a competent foreign language user--students leave the classroom with a solid base from which to continue their reading. Much student attention to the dictionary seems to come from fear of moving in the wrong direction by misinterpreting a word. Security about basic text information or direction helps reduce that dependence.

Skimming the beginning of a text may serve several purposes: to confirm student predictions from the title and/or illustrations, to activate appropriate schemata as students recognize text content and/or structure, to absorb students in the reading by showing them that it is humorous, suspenseful, interesting. Skimming involves reading as quickly as possible to get the gist of a text or part of a text. Students should know—or learn—that they need to read the title, consider the format, and glance relatively quickly through the text, looking most closely at the topic sentence of each paragraph to determine the author's main ideas. In class, the teacher provides immediate skimming objectives with questions on an overhead projector or the board: What is the structure? (narrative? essay? dialogue?) How do you know? (for dialogue: dashes or quotation marks indicating change of speaker, use of the second person, layout on the page) What is the conflict? What is the tone? When responding, students teach each other as those who answer the questions explain to the others how they knew.

If the teacher reads aloud, having students follow silently in their texts, they must skim quickly to keep up. This technique also ensures that most students finish at the same time. Alternatively, students read silently, raising their hands when finished or when ready to answer a question. This second format is clearly closer to real life reading; with it, however, some students are more likely to read too slowly and carefully or to daydream. In the final analysis, the goal is to encourage students to read swiftly for the stated purpose(s), not to look up words, and to ignore details temporarily; a combination of these two techniques may prove most serviceable.

Scanning is common in real world reading. We scan headlines or a magazine table of contents for interesting articles or those on a certain subject; we scan cookbooks for an exciting dessert; we scan classified ads for the right used car. Scanning involves reading a text or part of a text rapidly in order to find specific pieces of information. First deciding what the necessary information will look like (a date? a place? an explanation?), the reader then searches for only that sort of material. After finding a likely looking fact, the reader reads carefully the sentences surrounding it to decide whether it answers his or her need.

To help students practice scanning in a foreign language, the teacher again asks questions about information essential to the text or relevant to the students. At first, students should practice scanning with only short passages (e.g., the lead paragraph of a newspaper article); simple in one's first language, scanning can prove difficult in a foreign language. In fact, some students may find it worthwhile to practice scanning in the first language and then transfer their skill. Scanning helps students not only to glean essential information quickly but also to comprehend a text in general. Relating information gathered during scanning to predictions from the title or first paragraph helps students learn how to verify their predictions and inferences and enhances their reliance on those predictions. Insistence on scanning also reduces students' dependence on word for word translation.

Developing vocabulary. Since words certainly carry much of the meaning in a text, readers who do not have an adequate vocabulary for a particular text have difficulty skimming, scanning, or confirming predictions based on schemata. This difficulty is aggravated in foreign language reading because of the many cross-cultural aspects of vocabulary (Barnitz, 1985). For instance, although we do translate words from one language to another, they can rarely carry their cultural connotations with their translations. The French word *pain* conjures up different images than does the English word *bread.* Languages do not all have the same degree of specificity for specific words. The English term love must encompass the separate meanings of the Greek agape, philia, and eros. Expressions usually carry at least some cultural allusion. For example, "The Indians are on the warpath," may simply mean that the children are rowdy (Barnitz, 1985).

Thus, vocabulary development needs to be semantically based and may be considered an ongoing prereading activity, whereas introducing pertinent vocabulary just before reading a text may not be effective (Hudson, 1982; Johnson, 1982; Pak, 1986). Numerous vocabulary development techniques appear in the literature (see Chapter 2, note 2 for references). Johnson (1983) and Johnson and Pearson (1984) offer three first language variations of semantically oriented vocabulary activities: semantic associations, semantic mapping, and semantic feature analysis (also recommended for second language learning by Barnitz, 1985, and Hague, 1987). The *semantic associations* technique has students brainstorm all the words related to a text context or content area. The teacher and students then discuss the words, especially the new words, and organize them in some logical fashion. *Semantic mapping* is similar, but asks students to brainstorm words related to a concept crucial to the text

(Hague, 1987). The teacher and students organize these words into a visual map, grouping together those that relate to the same aspects of the concept (e.g., people at a bullfight, actions of the bullfighter, emotions aroused). In both of these activities, students can better learn how words compare with each other. Finally, the *semantic feature analysis* technique helps students focus in more detail on the distinctions between closely related words as they examine precisely what each word entails. Johnson's (1983) example analyzes tools (hammer, saw, scissors, etc.) to see which have certain attributes (e.g., wood, cloth, handle) and perform certain chores (e.g., pound, cut). Such activities help students perceive the uniqueness of most words.

Learning words in context has proven to be more effective than simply looking them up in the dictionary (Gipe, 1979). Thus, many *while reading* activities help students improve their knowledge of the foreign language lexicon. Because vocabularies vary among individuals, students should keep a record of useful words found while reading.

In conclusion. The choice of prereading activities depends on the text itself. Some texts closely follow a recognizable genre pattern or familiar story line; some have a particularly appropriate title or helpful illustrations; some require more introduction and background explanation than others; some have an absurd or ironic twist. Previewing a text with students should arouse their interest and help them approach reading more meaningfully and purposefully as the discussion compels them to think about the situation or points raised in a text. The prereading phase helps students define selection criteria for the central theme of a story or the major argument of an essay and improves their comprehension in several ways. First, students review or learn any background information and vocabulary needed to activate useful schemata. Secure in their understanding of the text beginning, at least, students can then recognize textual landmarks as they meet them. Finally, confident students are more likely to take risks in guessing word meanings and anticipating text content. They will be better strategy users while they read.

While Reading

Traditionally, foreign language learners have been left to read texts on their own, with little or no prereading orientation and no attention paid to their reading process. Yet, it is precisely while reading that they may lose the thread because of a word or verb tense misinterpreted. To intervene in a reader's process, we can ask questions about text segments, offer hints to aid comprehension, or have the reader talk about what he or she is thinking (see also Melendez & Pritchard, 1985). We do not yet know whether such intervention is beneficial or detrimental to a reader's comprehension and improvement in reading skill, but like most aspects of reading, the effects of intervention probably vary according to the individual. Certainly, those who read well in a foreign language do not need intervention. On the other hand, many students appreciate receiving help on strategy development both before and while they read in French (Barnett, 1988c; Kern, 1988). Depending on the text, students, and exercise, some strategy practice works best during class and some while students work independently.

Reading strategy practice and linguistic development form the core of the *while reading* phase. Proficient readers use a combination of reading strategies (Kern, 1988; Sarig, 1987); therefore, after first practicing discrete (single) strategies, students need to use strategies in conjunction with each other (synthetic strategy use). For this reason, it is helpful to pinpoint for students one or two pertinent strategies for each text studied and to help them practice those strategies directly. Initial practice in the first language may be valuable. Linked very closely with strategy use is students' linguistic proficiency. As we know, readers cannot use context to guess word meanings unless they already know many words in that context (see Jarvis, 1979); they cannot predict text direction unless they understand how adverbs and conjunctions function; they cannot follow references unless they perceive the relationship between relative pronouns and antecedents. Thus, working with reading strategies involves a clarification of foreign language vocabulary and grammar.

Recognizing individual reading processes. It is difficult but essential to realize and to remember that individuals have unique reading styles. For example, in pedagogical workshops, French and

Spanish high school teachers guessing the meanings of made-up words in Burgess' *A Clockwork Orange* (Phillips, 1985) vary greatly in their knowledge of Russian and their ability to apply it to morphology, in their experience with British culture, and in their willingness to risk guessing. Even in these rather homogeneous groups, background knowledge, schema-building capability, language development, cognitive skill development, strategy use, confidence, and the capacity for taking risks—in fact, the reading processes—are different. How can we handle at least equally wide disparities in the classroom?

First, as students work with reading strategies in class, they soon reveal their individual competencies; the more proficient in each case help those less expert, if only as models. The teacher can also note for individual students, whether formally or informally, their relative strengths and weaknesses. The teacher who can read with students individually will find the "Interviewer Guide for Reading Strategies" defined by Hosenfeld et al., 1981 (Figure 9) exceptionally helpful. Even without such scheduling luxury, however, the teacher who brings reading into the classroom can recognize individuals' strategy use. Those students, who realize in which ways they read effectively and where they can improve, are more likely to refine their reading skills where possible. The teacher may actually designate certain *while reading* exercises for students' specific problems.

Many teachable strategies for guessing word meanings are summarized in manageable form in Hosenfeld et al.'s (1981) "Interviewer Guide for Reading Strategies" (Figure 9). (See also Kern, 1988; Phillips, 1984, 1985; Swaffar, 1988b.) Grellet (1981) thoroughly explains and offers English practice with numerous reading skills and strategies, such as guessing word meanings through context and word formation, following reference words, predicting, and analyzing text organization. Although it lacks an index, this handbook contains a multitude of relevant exercise types. Meyer and Tetrault (1986) suggest using cloze passages to teach such strategies as predicting from knowledge of the world and the text, inferring content words, and analyzing syntax. Teachers who read French can find other exciting ideas in Capelle and Grellet (1979-1981). The sample activities below help students guess word meanings, acquire vocabulary, consider syntax and sentence structure, predict text content, read to learn new information, and use dictionaries efficiently.

Guessing word meanings. As was shown in Chapter 3, readers guess word meanings through a complex combination of context, background knowledge, and morphology (word families, cognates, word formation). To teach word guessing techniques, the teacher may present a detailed lesson context (cf. Hosenfeld et al., 1981), introduce clear-cut first language examples, or work only in the foreign language, using samples from assigned texts. (Although some current foreign language textbooks still handicap teachers by glossing all unfamiliar words, most students are willing to cover the glosses if told why.) By practicing word guessing with the class as a whole, the teacher can make several points:

(1) If there is adequate context, it is better to guess the meanings of unknown words than to reach immediately for a dictionary.

(2) Not all words are worth guessing (Lee, 1988a). Students begin to learn which words are minimally important to text meaning by analyzing many in class.

(3) Several routes to determining word meanings are available: context (including illustrations), cognates with words in other languages, the relationship of a word to familiar foreign language words, and word formation rules like those related to prefixes and suffixes (see below).

(4) It is vital to check the supposed meaning of a word against available context to see if it makes sense.

(5) Not all words can be guessed from context. Guesses can be logical but wrong (i.e., based on valid evidence that simply points in the wrong direction) and, also, poor but right (e.g., based on a false assumption but coincidentally correct). (See Hosenfeld et al., 1981).

(6) It is not always necessary to know the precise meaning of a word in order to get the gist of a passage.

At first, the teacher usually needs to direct students' guessing. To encourage guessing, the teacher has students write each guess, spot-checks their efforts, and gives credit simply for guessing. With this technique, overly cautious students become more willing to guess and less dependent on the "right answer." Calling quickly for a number of guesses, the teacher accepts all as legitimate without evaluating them immediately; guessing thus becomes more appealing. The teacher then asks why students guessed as they did. In answering, students express their thought sequence and show less proficient readers how to use clues. This discussion may take place in the first or foreign language (if the students have a common first language), depending on their level of foreign language proficiency.

Written word-guessing exercises can also help students while they read. To create these exercises, the teacher underlines or has students underline in a text words they probably do not know; the students then read to deduce what these words mean. As an option, the teacher may note relevant context clues and ask students to explain their guesses. Of course, students should read every text at least twice; to guess individual word meanings and also comprehend a text as an entity, they must read a text more than once. Individual readers can choose either of these techniques:

(1) The student quickly reads the entire text, or several paragraphs, to understand generally what is going on, checking vocabulary in a dictionary only when confused. After each quick reading, the reader rereads more carefully, guessing word meanings. During a final rereading, he or she expects to understand more and notes for clarification any passages that are still perplexing.

(2) The student reads the selection carefully once, guessing word meanings. The second time, he or she reads more quickly and concentrates on the central structure or major points of the text. During a final rereading, the reader puts it all together, also noting any confusing passages. Certainly, not all students work intensively and thoroughly. Yet if we do not recommend serious reading, few will achieve it on their own.

Training in using *word formation clues* includes specific practice in recognizing cognates, foreign language word families, inherent meanings of some prefixes and suffixes, and functions of compound words in the foreign language. For simple *cognate practice*, students underline cognates in a short text and guess their meanings. After demonstrating that they understand the concept of cognates and can recognize them, students read a text containing both false and true cognates, learning how to fit imagined meaning into context before accepting it. *Word families* are best studied in context, too, where differences in form and meaning between nouns, adjectives, and verbs are clear. Practice with texts includes finding words in the same family or those related to familiar words, marking their parts of speech, and comparing their meanings.

A list of common forms and meanings helps students learn how *prefixes* affect root word meanings. Since the meanings of many Indo-European prefixes are comparable, Appendix K lists basic English prefixes, standard meanings, and examples. Students can notice how the spelling of a prefix depends to a certain extent on the letters following it. For example, the original *cum* changes to *cor-* in correspondent (cor- / respond / -ent), which may be loosely translated as a person who responds (answers, talks, communicates) *with* someone else. *Suffixes* sometimes indicate word form; English words ending in *-ly* are normally adverbs; those ending in *-able* or *-ible* are probably adjectives. The relative paucity of widely applicable morphological rules unfortunately makes it difficult to generalize; repeated practice with available cases can, however, help students discern basic patterns.

Considering syntax and sentence structure. Beyond morphology, the efficient reader uses syntax and sentence structure to predict oncoming text. For example, *but* signals contrast; *consequently* signals a result. Other useful *function words* appear in Appendix J as cues to text structures. (See note for other ideas about discourse markers in reading.[6]) Obviously essential to comprehension and textual cohesion, function words are rarely cognates or related in form to other words and thus are best learned in context. Seeing such words contextualized by categories (e.g., words indicating contrast, words signalling a result, words explaining causes), students will eventually understand them spontaneously, as they do first language function words. They can also learn the difference between comparable, but not synonymous, expressions (e.g., *because* versus *because of* or *contrarily* versus *in contrast*). While reading, students underline or list all of a certain type of word, relating function words to text structures and predicting logical conclusions. For example:

Mr. Whipple is always optimistic; *in contrast*, his brother ...

a) doesn't like him.

b) is completely happy.

c) looks on the dark side.

Syntax also frequently determines the meaning of words as they are used in a sentence. For instance, *draft* can mean *draw* (verb), *draw up* (verb), *working* (adjective, as in *draft horse*), *call to military service* (noun or verb), and *beer* (adjective used as noun). Knowing how *draft* is used in a particular sentence eliminates some of these choices. Thus, although vocabulary is of paramount importance, recognizing the grammatical function of an unknown word may help students understand it. Students can practice discerning from context meanings and functions of problematic words. They recognize false cognates, words with multiple meanings, and new words related to familiar words. When students must decide word function, they rarely make an otherwise common error of assigning the word the first translation that occurs to them, and then altering the syntax to correspond to that meaning.

Finally, syntax can be troublesome, especially with regard to *reference words* (e.g., relative pronouns, demonstrative adjectives and pronouns, object pronouns, possessive adjectives). How learners manage reference words depends to a certain extent on their first and foreign languages. Foreign language reference words might be syntactically difficult, might encourage erroneous first language transfer, or might be skipped as unimportant. Too many American students seem, in fact, unaware of how some reference words function in English; in the foreign language, they tend to disregard these small, apparently meaningless words. To analyze and improve students' capacity to follow reference words, the teacher asks students to find the word or idea to which each underlined reference word refers (for other suggestions, see Grellet, 1981; Williams, 1983).

Depending, too, on how students' first and foreign languages compare, the teacher may need to explain the difference between *anaphora*, reference to something preceding the reference word, and *cataphora*, reference to something following the reference word. In the following excerpt, "it" (referring to "to have to go to the Poor Farm") is an example of cataphora; "his," "there," and "This" are anaphoral:

> *It* was humiliating, degrading, and shameful to have to go to the Poor Farm, and any child in the county would rather die than have a relative of *his* wind up *there*. *This* contributed to making Mr. Lum Thornton as fascinating and puzzling as the revolving barber pole.

(From Ferrol Sams, *Run With the Horsemen*, 1982, p. 75)

Little research has been done on the relative difficulty of these two types of reference; Barnett (1988a) finds virtually no difference in American students' ability to identify in French texts antecedents for either anaphora or cataphora.

Predicting text content. Further research would also help discover why many students predict text content less frequently than they use other reading strategies. Although first language readers normally have expectations about forthcoming text content, many foreign language learners cannot formulate predictions even when asked to do so. Several explanations are possible. Some students seem not to expect foreign language texts to make sense; many do not instinctively read titles or authors' names or think about illustrations; other students may be so uninterested as not to care what a text might say. Prediction requires regarding a text as a whole rather than as individual words and sentences; to predict, a reader must be confident about what he or she has understood so far. Whatever the problem, teachers need to encourage learners to predict text content and direction; otherwise, readers can rise neither to the efficient reading defined by models of interactive text processing nor to cultural or literary analysis.

During the prereading phase, students often predict text content by considering text source, illustrations, and title, by skimming, by reviewing pertinent schemata, and so on. For some texts, readers can also predict text development while reading. In demonstration, let us consider first a fictional text, "The Black Cat" by Edgar Allan Poe, and then a standard nonfiction form, the classified ad (see also Adamson, 1980; Pakenham, 1984).

Before beginning "The Black Cat," readers might well have certain expectations based on their knowledge of Poe as a creator of suspense and terror. Or they scrutinize the title: Could this be an animal story? a fable? a story about witches or black magic? a superstition? (These possibilities involve, of course, cultural awareness of black cats as a bad luck omen.)

As always, Poe sets the tone from his first words: "For the most wild yet most homely narrative which I am about to pen, I neither expect nor solicit belief." Such a statement is rife with possibilities and foreshadowings, and students again learn from each other if the teacher encourages brainstorming about this sentence. To continue students' predicting while reading, the teacher asks them to stop at specified points during their first reading to imagine what might happen next or why Poe wrote what he did. Such an exercise is easy to create. The teacher notes when first reading a new text where he or she naturally stops to predict future occurrences against which to check subsequent reading. In "The Black Cat," for instance, the narrator's contrast between animals' devotion and man's "paltry friendship" hints, as early as paragraph 2, that an animal will repudiate him. In the middle of the story, his growing dislike for the cat announces some dreadful fate for the cat. Finally, the narrator's extreme joy at the second cat's disappearance prompts the thoughtful reader to prophesy some momentous reappearance. The teacher may elicit students' predictions by simply marking where they would be likely or by noting clues in the text. As a variation, the teacher assigns only part of a text for the next class; students write their own ending or imagine ensuing events. Comparing their answers with those of classmates, students stretch their imaginations.

Working with classified ads or other standard text forms, students perceive how knowledge of text format and content enables them to understand more than actual words say. Knowing the category of a particular advertisement, a reader expects to be offered an apartment to rent, a used car to buy, or an interesting person to meet. A prereading conversation can define identifying characteristics of certain categories; students then use those characteristics to analyze ads. Compare these two ads:

PLYMOUTH '78, Station Wagon. Runs great. Air. Must sell. 973-2473.

32 yr. young female. Sense of humor, independent, self- sufficient has a variety of likes seeks male of intellectual quality, down to earth, 32-42 for sharing healthy relationship (music, movies, etc.). 978-4374, message.

To the reader who recognizes a used car ad, the mysterious single word "air" makes perfect sense; the reader who knows this ad appeared in July might even have predicted its inclusion. The run-on sentence of the second advertisement will not puzzle a reader who comprehends the vocabulary and is familiar with personal ads. Working as a class or in small groups, students categorize different texts, explaining their decisions. If they then rewrite ads in standard prose, they are expressing predictions they made while reading. When language learners can predict spontaneously, they have learned to expect and search for meaning in a foreign language text.

Reading for information. Frequently, even in elementary courses, students read foreign language texts in order to learn more about the target culture or history. Although clearly practical, reading for information brings its own difficulties: unknown terms, cultural allusions, and sometimes unfamiliar text structure. As Dubin (1986) notes, a useful way to understand such texts can be the SQ3R approach formulated by Robinson (1962): survey, question, read, recite, review.

As Robinson explains, the student spends a minute *surveying* a chapter by glancing over the headings and by reading the final summary paragraph, if possible. Next, the student turns the first heading into a *question*, thus eliciting useful background knowledge and creating a purpose in reading. When *reading*, the student searches actively for the answer to the question. After reading each section, the student *recites* the answer to the question, giving an example and perhaps writing cue phrases in outline form. The student who cannot recite the answer is encouraged to read the section again. Each text section is treated in the same manner. Finally, the student *reviews* the notes of main points and checks memory of them by reciting the major ideas under each heading without reading the notes. With foreign language texts, students should note phrases or sections which are linguistically or culturally confusing. The teacher may, of course, choose to clarify these during the prereading phase.

Using the dictionary. Efficient dictionary use is a strategy in itself and crucial to reading with understanding. Students need to know when to use a dictionary (and which kind) and how to use it. Readers should check a dictionary when an important word or phrase is not clear from context, but foreign language readers routinely have difficulty deciding which words are essential. As the think-aloud results from the experiment on guessing word meanings show, some students demand the exact meaning of every word, others accept the first meaning that comes to mind, still others skip all unknown words, and the rest combine these qualities in different measure.

To encourage most students to guess when reasonable and to resort to a dictionary when expedient, the teacher reads several passages with them, discussing whether each unknown quantity is indispensable to an acceptable understanding. Sometimes part of speech loosely indicates the importance of a word. Nouns and verbs usually carry basic meaning; descriptive adjectives and adverbs are normally less critical to a global understanding, although they may signify a change in tone or point of view. Function words, like conjunctions, prepositions, and some adverbs, may explain key relationships. As a basic policy, a reader who is perplexed after two or three readings should check some words in a dictionary.

Having decided to examine a dictionary, a reader must know how to find the best translation quickly. To practice, students work with reading passage context to check word meanings, identifying parts of speech and confirming suspected meanings in context. Students may also verify translations in the first-language section of a bilingual dictionary to see how context determines word meaning. Of course, using a dictionary written entirely in the foreign language is preferable for students with adequate language facility. Beginning language learners are frustrated by chasing parts of a definition throughout a dictionary, but they can eventually be trained to use a monolingual dictionary. First checking words in a bilingual dictionary, students confirm suspected meanings in a monolingual dictionary where they confront sometimes wordy and technical definitions with the expectations provided by the bilingual dictionary. Marking dictionary words as they are looked up helps many language learners increase their vocabulary as a corollary to their reading.

In conclusion. Helping students employ strategies while reading can be difficult because individual students control and need different strategies. Still, the teacher can pinpoint valuable strategies, explain which strategies individuals most need to practice, and offer concrete exercises. Applying specific strategies to each text enables students to master discrete strategy use before attempting to synthesize strategies for effective reading. Considering a number of reading strategies at once can be overwhelming, but the teacher's coupling of appropriate strategies with texts both enhances students' capacity for understanding and gives each strategy a logical field of play. Once students become aware of the complex nature of reading, however, they become enthusiastic about improving their strategies.

Postreading

After reading, teacher and students ascertain how well the text was comprehended. Since traditional comprehension checks generally focus on myriad text details, many students learn to answer not by understanding the text well but by looking progressively through a text, following the questions as they go. Phillips (1985) shows how learners can answer comprehension questions without processing meaning:

Text:

The gloopy malchicks scatted razdrazily to the mesto.

Sample questions and answers:

What is the sentence about? (malchicks)
What are they like? (They are gloopy.)
Where did they go? (to the mesto)

Moreover, such questions chronically ask about inconsequential details a native reader would not normally remember. Comprehension questions leading to a blow by blow retelling of a story or article may provide good oral practice, but they do little to verify true comprehension, and they inherently inform learners that foreign language texts are not very meaningful.

The postreading phase of this lesson plan has, instead, real world objectives. The type and amount of comprehension required depends upon what a native reader would gain from understanding text facts and from making inferences. Evaluating what they read, educated native readers can justify their opinions. In addition, adequate reader comprehension should proceed, as much as possible, from productive application of pertinent reading strategies. For instance, to discuss a story for which they predicted future happenings, small groups of students compare their predictions with actual story events. In this way, students see that their predictions are important; they summarize main story actions, and they resolve misunderstandings in consultation with their peers.

Exercise types. To establish realistic objectives, the teacher must read each text the first time as a native speaker would, imagining in what context and with what objectives the text would normally be read. Different texts demand different reading goals. One reads a newspaper article to find out the facts; the classified ads to see what is for sale or to search for something needed; an essay to understand a different point of view or to expand one's horizons; a short story to be amused, to meet interesting characters, and/or to gain insight on life; a bus schedule to see what time a bus will leave or arrive. After that first reading, the teacher notes what has been remembered from the text, why the text is worth reading, and the comprehension strategies used. The postreading phase results from these decisions.

Here are a few sample activities to match text types listed above:

- Newspaper article: Students list the facts or complete a chart or questionnaire with the facts.

- Classified ads: Students decide which apartments they will call about and tell why. Or, they look for the advertisement that best suits the teacher's need for a used car.

- Essay: Students decide which on a list of statements best expresses the author's point of view. Students with better language proficiency summarize the author's points.

- Short story: Students identify main characters from descriptions given or describe the characters. If story theme is most important, students first answer questions designed to illuminate the theme. Students are asked about the nature of the misunderstanding between the two main characters. "What does each of the characters want to do, and what finally happens?" "Who did the heroic deeds, and who received credit for them?"

- Bus schedule: Students give necessary information. They answer questions such as, "When does the San Francisco bus leave?"; "When does it arrive?"; "Does one need to take a lunch?"; "What is the fare?"

Normally, students write their answers to postreading exercises. They may then refer to their notes for the discussion (which may take place days after they read a text), and the teacher has the option of collecting assignments for individual checking or correction.

Appropriate strategies practiced with each text help students comprehend necessary information:

- Newspaper article: scanning, using text structure

- Classified ad: using background knowledge, predicting, scanning, guessing word meanings

- Essay: predicting, following text cohesion, guessing word meanings

- Short story: predicting, following text cohesion

- Bus schedule: scanning, using background knowledge

Grellet (1981) offers probably the most complete compendium of comprehension exercise types; she also explains the benefits of each exercise, links it to a reading strategy, and demonstrates it with English texts. An attempt to duplicate her efforts would be redundant and futile, but a list of her exercise types reveals the variety of activities possible and may generate new approaches. Figure 10 parallels Grellet's order of exercises.

To expand the usefulness of her volume, Grellet defines and illustrates 25 question types as used for reading comprehension, including such standards as multiple-choice and sentence completion, as well as newer methods such as inferring what happened before the text began and deciding whether characters might have made an imaginary statement. Experience working with students tackling innovative comprehension questions has shown that, as long as directions are clear and expectations reasonable, such queries interest students in extracting significant information. As a result of their imaginative interaction with a text, students feel more confident about what they have understood and are more willing to participate in class discussions.

From comprehension to analysis. During class, students receive feedback on postreading activities and discover in general how well they have understood the text. Since simply "going over" questions and correct responses can be boring, varying the formats is advisable. Of course, when a text is relatively difficult or contains vital chronology, facts, or issues, then a review of students' answers is indispensable. Asking students to compare their ideas in pairs or small groups and to summarize discrepancies is especially useful when the reading purpose is to make a decision based on text information. When a text is relatively simple, focussing on one or two major points during class (and perhaps individually checking students' performance on all questions) is probably more expedient. Swaffar (1988a) suggests that students review text content by summarizing who, what, when, and where.

Moving beyond comprehension questions, discussions help students analyze texts that warrant analysis. Analytical questions provoke critical thought and encourage students to compare ideas and reactions (see also Sacco, 1987). Such discussion questions do not normally require written answers (although they are valuable for essay examinations) but rather should induce students to think about what they have read. It is usually best for students to consider them during and after their reading. Analytical discussion questions differ from comprehension questions, as exemplified in the follow-

To check understanding of:	Exercises
Chronology	Reorder pictures describing text
	Reorder text to match pictures in correct order
	Reorder events according to text
Main information	Match information and routes on a map
	Identify correct diagram of information
	Match articles and headlines
	Use text information to make decisions (e.g., "Where would you vacation?")
	Fill in a table or document with text information
Details	Match precise drawings with parts of a text describing them
	Complete, or draw, a diagram or map according to the text
Text organization	Groups of students with different text passages put them in order
Information and evaluate it	Compare several passages on same subject
Character relationships	Identify correct diagram of relationships

Figure 10
From F. Grellet, (1981). *Developing Reading Skills: A Practical Guide to Reading Comprehension Exercises.* Cambridge: Cambridge University Press.

ing example.

Classified Personal Ads

COMPREHENSION EXERCISES:

(1) Students find an interesting ad and tell why it appeals to them.
(2) Students rewrite one or more ads in standard prose.
(3) Students find ads placed by people looking for certain types of partners.

DISCUSSION QUESTIONS:

(1) What are the advantages and disadvantages of personal ads? Would you use them? Why or why not?
(2) Why are so many abbreviations used? Is there a reason beyond the simple convenience of saving space?
(3) Compare personal ads with other ways of meeting people. Which make the most sense to you, and why?

Although such discussion questions have accompanied reading texts for years, they are more effective when linked logically to texts through comprehension questions; that is, information necessary to analysis is elicited by comprehension exercises. With this connection, students' understanding leads directly to text analysis. Furthermore, class discussion proceeds naturally from determining facts to exploring deeper ramifications of texts. In the final analysis, the goals of most real world reading are not to summarize text content or to memorize an author's point of view but rather to see into another mind, to compare one's own understanding with someone else's, or to mesh new information with what one already knows. Foreign language reading instruction must go beyond detail-eliciting comprehension questions to recognize legitimate reading purposes and to give learners a reason to read beyond the assignment for the next class.

Follow-up. Beyond analysis, language learners need to relate creatively and imaginatively to a text read and understood. Like exercises in preceding phases of this lesson plan for interactive reading, some follow-up activities parallel as much as possible authentic reactions to a text. After reading a story, people tell what they liked and did not like about it, or they compare their views of characters' motivations with friends' understanding. After studying a train schedule, one buys a ticket. After reading a newspaper article, one writes a letter to the editor. After reading an article or essay in an academic environment, one summarizes the author's lines of argument. Thus, we can follow reading with natural responses to each text. Other follow-up activities emphasize the play aspect of language and language learners' creativity: role-play situations, simulations of cultural experiences, and some composition topics. Going beyond a text, readers recast or transform various text features for a new setting or form.

In authentic language usage, skills integrate with each other. A speaking/listening activity precedes or follows a reading practice; writing accompanies or closely follows reading. Moreover, efficient native readers know and use favorite comprehension strategies. These two aspects of language use—strategy transfer and skill integration—are the essence of a productive follow-up phase. Thus, using Phillips' (1984, 1985) terms *integrative* and *transferable*, we can define and exemplify several ways to help students extend their reading ability and use different skills naturally.

Transferring skills. As Phillips (1984) explains, the transferable activities stage goes beyond a particular reading passage and helps learners use successful cognitive strategies with comparable texts. Students who learn how to skim a magazine table of contents to find articles relating to the United States skim a newspaper page to decide which articles deal with medical breakthroughs. After an introduction to the possible uses of flashbacks, students read a different story containing flashbacks. After gaining an insight into one philosophical essay structure, students read a similarly structured treatise.

To create transferable follow-up exercises, the teacher provides other texts to which previously taught strategies could be applied, thereby recycling strategies to maintain students' awareness of them. Especially at the beginning, the teacher makes sure students know which strategy they should practice, but little prereading work is necessary. In fact, some strategies and texts are particularly suited to valuable independent work. When prepared to understand the text, students do so and feel more confident about their reading. Finally, students who have approached and understood texts autonomously have read in the foreign language as they will after leaving the teacher's guidance.

Integrating skills. As explained above, reading can be constructively integrated with the rest of the language course. Essential elements are task authenticity or imagination; what students do in reaction to reading either must be realistic or must arouse their creativity.

The writing skill is most regularly integrated with reading. Students react to texts with pastiches, summaries, endings, analyses, a new version in another form (e.g., play, poetry, dialogue), and so on. This alliance between reading and writing, if carefully handled, is immensely helpful. Reading well-written style contributes to good writing, and both reading and writing can be considered composing processes (Pearson & Tierney, 1984); therefore, students extrapolate, both consciously and subconsciously, from their practice in the two skills. Their reading enables them to assimilate turns of phrase and idiomatic expressions difficult to memorize in isolation; their writing alerts them to syntactic and structural situations they then recognize more easily when reading (see also Lee, 1987b, and Spack, 1985). Reading often leads to writing in the real world: friendly or business letters, an answer to a letter in an advice column, a note in response to a telephone message, a complaint about a proposed ordinance, one's own personal classified ad, or a response to one.

Creative writing has long been a standard academic response to reading. To continue student-text interaction, the teacher correlates the composition assignment with the text read and strategy practiced. For instance, if text structure was emphasized, students use the same structure to write about a different topic: a day full of interruptions (chronological but disjointed structure), a persuasive essay organized by general statement and example, a description using comparison and contrast. If text genre is important, students write their own folktale, mystery, or spy story; at a more advanced level, they rewrite the text in a different genre. Students who analyzed characters' motivations rewrite some scenes from a different character's point of view. By relating the writing assignment closely to the text studied, the teacher helps students absorb cultural allusions and improve their writing style.

The speaking skill can also be legitimately combined with reading. Academic discussion of a text (explained in the postreading section) allows students to voice their reactions to, analyses of, and opinions of a text. To preserve students' interest in a text and to confirm that the foreign language is indeed a vehicle of meaningful communication, teachers must direct authentic and interesting discussions. Authenticity follows naturally when prereading and postreading derive intelligently from important aspects of the text.

Creative speaking can take the form of role-play, including acting, interviewing, debating, simulating, and masquerading. Students might reenact part of the text or imagine a variation on the action. They may also move farther from the text to dramatize interviews in which they argue the perspectives of characters or authors without necessarily using their words. Role-play preparation may take place quickly during class or at more length outside of class, depending on the text, the students, and the teacher's objectives.

Integrating the listening skill with reading (aside from listening to others speak) requires authentic listening materials. Yet, linking listening with reading repays the effort involved since these receptive comprehension skills require many of the same comprehension strategies. Hence, listening practice can be used to transfer reading strategies to different texts. Reader schemata are equally vital to understanding. Guessing word meanings is still necessary when listening, but the listener normally has fewer cues. Skimming and scanning function similarly in listening and in reading. To skim something heard, the listener notes key words to get the gist; to scan, the listener seeks the type of information needed. (See Byrnes, 1985, for extensive comparison of reading and listening and for pedagogical applications.)

With the increasing number of authentic video and audio tapes, teachers can more easily acquire listening materials related to specific reading passages for realistic language practice. We frequently learn the same news from an article and from a television or radio broadcast. We see films and read or hear reviews of them. We read a critic's arguments and then hear her discuss them with a moderator. Few programs that join listening and reading exist, but the teacher who develops coherent materials can use them repeatedly.

Conclusion

This reading lesson plan is designed to help foreign language students interact with authentic texts by using their cognitive skills, their knowledge about the world, their first language, the foreign language, and written text. Since few textbooks incorporate all the essential aspects of *prereading, while reading, postreading,* and *follow-up* activities, this text suggests how teachers can approach a text naturally, with as little preparation as possible. Certainly, not all these recommendations—and perhaps not all the lesson plan phases—can be used with any specific text. But approaches and exercise models may be applied to a variety of texts. By working with them, students learn to treat foreign language reading as a meaning-ful activity and to use every method at their command to create sense from texts for themselves. As a result, they participate more actively in class and in their own language learning.

5

Beyond the Reading Lesson

Several considerations in teaching foreign language reading exist beyond the basic lesson plan and general methodology just detailed. Given current reading textbooks (cf. Beatie *et al.*, 1984), teachers must often choose appropriate readings for their students, whether by selecting texts from authentic sources, by adapting the available reading textbook, and/or by directing students to discover reading material interesting to them. Most teachers need to test or assess students' reading ability in some measurable way aside from the postreading phase for each text. In many foreign language departments, reading comprehension is the forerunner to literary and cultural analysis. We consider how this transition takes place. Finally, for teachers who want to learn more about the process of reading in a foreign language or who want to improve their teaching by analyzing students' reading processes, methods of eliciting and using readers' think-aloud and recall protocols are discussed.

CHOOSING READING TEXTS

Text selection criteria have become less dependent on readability formulas based on text length, sentence length, or vocabulary/new-word density; more important are reader interest, type of text, text structure, authenticity, and the match between reader and text schemata, (Bernhardt, 1984; Cates & Swaffar, 1979; Schulz, 1981).[1] More comprehensible texts tend to be those with a clear and identifiable structure/genre, familiar or approachable content, and a reasonable level of sentence complexity. With appropriate prereading activities, students can acquire the information necessary to approach an otherwise too-difficult text. By asking the right postreading questions, the teacher can ask students to understand a sensible amount of an otherwise demanding text. As long as a text remains within students' general competence, the challenge it offers comes more from the tasks required than from the text itself (Ervin,

1988; Grellet, 1981). Teachers may also choose to "reconstitute" an authentic text by adding features such as headings and glossing for increased comprehensibility (see Dubin, 1986, for ESL examples).

Authentic texts are vital; they motivate students, offer a real context, transmit the target language culture, and prepare students to read outside the classroom (cf. Grellet, 1981; Swaffar, 1985). As stated above, authentic texts are considered to be those written for native speakers, those "whose primary intent is to communicate meaning" (Swaffar, 1985, p. 17). They can be found even for elementary language courses: advertisements, simple poems, questionnaires, letters, and menus (Beatie et al., 1984; Meyer & Tetrault, 1988; Rogers & Medley, 1988). Simplified texts are not necessarily easier to read; the standard "simplification" process often destroys useful references and redundancies and alters the author's intended meaning (Grellet, 1981; Rivers, 1968).

Adapting The Textbook

Despite some changes since Beatie, Martin, and Oberst's 1984 survey of French, German, and Spanish first-year/four-skills textbooks, many foreign language textbooks still contain weak reading sections. Beatie et al. found that one quarter of the college textbooks surveyed had no postreading comprehension exercises, and few had prereading activities. Many high school textbooks offer neither. Within a single textbook some texts are authentic, but others are not. Thus, the teacher who wishes to develop students' reading strategies must adapt available materials, and work as much as possible with authentic texts.

Creating prereading activities for four-skills textbook readings is relatively easy because the readings are normally tied to the chapter or lesson topic and vocabulary. A class discussion can establish schemata and lead into reading. Photographs and other realia topically related to the reading, although rarely connected directly to the passage, are useful for prereading because they allow the reader to predict text content, give cultural details, and identify settings. Textbook authors and publishers, now more informed about the need for authentically reproduced realia, are presenting texts in their original formats. Teachers can exploit the size of type, accompanying designs or acronyms, or essential abbreviations; to highlight the reality of texts, teachers can sometimes display an issue of the magazine or newspaper in which the reading originally appeared.

Yet, other obstacles remain. First, as noted in the preceding chapter, students cannot practice guessing word meanings if all the unknown items are glossed. For classroom practice, the teacher can present paragraphs without glossing on an overhead projector. Students are also willing to cover textbook glosses for short word-guessing exercises. Second, excerpts from literary works can be troublesome, sometimes requiring more in the way of introduction and preparation than they offer in interest and literary value. Some teachers choose, instead, to work with a novelette for several weeks or to read short, self-contained stories, articles, essays, and/or poems. Third, most textbooks are still limited only to cultural or literary texts; the teacher who wishes to expand the curriculum must provide the other type. In many cases, then, the serious foreign language reading teacher must transform available texts and exercises to facilitate students' reading skill development.

Self-Selected Reading

Although not often explored experimentally, the impact of reader interest on comprehension implies a value in allowing readers to select their own texts. Self-selected reading should motivate foreign language students as it does first language students, who frequently prove to read more and better when allowed to read what they prefer (Krashen, 1988). Students can then choose topics for which they have some knowledge and interest. Dubin (1986) also notes the motivational value of *unanticipated texts*, those that learners do not expect to find in a classroom, for example, reviews of current movies, or catalogues.

To integrate self-selected reading within a standard reading program, the teacher needs to suggest sources of reading material available in the classroom or school library: magazines, newspapers, short stories, poems. Introductory classwork with various types and sources of reading texts should circumvent students' choosing material that is too difficult and frustrating. Allowing students occasionally to select texts furnishes a more natural purpose for reading than is usually possible in the classroom. The relevance of a reading topic and its interest for the reader are very important (Dubin, 1986). Follow-up writing or speaking activities are also

146

legitimate; students summarize what they have read either for a friend (as in a letter), as an editor (for a publication like *Reader's Digest*), or in an academic setting. Self-selected reading should not monopolize students' reading, however; directed reading, a good source of comprehensible input, provides the same cultural information to all students and introduces a variety of text types and topics.

TESTING READING

Classroom testing of students' reading skill development is the focus here; standardized reading tests, computer-assisted reading, and criteria for developing valid and reliable tests have been explored elsewhere.[2] Traditionally, reading tests have examined what has been read or studied rather than what skills are developing. Asking students about texts that have been read and discussed in class tests their listening comprehension and memory as much as, sometimes more than, their reading skills. Asking them to answer in the foreign language tests the students' ability to produce written language and may actually conceal their complete understanding (cf. Lee, 1987a). To test whether students are improving their reading ability, teachers must ask students to use new texts and to demonstrate the strategies that they have practiced. Students must show that they can understand a text on their own (cf. Liskin-Gasparro, 1984; Swaffar & Arens, forthcoming). This sort of testing is, moreover, part of the learning process because it not only reinforces but also extends what has been taught (Lee, 1988a).

Testing reading, then, means asking students to read an authentic text that is unfamiliar but similar in some way to texts practiced as classwork. Test tasks reflect as closely as possible real world reactions to reading that particular text, just as they do in the postreading phase. Students' work with the original text provides or activates schemata relevant to the second text; strategies necessary for comprehension should also be comparable. Both strategy use and comprehension are tested much as they have been practiced in class. In this way, students see the immediate importance of new reading strategies, and they soon learn that they will be asked to comprehend written text independently rather than to reiterate what has been said about a text in class. On the test as in practice, required strategies and comprehension must reflect what a normal native reader would typically do with the text. Essential cultural information taught with practice texts can realistically be tested here, too, as students relate the new text to the one studied, comparing or contrasting viewpoints, summarizing arguments, or listing new information. Eliciting information from practice texts may serve simultaneously as a test of student assimilation of cultural facts and as a prereading activity for the new text.

To demonstrate these principles of testing reading, two short English texts appear below. In our hypothetical situation, the first would be used as reading practice and as information about Gothic cathedrals in general and about Notre Dame de Paris; the second would be used to test what students have learned and what they comprehend from reading it. In normal circumstances, these texts would probably continue for several more paragraphs; excerpts serve as examples here. The exercises sampled relate only to the reading test; it is assumed that students will have worked with a practice text, doing *prereading, while reading, postreading,* and *follow-up* activities. Of course, not all the exercises offered would appear on one test; sample questions are meant to show various possible options. The level of questions actually used depends on students' proficiency.

BEGINNING OF THE PRACTICE TEXT:

Only slightly later than the Cathedral of Laon, Notre Dame de Paris occupies a pivotal point in the history of Gothic architecture. One of the first cathedrals of truly colossal scale—the vaults of the nave have leapt from a height in the 70s to nearly 110 feet in one bound—it is also not only the last and greatest of the line of cathedrals with tribune galleries, but the probable birthplace of the true flying buttress, introduced over the nave aisles in about 1180.

(W. Swaan, *The Gothic Cathedral,* New York: Park Lane, 1981, p. 110)

**From what period of architecture does Notre Dame de Paris date?

**Give two reasons why Notre Dame de Paris is important to the history of architecture.

Excerpt of test text:

[Shown with Plate 108, a photo of the southern rose window; the vocabulary item "rose window" should already have appeared in class practice.]

The new transeptal fronts of Notre Dame are among the most splendid examples of the *Style Rayonnant,* so-called from the characteristic 'radiating' tracery of the enormous roses and rosettes that are such favoured motifs (Plate 108).

It is only in the two great roses of the transepts and that of the west front that Notre Dame has retained any of its original glass. That of the western and southern roses has been much restored, but the northern rose has come down to us virtually intact. The filigree delicacy of the tracery and the glorious color of the glass, predominantly blue and incorporating no less than eighty subjects from the Old Testament, are both outstanding; their combination is unique and overwhelming in its emotional impact.

(W. Swaan, *The Gothic Cathedral,* New York: Park Lane, 1981, p. 112) (See the sample strategy exercises, pp. 150 - 152.)

Grading criteria can be difficult to define, especially with such open-ended questions as (a) and (b) on p. 152. Interrater reliability on such questions has proven to be hard to control (Kreeft & Sanders, 1983). Although grading may pose problems in multisection courses, the motivational value of authentic reading tasks must not be ignored in an effort to regiment grading practices. A judicious combination of objective, discrete-point items with more provocative, realistic questions clarifies many grading dilemmas while

(text continues on p. 153)

Sample Strategy Exercises

a) Guessing word meanings (with clues):

--What part of the words *transeptal* and *transepts* partially

explains their meaning?_____ To what do these

words refer? _____

--What other word in the text means the same as *rayonnant*?

_____

--What word does the photo explain? _____

--What familiar word is contained in the word *tracery*?

_____ To what does *tracery* refer?_____

b) Guessing word meanings (without clues)/ Identifying grammatical
category of words:

--Complete the chart below to figure out the meanings of the
underlined words. The first word has been done as a model.

Words	Part of Speech	Clue(s)	Meaning
transepts	noun	trans= across roses are in the transepts	halls crossing the main hall
rayonnant			
tracery			

c) Analyzing text cohesion:

--Where does the original glass still remain? _____

--What combination is "unique and overwhelming in its

emotional impact?" _____

--To what do these words [underlined in the text] refer?

that (line 7): _____

That (line 8): _____

their (line 14): _____

it (line 15): _____

d) Recognizing main ides:

--The topic of the second paragraph is _____.

OR, as multiple choice:

--The topic of the second paragraph is

a) transepts   b) windows   c) the Bible   d) tracery

e) Recognizing text function:

--Give two words or phrases that indicate an objective
description of Notre Dame:

_____   _____

-- Give two words or phrase that indicate the author's feelings about Notre Dame:

_____   _____

At a higher level:

-- Is the author more objective or emotional in his description of Notre Dame? Give reasons for your choice.

Sample Comprehension Exercises (including inference and general understanding):

a) What is the author's tone? Give one example from the text to support your answer.

b) What does the author think of Notre-Dame de Paris? Give an example from this text and from the passage we read in class.

c) Give three facts this text tells you about Notre Dame.

d) [Omit the textual reference to Plate 108.] To which paragraph does the photo relate? How do you know?

e) [For a more detailed understanding of the text, provide a simple floor plan of Notre Dame from the book.] Label the floor plan with four of the areas discussed in the text.

maintaining student interest and test validity. Questions must address relevant information and will vary according to text type and purpose. Questions may be in the first or target language; foreign language questions should not come directly from the text, however, or point to the correct answer. Answers in the first language usually demonstrate reader comprehension of the text better than do foreign language answers. As most teachers know, many language learners can correctly answer some comprehension questions in the foreign language without entirely understanding the tested material. For this reason and to avoid testing production at the same time as comprehension, it is recommended that students answer in their native language if the teacher understands it. Asking readers to quote segments from a text encourages more superficial reading than does answering in the first language (Cohen, 1986).

Some specialists have offered different types of reading assessment items: cloze (Greenewald, 1979), recall protocols (Bernhardt, 1983), different question types (Grellet, 1981; Phillips, 1985). Varieties and uses of cloze passages are detailed in Chapter 2, note 1. (See below for Bernhardt's suggestion that recalls can give insights into readers' comprehension processes.)

From Reading Comprehension To Literary or Cultural Analysis

For many, the study of foreign language literatures and cultures is vital to the liberal arts or humanities curriculum, developing critical thinking skills and leading to an understanding of other peoples otherwise unknowable. Students and faculty read literature with pleasure and believe that analyzing it creates deeper understanding and appreciation of diverse cultures and of different world views. Reading great literature also furnishes fine models of written language for developing composition skills (cf. Spack, 1985). In the preceding chapter, we saw how students go beyond factual comprehension and react to texts; in this section we assume basic reading comprehension as learners move further toward critical evaluation of suitable texts. (For other pedagogical suggestions, see note. [3])

Although many first and foreign language teachers begin teaching textual analysis by explaining conceptual terms for figurative language (e.g., "symbol," "metaphor," and "assonance"), this terminology is meaningless unless readers' schemata become involved. That is, one's understanding of literary concepts may depend upon contacts between one's past experiences and what appears in a text. No one who has learned to read is a *tabula rasa*; even children exclaim, "Oh, you're just making that up!" when a story does not match their schemata. Thus, readers are, by definition, ready to assess textual meaning on levels deeper than surface words.

Looking again at Edgar Allan Poe's tale "The Black Cat", we see several schemata essential not only to understanding but also to analyzing the narrator's actions and feelings and thus to grasping Poe's point:

> black cats: their intelligence, reputed independence, and association with the occult and witchery
>
> storytellers: their possible bias and unreliability
>
> pets: devoted, faithful, requiring owner responsibility (a cultural concept uncommon in non-Western civilizations)
>
> alcoholism: to which the narrator makes rather subtle allusions;
>
> the concepts of right and wrong, of sin, and of conscience

The experienced, analytical reader catches all this at reading speed, processes it, and keeps it in memory in order to interpret it. The non-analytical but comprehending reader, on the contrary, reads in a straightforward fashion, as though text were a compilation of facts and details. To make the transition to analysis, this comprehending reader needs encouragement and direction. Readers can analyze what underlies the surface statements of "The Black Cat" by taking advantage of their life experiences and knowledge. After checking that surface comprehension has taken place, the teacher asks what is striking or unusual about the story. Most of the details and reactions thus elicited will figure in a critical evaluation of the story because of students' natural ability to make value judgments according to society's norms. Of course, students with no previous training and little inherent discernment might begin at a surface level of analysis. For these, a dialogue like the following can prove effective:

Teacher: What strikes you about "The Black Cat"?

Student: Not much. It seems like a murder story to me.

T: OK, do you think it's a typical murder story? Do you see any ways in which it's different from other murder mysteries you've read?

S: Well, the murderer tells the story.

T: That's right; the narrator is the murderer. What do you think about that? How much can you trust a murderer to tell the truth?

S: I think the guy's crazy.

T: So you might not want to trust everything he says; he might be an unreliable narrator. But why do you say he's crazy?

S: Well, the way he treats the cat, for one thing.

T: A good point. But why do you say he's crazy and not just mean? Does he say anything about what he does?

S: He sort of blames it on drinking, and he says he doesn't know why he does it.

T: Yes, he harms the cat despite himself, knowing it's wrong. What do you think about that? Do people often act worse than they mean to?

S: I think that happens a lot. You try to do the right thing, but sometimes it doesn't work out.

T: Right. In some ways, the narrator is a lot like us and somehow arouses our sympathy. So, which do you think is more important in this story: the murder or the narrator's character?

S: The narrator spends a lot more time talking about himself than he does murdering his wife. What he thinks is more important.

Introducing technical and figurative expressions when appropriate, the teacher helps this student relate Poe's themes to what the student knows about life and about stories; through these comparisons, readers see what Poe has highlighted.

Figurative terms (e.g., *simile, allusion, hyperbole*) and technical vocabulary (e.g., *point of view, stanza, protagonist*) are defined automatically as examples arise in discussion. Students who proffer such terms are asked to explain them, revealing whether they truly understand while clarifying new concepts to classmates. Descriptive terminology has too often been accompanied by a mystique which can alienate more literal readers; if used in context to identify deeper meanings or to elaborate concepts, it fulfills a useful function. Figurative language and literary devices (e.g., the unreliable narrator or an omniscient point of view) are but means to examine meaning indirectly beneath the surface meaning directly expressed. As small spotlights, they focus readers' attention on what the writer most wants to say.

Strong figurative language and accessible themes unify the understanding of various readers, whose reactions depend to a great extent on cultural norms, on the power of social prescriptions and proscriptions. This close affiliation between literature and the culture in which it is created make analytical reading an exercise in both literary and cultural understanding. All that has been suggested above applies equally well to analyzing cultural bias in nonfiction texts. Learners who do not know the cultural assumptions underlying a writer's point of view or statements can infer many of them by comparing the text with their own cultural understandings (cf. Byrnes, 1988, on teaching culture by analyzing foreign language texts about American culture). To interest the average reader in literary and cultural analysis, we must demystify analysis and teach it for what it is: the logical evaluation of what a written text says in light of what the reader knows. With the right questions, any thinking person can be brought to analyze subsurface meanings in a text.

ANALYZING READERS' PROCESSES

Direct views of readers' processes, from either think-aloud protocols or recall protocols, are revealing. (See Allerson & Grabe, 1986, on focused teacher observations and student/teacher conferences.) Teachers who want to learn more about the foreign language reading process or to teach better may wish to analyze their students' reading. Although the data obtained from the think-aloud process must be verified with other objective techniques in order to be statistically useful (Ericsson & Simon, 1980), think-aloud protocols can be helpful in an instructional situation (Casanave, 1988).

They do help the listener perceive a reader's mental activity: strategies attempted successfully and unsuccessfully, the role of translation, and the level of reader confidence. Written recall protocols show how individual readers reconstruct a text: what they remember, how they interpret vocabulary and grammar, which schema(ta) they invoke, how meaningfully they read.

The time needed to use either type of protocol can be minimal. As homework, students can think aloud about a text into a tape recorder or they can read a short text and write recalls of it in as little as twenty minutes. Analysis, although more time-consuming, helps the teacher recognize learners' strengths and problems, individual reading styles, and the complexity of reading in a foreign language. Thus, analysis is an excellent basis for an individualized reading curriculum. Yet, few teachers can individualize instruction to any great extent, given the demands of class size and teaching loads. Each teacher may adapt the above suggestions as necessary, while remembering that the individual nature of the reading process demands that effective instruction be "reader centered and reader generated" (Bernhardt, 1986c, p. 108).

Using Think-Aloud Protocols

The teacher or researcher who listens to a student think aloud while reading gains insights not available from traditional reading lessons. Methods for eliciting and recording think-aloud data vary. For instance, self-observation may be done immediately (*introspection*) or after some delay (*retrospection*); students may or may not be trained about the type of data they should provide; the teacher or researcher may or may not ask leading questions; subjects may speak or write their self-reports. (Cohen & Hosenfeld, 1981, present a detailed methodology for gathering mentalistic data.) For instructional applications, the quickest and easiest method is probably the most practicable.

Hosenfeld et al. (1981) advocate teaching students to think aloud, or self-report, as they read (see also Hosenfeld, 1979). The teacher then uses the "Interviewer Guide for Reading Strategies" (Figure 9) to designate each student's use of reading strategies as satisfactory, unsatisfactory, or non-existent. Hosenfeld et al. suggest working with students individually, as they read silently during class. In a few minutes, a teacher can check the first thirteen strategies, with more time; all twenty. A baseline thus established, the teacher can decide more specifically which reading strategy practice will most benefit the class and/or individual students. Since a reader's strategies interact with each other and with texts in a most complex fashion, they cannot be hierarchized. Thus, the decision about which strategies to teach first depends most on the learners. (See Bereiter & Bird, 1985, for a first language model of teaching comprehension monitoring and ways to improve strategy use.)

An alternative use of think-aloud protocols for the teacher with extremely limited time is to concentrate on working only with weaker readers. Students with poor comprehension may be able to tap effective strategies if, from an analysis of their strategies, they learn where they are going wrong. Transcripts, essential for an experimental study, are not indispensable to obtaining a global view of an individual's reading process. By simply listening to a student thinking aloud during a short reading, the teacher can get a general idea of strengths and weaknesses. Students may also listen to the tape recordings of their own reading, and then tally their strategies on a checklist like the one provided by Hosenfeld et al. (1981) or Sarig (1987). In any case, unravelling some of a learner's strategies normally makes that learner more aware of efficient and inefficient processing and, therefore, more willing to try new techniques.

Using Written Protocols

Readers' written recall protocols give a teacher different insights into how students are reading. Because readers create their own meaning for any text, the teacher's reconstruction of an assigned text may not parallel those of the students, especially any based on misunderstandings (Bernhardt,1986a). As Bernhardt explains, the student whose understanding of a text diverges greatly from that of the teacher is likely to say nothing during class discussions. Thus, the teacher has little opportunity to help the learners who most need help.

Having students write recall protocols is useful. Students' reconstructions of the target text show precisely what it means to them, where they have miscomprehended, and how their schemata have interacted with the text. (For German examples, see Bernhardt, 1986c; Bernhardt & James, 1987.)

Bernhardt (1986c) offers the following outline for using the recall protocol procedure successfully in classroom instruction:

1. Select an unglossed text of perhaps 200 words.

2. Tell students that they may read the text as many times as they like and that they will then be asked to write in English as much as they can remember.

3. Give students time to read the text several times.

4. Ask the students to write everything they remember without looking at the text.

5. Collect these protocols and use them as the basis of a future lesson plan that addresses cultural, conceptual, and/or grammatical features interfering with comprehension.

A short sample of text from "Prisonnier de guerre" (Appendix A) and several student recalls from the experiment on guessing word meanings demonstrate possible analyses of readers' processes and problems (see Figure 11).

A comparison of the recalls of Students 1 and 2 illustrates the different levels of specificity at which people read and remember. Both are correct, but Student 1 may be avoiding reading at a level necessary for analysis or deep understanding. The responses of Students 3 and 4 show a common confusion about the role of "dogs" here, probably because of misapprehension of the relatively infrequent past conditional tense. Close reading of this paragraph in class might be indicated. These two recalls also reveal different reader schemata at work. Student 3 correctly interprets "not fit for a dog," whereas Student 4 seems to imagine a more grisly sort of dog food. These readers need to give more careful attention to speakers' voices.

Of course, teachers of normally large classes cannot often work individually with students on specific problems like those above. An analysis of students' recalls of short texts can, however, highlight important syntax, vocabulary, or cultural information that is later decoded with the teacher's help. Moreover, having students commit

From "Prisonnier de guerre":

 —Vous ne serez pas mal dans ce camp-là, a dit le gendarme. Je ne parle pas de la nourriture, bien sûr. Avant la guerre les chiens n'en auraient pas voulu. Mais pour le reste, c'est le meilleur camp de concentration qui soit en France, à ce qu'on assure. C'est le camp des Allemands.

 ("You won't be bad off in that camp," said the gendarme. "Of course, I'm not talking about the food. Before the war, dogs wouldn't have eaten it. But, otherwise, it's the best concentration camp in France, from what they say. It's the camp of the Germans.")

Student recalls of this passage:

Student 1: The three of them talked about the concentration camp where Gerbier was going.

Student 2: The guard told G. that he wouldn't find the concentration camp too bad. The food wasn't great (Before the war dogs didn't want it), but it was the best camp in France.

Student 3: They went to a camp in Germany that wasn't fit for a dog for some but for others there was no better place.

Student 4: They got to the concentration camp and the guards told him he was at the best one in Germany; he heard dogs in the background that were well fed and he did not ask about the nourishment.

Figure 11

themselves to a reconstruction of a text which they can then compare, even independently, to the standard reconstruction discussed in class must help them improve their reading (cf. Bernhardt's [1987b] argument that teachers need to know students' conceptual representations of texts). Again, the teacher can analyze and use students' recall protocols to the extent that proves possible and worthwhile. Discussing with students two different protocols (perhaps from another class) and what they show about how and what the readers comprehended cannot but enlighten learners about various sources of misunderstanding and diverse ways to approach foreign language reading.

CONCLUSION

Today, we are more aware than in the past that all four skills, together with cultural awareness, are essential to language learning. Reading is central in several ways. Appropriate texts provide comprehensible input from which learners assimilate grammar and vocabulary. Closely related to writing, reading promotes analytical and cognitive skill development as readers grapple with both surface meaning and deeper understanding. Similar to listening in the way readers' schemata affect comprehension, reading encourages thoughtful strategy use. The skill most easily maintained after the end of formal education, reading affords insights into other cultures and foreign literatures; it offers another view of life that could otherwise be gained only by extensive travel.

The reading skill is an attractive focal point for many teachers and researchers because of its benefits and its fascinating complexity. Although we know a great deal about the second language reading process, much remains to be studied, both to expand our theoretical base and to improve our language teaching techniques. The teacher or researcher concerned with understanding learner strengths and difficulties and dedicated to refining methodologies is the most qualified person to analyze the learning process. When teachers question why students do what they do, and when researchers apply their theories to classroom learning, teaching and research become truly intertwined and mutually supportive. By pondering and examining the complexity of the reading process— or the process involved in any language skill—the teacher/researcher better understands, and thus works more effectively with language learners' problems, challenges, and capabilities.

161

Notes

Part I, Chapter 1

[1]Suggestions that increased vocabulary learning improves foreign language reading come from, for instance, Cowan, 1974; Greenewald, 1979; Henning, 1975; Kruse, 1979; Yorio, 1971. Later comes encouragement to teach vocabulary primarily in context: e.g., Bensoussan, 1986; Clarke & Silberstein, 1977; Crow, 1986; Hague, 1987; Kern, 1988.

[2]See Hudelson, 1981, for a collection of work relating miscue analysis to second language reading; see also Allen, 1976; Connor, 1981; Rigg, 1977. For applications of first language psycholinguistic theory to second language reading, see Barnitz, 1985; Coady, 1979; Grove, 1981; Renault, 1981. For second and foreign language reading research with a psycholinguistic perspective, see Barnett, 1986; Bialystok, 1983; Clarke, 1980; Connor, 1981; Cowan, 1976; Cziko, 1978, 1980; Eskey, 1973; Ulijn, 1984.

[3]For pedagogical models with a psycholinguistic orientation, see, for example, Aspatore, 1984; Bar-Lev, 1980; Been, 1979; Bertin, 1987; Cates & Swaffar, 1979; Clarke & Silberstein, 1977; Elias, 1975; Eskey, 1979; Gremmo, 1980; Kellerman, 1981; Loew, 1984; Moody, 1976; Phillips, 1984, 1985; Robinett, 1980; Saville-Troike, 1979; Swaffar & Woodruff, 1978; Woytak, 1984; Yorio, 1971. For suggestions of prereading activities, see Beatie et al., 1984; Omaggio, 1984; Phillips, 1984; Renault, 1981; Schulz, 1983; Spinelli & Siskin, 1987; Swaffar, 1981.

[4]For more information on the role of schema theory in the realm of second language reading, see especially Carrell, Devine, & Eskey, 1988; additional references appear in the schema theory section in Part I, Chapter 2.

[5]See, for instance, Benedetto, 1985; Bernhardt, 1986a; Clarke, 1980; Cziko, 1980; Hudson, 1982.

[6]See, for example, Connor, 1978; Rigg, 1977; Steffensen, 1987.

Part I, Chapter 2

[1]A cloze passage is a text from which some words have been replaced with blanks. The deletion may be mechanical, for every nth word (normally not more frequently than every fifth word), or rational (the preparer chooses to delete particular words in order to test for certain types of words or processing strategies). The reader may be given multiple-choice alternatives or asked simply to fill in the blanks; in the latter case, the scoring criteria may be either exact replacement of the original word or completion with any logical or acceptable word. The researcher then studies what the reader puts into the blanks; clearly, the blank cloze procedure gives no explicit insight into why completions are made the way they are, leaving the researcher to infer subjects' thought processes. Originally created as a test of first language readability, foreign/second language cloze tests are used to teach and test reading and to study the reading process (e.g., Barnett, 1986: Clarke, 1980; Cziko, 1980; Oller, 1973; Stansfield, 1980).

Yet, because performance on cloze tests clearly depends on the interaction of a number of separate skills (e.g., language proficiency, cognitive skill, familiarity with text topic, ability to draw inferences), numerous questions have been raised about exactly what cloze tests examine. Cloze performance can be improved by encouraging students' inferencing behavior through classroom training (Bialystok & Howard, 1979). Cognitive style may affect cloze performance; that is, field independent individuals complete a cloze passage more easily than field dependent individuals (Stansfield & Hansen, 1983).

For an explanation of miscue analysis, see the section on Goodman's psycholinguistic model, Chapter 1. Hudelson, 1981, offers a collection of work relating miscue analysis to second language reading; see also Allen, 1976; Connor, 1981; Dank & McEachern, 1979; Rigg, 1977.

Eye movement studies, in which comprehension processes are inferred from what the eye does, are explained with respect to the Just and Carpenter model, 1980, in Chapter 1. Such studies in second and foreign language reading include Bernhardt, 1987; Muylaert et al., 1983; Oller, 1972.

For the recall protocol procedure, readers read a text (either during a limited time period or as many times as they like) and then write down, most often in their native language, as much of the text as they can remember. Each recall protocol is compared to a propositional analysis of the original text prepared by the researcher, and readers receive credit for propositions correctly remembered. (For methods of propositional analysis from work in first language learning, see Meyer, 1975, and Deese, 1984.) Foreign language reading research using recall protocols includes Barnett, 1986, 1988a,b; Bernhardt, 1983, 1988, in press; Lee, 1986b; Wells, 1986; see also the experimental design explained in Chapter 3.

The think-aloud procedure is a metacognitive measure in that it asks the reader to be aware of his or her own skills and strategies while reading. Although the details of the task may vary (see Cohen & Hosenfeld, 1981, and Cohen, 1987, for a thorough overview), the think-aloud technique generally has the reader think aloud (in either native or target language) while reading silently. The introspective approach is similar, except that subjects are asked to reflect upon their operations as they perform them; the retrospective approach has them reflect some time after they have performed the operations. Although there is still suspicion that having readers voice their strategic or comprehension processes as they read may interfere with the reading process, such mentalistic data is becoming more popular and more accepted. For second and foreign language think-aloud studies, see Cohen et al., 1979; Hosenfeld, 1976, 1977a, 1977b, 1979; Kern, 1988; and later in Chapter 3 of this volume. See Ericsson and Simon, 1980, for a discussion of the validity of verbal report data in first language studies.

See Johnston, 1983, for an explanation and evaluation of all these process analysis procedures in first language reading.

[2]For theoretical ideas on the relationship of vocabulary to reading comprehension, see, for example, Alderson & Urquhart, 1984; Carrell, 1987b; Cowan, 1974; Greenewald, 1979; Williams & Dallas, 1984. For pedagogical suggestions on increasing reader vocabulary to improve comprehension, see, for instance, Barnitz, 1985; Crow, 1986; Hague, 1987; Holley, 1973; Kruse, 1979; Pakenham, 1984; Parry, 1987;

Saragi et al., 1978.

Part I, Chapter 3

[1]These specialists are among those calling for teaching strategies to improve reader's comprehension: Aspatore, 1984; Beatie et al., 1984; Byrnes & Fink, 1985; Cates & Swaffar, 1979; Grellet, 1981; Hosenfeld et al., 1981; Loew, 1984; Omaggio, 1986; Phillips, 1975, 1984, 1985; Schulz, 1983; Swaffar, 1985; Tyacke, 1981; Woytak, 1984; Zvetina, 1987.

[2]For definitions of mentalistic research methodologies, see note 1 in Chapter 2 of this work. For a thorough explanation of terms and procedures, see Cohen & Hosenfeld, 1981. For support of mentalistic methodology as a research technique, see Casanave, 1988; Cohen, 1984, 1986; Connor, 1987; Faerch & Kasper, 1987, in second language; Ericsson & Simon, 1980, in first language. For a detailed analysis of the importance of metacognitive skills in first language reading, see Baker and Brown, 1984, and Flavell, 1981.

[3]Cf. Groebel (1981) who finds that second language students' hierarchy of strategy use does not match their teachers' preferences; Phifer and Glover (1982) find that college students do not correctly perceive first language reading strategies.

[4]Carton (1971) specifies three different types of contextual cues. Intralingual cues are morphological and syntactic cues contained within the target language. Interlingual cues include what can be inferred by comparing the second language to other known languages: e.g., cognates or regularities of phonological transfer. Extralingual cues are those derived from the reader's real world knowledge about the text topic.

Carrell (1983) considers context from a schema-theoretic point of view. For her, context refers to a reader's prior knowledge that a text is about a particular topic. Transparency refers to the degree to which the lexical items in a text reveal its topic. Familiarity is the amount of knowledge about the topic the reader brings to the text. Hence, she very nearly equates background knowledge with context.

For Bialystok (1983), context is relative to the reader. She posits three types of inferences attributable to three different sources of knowledge: implicit knowledge, the unanalyzed, intuitive information the learner has about the target language; other knowledge, information about other languages and the learner's general world knowledge; and context, both the linguistic and physical aspects of a situation which provide cues to meaning.

[5]For recommendations that students be taught how to guess word meanings from context and for appropriate classroom activities, see Alderson & Alvarez, 1978; Bensoussan & Laufer, 1984; Bramski & Williams, 1984; Carton, 1971; Crow, 1986; Clarke & Nation, 1980; Clarke & Silberstein, 1977; Goodrich, 1977; Hagboldt, 1926; Hill, 1978; Honeyfield, 1977; Hosenfeld et al., 1981; Jarvis, 1979; Jensen, 1986; Nuttall, 1983; Siebert, 1945; Phillips, 1984, 1985; Stoller, 1986; van Parreren & Schouten-van Parreren, 1981; Weible, 1980; Woytak, 1984.

[6]To check the level of text difficulty, both texts were given to a pilot group of French 202 students (N = 30) a month before the experiment. For each text, students answered three types of questions in English: background knowledge questions

(Appendix D), multiple-choice comprehension questions, and open-ended comprehension questions (Appendix G). Pilot group students showed strong background knowledge of both text topics: 88.4% correct for "Eastwood;" 73.3% correct for "An 2000." The fact that the "An 2000" score is relatively low is due in part, at least, to poor response to a question asking about the general topics of *Le Figaro* Magazine. Only about half the students answered it correctly; for the experiment, the more appropriate question about what computers can do replaced it. The multiple-choice comprehension question scores for each text showed better than average comprehension (79.2% for "Eastwood;" 74.8% for "An 2000"), as did the answers on the more open-ended questions: nearly all the students were able to give the gist of the texts. These two texts appear to be reasonably difficult but comprehensible for French 202 students.

[7]To develop the two strategy-use instruments, the students in the pilot phase were asked, before they read the texts, to give the English meaning, a cognate, and the part of speech for 126 words listed alphabetically from both texts. All the words possibly unfamiliar to French 202 students were included in this list. All students completed this section although none offered meanings or cognates for every word. The tally of their responses yielded about two dozen words from each text unknown by more than one student in the pilot phase. Twenty of these words from each text became the target words to be defined in the strategy-use segment of the experiment. Many of the multiple choice possibilities for each word (Appendix F) were taken directly from the pilot students' guesses. Other criteria in the selection of distractors were English words that looked like or were cognates of the target word, words relating to other parts of the context surrounding the target word, and antonyms of the true meaning of the target word. In general, the distractors were of the same part of speech as the target word.

[8]To generate the questionnaire on perceived use of strategies (Part 6), the researcher compiled a list of many text-level and word-level strategies generally recommended as useful by specialists. Less effective strategies were alternative choices. First, an early version of the questionnaire was pretested with 61 fourth-semester French students: they chose all the strategies that described what they did while reading, added other strategies and techniques they used, and deleted strategies that did not describe their reading (see Barnett, 1988a). Depending on student answers, a few questions and choices were eliminated, and strategies suggested by a number of students were substituted for those proposed by the researcher. In the final version (Appendix H), possibilities within each question appeared in scrambled order so that no correct sequence of choice would be implied. All strategies generally considered effectual were accepted as correct. The questionnaire was in English to ensure students' comprehension.

[9]Because the experiment could be administered only during regular class time, available time was limited. Timing for the various parts was as follows: The subjects had five minutes to answer the eight background knowledge questions about World Wars I and II. Then the subjects were told that they had ten minutes to read "Prisonnier de guerre," after which the story would be collected and they would have ten minutes to write their recall of it in English (see Lee, 1986b, for a discussion

of using the native language for written recalls). Subjects then had twenty-five minutes to answer the background questions about either "Eastwood" or "An 2000" and to read the text and choose appropriate word meanings. They were not allowed to return to the background knowledge questions once they had begun the text. In the strategy-use section, they were encouraged to read the text through once before beginning to choose word meanings. Finally, the subjects completed the perceived-strategy-use questionnaire in seven minutes, choosing the one strategy in each situation that best described their reading habits and answering all questions. The teaching assistants reported that most of their students had ample time to complete each portion of the experiment.

[10]In order to retain as much as possible the syntactic character of the relations within propositions, the propositional analysis was performed according to the rules set forth by Deese, 1984. In effect, this method separates basic subject-predicate relations and the words and phrases modifying them. If, however, the modifying phrase does not contrast with any other modifier, it remains part of the subject-predicate phrase. Thus, "the police van stopped in front of an isolated farm" is treated as one proposition. Implicit propositions or parts of propositions needed to complete this outline appear in capital letters in parentheses; they provide a context for subordinate propositions (see Appendix C). I appreciate the help of James Deese and of his colleagues, Thomas H. Estes and Elizabeth Wetmore, with this propositional analysis. Heartfelt thanks go to Brenda Loyd for her gracious help with the statistical analyses. I also thank Renée Severin for her help in scoring the recall protocols. Interrater reliability was 87.5%.

Part II, Chapter 4

[1]For pedagogical approaches to second language reading in specific and general contexts, see Dubin, Eskey, and Grabe, 1986. For myriad suggestions on teaching reading to EFL students with various cultural backgrounds, see Nuttall, 1983. For an ESL application of the Language Experience Approach (LEA), in which learners create orally texts which they then learn to read, see Dixon and Nessel, 1983. For summaries of various methods, see Barnitz, 1985.

[2]See Swaffar, 1985, for a thorough definition of authentic materials; Bertin, 1987, also advocates presenting texts as they originally appeared; Rogers and Medley, 1988, define authentic language samples as those that reflect naturalness of form and appropriate cultural and situational context.

[3]Reading specialists who propose a multiphase reading lesson plan and offer appropriate exercises include Jensen, 1986; Melendez & Pritchard, 1985; Phillips, 1984, 1985; Rathmell, 1984; Rogers & Medley, 1988. For a model of a reading lab, an independent reading program designed to prepare ESL/EFL students for the extensive reading required by their studies, see Stoller, 1986.

Various other methods have also been proposed. The ECOLA approach (Extending Concepts Through Language Activities) is a first language reading/writing technique that involves reading for a purpose and writing in response to texts, considering the original purpose (Smith-Burke, 1982). Offering an admittedly unconventional method, Burling (1982) proposes a foreign language reading course in which students read interesting French stories transposed into English words following French syntax. As students learn grammar rules, the English words are translated into French until the entire text appears eventually in French.

[4]In addition to those reading specialists listed in note 1, others have offered numerous specific activities for each phase:

For prereading, see Beatie et al., 1984; Dubin, 1986; Henry, 1984; Langer, 1981; Medley, 1977; Meyer & Tetrault, 1988, for a variety of languages; Omaggio, 1984; Renault, 1981; Schulz, 1983; Siskin, 1987 (for French); Spinelli & Siskin, 1987 (for French and Spanish); Swaffar, 1981 (for German); Swaffar, 1985.

For exercises while reading, see Nuttall, 1983, for a variety of activities and approaches; Pakenham, 1984, on developing readers' expectations; Pierce, 1979, on teaching text organization and redundancy; Swaffar, 1981 (for German); Tuttle, 1981, on teaching students to infer from cultural knowledge. The Directed Reading-Thinking Activity (DR-TA) (Stauffer, 1980) is a first-language technique that should work with readers who have some degree of language proficiency. Students predict (that is, set purposes and make hypotheses), read (process ideas), and prove by giving evidence to confirm their purposes and hypotheses.

For strategy practice, see Alderson & Alvarez, 1978; Been, 1979; Bramski & Williams, 1984; Clarke & Nation, 1980; Grellet, 1981; Hosenfeld et al., 1981; Jensen, 1986, and Mahon, 1986, for development of reading rates; Kern, 1988; Mackay, 1979; Nuttall, 1983; Renault, 1981; Stoller, 1986; Swaffar & Woodruff, 1978; Tyacke, 1981; van Parreren & Schouten-van Parreren, 1981; Walker, 1982; Westphal, 1979 (for French); Byrnes, 1985, and Omaggio, 1986, for collections of ideas.

For postreading, see Munby, 1979, for multiple-choice questions to teach students to infer correctly.

[5]Pedagogical suggestions for activating readers' schemata appear in Carrell, 1984; Carrell, 1985 (training in text structure); Carrell, 1988a; Carrell & Eisterhold, 1983; Dubin, 1986 (especially, building background knowledge through "reading-in-depth"); James, 1987; Melendez & Pritchard, 1985. Bensoussan (1986) demonstrates how readers' misapplied schema can result in miscomprehension. Au (1979) presents the Experience-Text-Relationship (ETR) Method, which can be useful for developing prior knowledge and dealing with cross-cultural schemata. Students share their experiences and knowledge that relate to the text being read both before, during, and after they read.

[6]See Williams, 1983, for another categorization of discourse markers; see Bensoussan, 1986, on the importance of understanding logical connectors; see Berman, 1979, on approaching a text through its syntax.

Part II, Chapter 5
[1]The question of readability may become prominent again, however, as we search for norms to test second language reading proficiency (Swaffar, personal communication, August, 1988). New readability formulas will probably depend on text cohesion and organization of macropropositions as well as on sentence length and vocabulary.

[2]For information on the ACTFL Computer-Adaptive Reading Test, see Dan-

donoli, 1987; Hummel, 1985; Kaya-Carton & Carton, 1986; Lowe, 1984. For more generic information on computer-assisted reading, see Dever, 1986; Pusack, 1984; Wyatt, 1984. For basic information on language test development, see Valette, 1977. For specifics about reading test development see Canale, 1984; Jones, 1984. For sample test items, see Grellet, 1981; Munby, 1979 (to teach students to infer); Omaggio, 1986. For information on ESL/EFL standarized, placement, and achievement tests, with a focus on reading programs, see Allerson and Grabe, 1986.

[3]Allen, 1975, provides insights into how considering the linguistic elements of a text helps clarify assessments of literary craftsmanship; Bretz & Persin, 1987, offer the outline of a course in which presentation of critical literary theories intermingles with work on reading comprehension; Birckbichler & Muyskens, 1980, suggest means of involving students personally in interpreting and appraising texts; Kramsch, 1985, offers a methodology within a framework of discourse analysis for analyzing German literary narrative; Littlewood, 1975, weighs the relationship of literature to language teaching and discusses text selection criteria; Prince, 1984, considers the difficulty of understanding the cultural, social, and historical dimensions of a literary text; Schulz, 1981, proposes ways to predict text readability and reduce students' frustration.

Glossary

affective factors, those relating to a learner's feelings or emotional reactions

coherence, the way in which ideas and meanings in a text relate to each other

cohesion, the semantic functions realized in the surface-level features of the text. For a list of cohesive ties as defined by Halliday and Hasan (1976) see pp. 62-63.

context, the inherent relationship of surrounding words, phrases, and sentences to any particular word or expression within them

EFL, acronym for the field of English as a Foreign Language, in which learners study English while living in their first language culture

ESL, acronym for the field of English as a Second Language, in which learners study English while living in an English- speaking community

extensive reading, the reading of longer texts for global understanding, normally on one's own, frequently for pleasure; often juxtaposed with **intensive reading**

fixate, in eye-movement studies, the verb used to describe the motion of the reader's eyes as they fix on (look at) each word

fixation time, in eye-movement studies, the amount of time during which the reader's eye looks at each word (usually measured in milliseconds)

FL, acronym for Foreign Language, implying an academic learning situation in which Americans study another language while living in the United States

graphophonemic, describing the written form of basic units of sound (phonemes) in a language

intensive reading, the close and careful reading of shorter texts or parts of long texts, to extract specific information; often juxtaposed with **extensive reading**

lexicon, vocabulary of a language or of a text

mentalistic data, information obtained by having learners talk about their thought processes as they perform various tasks

metacognition, the knowledge of one's own cognitive processes (e.g., how one learns or how one reads) and a learner's self-regulation of those processes

miscue, an observed oral reading of printed text that does not conform to what is printed

phonemes, basic units of sound in a language

protocol, literally, a statement of an observation without any interpretation attempted; in research methodology, subjects' statements of either what they understand from a text or what they are thinking as they process a text

psycholinguistic, related to the study of the relationships between language and the behavioral characteristics of language users; commonly used to refer to the interrelationship of thought and language

reader-based variables, the aspects of reading that come from the reader rather than the text (e.g., background knowledge of the world and texts, cognitive development, interest and purpose in reading, strategy use)

reliability, the measure by which is expressed the chance that any two people will rate or score a test or test item in the same way. For example, an objective, multiple-choice test with one defined answer for each item has 100% reliability, whereas a subjectively scored essay item will probably have a lower reliability (cf. **validity**).

schema theory, a theory that holds that present experiences are interpreted in terms of past experiences and prior knowledge. According to schema theory, a text does not carry complete meaning in itself but rather provides guidance to listeners or readers as to how to construct the intended meaning from the knowledge they already have and how to add to that knowledge.

schema(ta), the organization(s) of knowledge structures or concepts an individual has because of previous experiences. Schemata which relate to text topics, such as events and scenes, are called **content schemata;** schemata describing or defining the hierarchical rhetorical organization of a text are called **formal** or **textual schemata.**

semantics, the meaning of text, as expressed through its lexicon and syntax

syntax, the rules that govern the formation of sentences and phrases from words

text-based variables, the aspects of reading that come from the text rather than the reader (e.g., vocabulary, syntax, rhetorical structure, cultural content)

think-aloud, a metacognitive measure that asks the reader to be aware of and voice his/her own skills and strategies while reading

validity, the measure by which is expressed the degree to which a test item actually checks what it is supposed to test. For instance, a test of reading on which 75% of the points depended on summarizing class discussions of texts would have low validity (cf. **reliability**).

Appendices

APPENDIX A

Background Knowledge Questions: "Prisonnier de guerre"
Please answer the following questions on the red computer-scorable answer sheets. Fill in the circles completely with dark marks using a #2 pencil. You have five minutes to complete this section.

1. In World War I,
   a. France lost
   c. France and England were enemies

   b. France was neutral
   d. France and Germany were enemies

2. In World War II,
   a. France lost
   c. France and England were enemies

   b. France was neutral
   d. France and Germany were enemies

3. World War I ended with the
   a. Treaty of Utrecht
   c. Treaty of Lyon

   b. Treaty of Paris
   d. Treaty of Versailles

4. During World War II,
   a. the French occupied Germany

   c. the Germans occupied France

   b. the French occupied England
   d. the Americans occupied France

5. The Vichy government was in

   a. Belgium
   c. France

   b. Switzerland
   d. Germany

6. The Vichy government was under the domination of the
   a. Belgians
   c. French

   b. British
   d. Germans

7. The term "French underground" refers to
   a. French spies in Germany
   b. French fighting against German occupation
   c. French soldiers on the Maginot line

    d.   French spies allied with the Germans

8. The term "drôle de guerre" refers to
    a.   the beginning of World War II when a lot of fighting took place
    b.   the beginning of World War II when a little fighting took place
    c.   the end of World War I when the Allies were winning
    d.   the end of World War I when the Americans were in Europe

APPENDIX B

"Prisonnier de guerre" par Joseph Kessel

Il pleuvait. La voiture cellulaire montait et descendait lentement la route glissante qui suivait les courbes des collines. Gerbier était seul à l'intérieur de la voiture avec un gendarme. Un autre gendarme conduisait. Celui qui gardait Gerbier avait des joues de paysan et l'odeur assez forte.

Comme la voiture s'engageait dans un chemin de traverse, ce gendarme a observé:

—On fait un petit détour, mais vous n'êtes pas pressé, je pense.

—Vraiment pas, a dit Gerbier, avec un bref sourire.

La voiture cellulaire s'est arrêtée devant une ferme isolée. Gerbier ne voyait, par la lucarne grillagée, qu'un bout de ciel et de champ. Il a entendu le conducteur quitter son siège.

—Ce ne sera pas long, a dit le gendarme. Mon collègue va prendre quelques provisions. Il faut se débrouiller comme on peut par ces temps de misère.

—C'est tout naturel, a dit Gerbier.

Le gendarme a considéré son prisonnier en hochant la tête. Il était bien habillé, cet homme, et il avait la voix franche, la mine avenante. Quel temps de misère . . . Ce n'était pas le premier à qui le gendarme était gêné de voir des menottes.

—Vous ne serez pas mal dans ce camp-là, a dit le gendarme. Je ne parle pas de la nourriture, bien sûr. Avant la guerre les chiens n'en auraient pas voulu. Mais pour le reste, c'est le meilleur camp de concentration qui soit en France, à ce qu'on assure. C'est le camp des Allemands.

—Je ne comprends pas très bien, a dit Gerbier.

—Pendant la drôle de guerre on s'attendait, je pense, à faire beaucoup de prisonniers, a expliqué le gendarme. On a installé un grand centre pour eux dans le pays. Naturellement il n'en est pas venu un seul. Mais aujourd'hui ça rend bien service.

—En somme, une vraie chance, a remarqué Gerbier.

—Comme vous dites, Monsieur, comme vous dites! s'est écrié le gendarme.

Le conducteur est remonté sur son siège. La voiture cellulaire s'est remise en route. La pluie continuait de tomber sur la campagne limousine.[1]

* * * * *

Gerbier, les mains libres, mais debout, attendait que le commandant du camp lui ait adressé la parole. Le commandant du camp lisait le dossier de Gerbier.

"Toujours la même chose, pensait-il. On ne sait plus qui on reçoit, ni comment les traiter."

Le commandant ne regardait pas Gerbier. Il avait renoncé à faire une opinion d'après les visages et les vêtements. Il essayait de deviner entre les lignes dans les notes de police, qui lui avaient remises les gendarmes en même temps que leur prisonnier.

"Caractère indépendant, esprit vif; attitude distante et ironique," lisait le commandant. Et il traduisait: "à mater." Puis: "Ingénieur distingué des ponts et chaussées," et, son pouce dans la joue, le commandant se disait: "à ménager."

"Soupçonné de menées gaullistes"—"à mater, à mater." Mais ensuite: "Libéré sur non-lieu"—"influence, influence . . . à ménager."

Alors le commandant a déclaré avec une certaine solennité:

—Je vais vous mettre dans un pavillon qui était prévu pour des officiers allemands.

—Je suis très sensible à cet honneur, a dit Gerbier.

Pour la première fois le commandant a dirigé son regard lourd et vague, d'homme qui mangeait trop, vers la figure de son nouveau prisonnier.

Celui-ci souriait, mais seulement à demi; ses lèvres étaient fines et serrées.

"A ménager, certes," a pensé le commandant du camp, "mais à ménager avec méfiance."

*   *   *   *   *

Le garde-magasin a donné à Gerbier des sabots et un bourgeron de bure rouge.

—C'était prévu, a-t-il commencé, pour les prisonniers . . .

—Allemands, je le sais, a dit Gerbier.

Il a enlevé ses vêtements et a enfilé le bourgeron. Puis, sur le seuil du magasin, il a promené ses yeux à travers le camp.

---

[1]limousin: adjective referring to Limousin, a province in the Massif Central region of France

APPENDIX C

Propositional analysis of the first five paragraphs of "Prisonnier de guerre"

1. It was raining.

2. The police van (WAS MOVING ALONG) the route

3.   was going up

4.   was descending

5.   slowly

6.   the slippery route

7.   the route which followed the curves of the hills.

8. Gerbier was inside the van

9.   alone (NO OTHER PRISONERS)

10.   with a gendarme.

11. Another gendarme was driving.

12. The one who was guarding Gerbier had (TWO THINGS)

13.   the cheeks of a peasant.

14.   a pretty strong smell.

15. As the van entered a crossroad, this gendarme observed:

16.   "We're making a small detour,

17.   but I think (SOMETHING)

18.   you're not in a hurry."

19. Gerbier said (SOMETHING)

20.   with a brief smile

21.   "Not really."

22. The police van stopped in front of an isolated farm.

23. Gerbier saw (SOMETHING)

24.   through the grilled (small) window

25.   only a bit of sky

26.   and a bit of field.

Sample student recalls of the first five paragraphs of "Prisonnier de guerre" scored according to the propositional analysis. The students whose recall protocols appear here all took part in the follow-up think-aloud procedure (see sample think-aloud protocols in Appendix I).

Recall of DR (Total score: 42)

It was raining (1). The limousine was travelling along (2) the glistening roads (6), mounting (3) and descending (4) the hills and valleys (7). Gerbier was alone (9) in the interior of the car (8) with one guard (10) (a very powerful one); another was driving (11).

"We are going to make a stop," (16) says the guard (15). "I doubt that you're in a hurry." (17, 18)

"Not really," (21) replies Gerbier (19) with a small smile (20).

Recall of AP (Total score: 10)

It was raining (1). A car followed (2) the slippery road (6) that twisted through the hills (7). Gerbier was alone (9) in the back (8) with a policeman (10). Another policeman was driving (11).

The car arrived at a deserted farm (22).

Recall of RW (Total score: 7)

It was raining (1). They were driving (2) on a hilly road (7). They stopped (22) so the guard could get provisions (30).

APPENDIX D

Background Knowledge Questions

"Clint Eastwood sur les traces de Reagan"

Answer these questions on the computer-scorable answer sheet <u>before</u> you begin reading:

1. Clint Eastwood is
   a. a rock singer
   b. a movie director
   c. a movie star
   d. a Broadway actor
2. Clint Eastwood lives in
   a. France
   b. California
   c. New York
   d. Colorado
3. Clint Eastwood recently ran in an election for
   a. state senator
   b. U. S. senator
   c. governor
   d. mayor
4. Did he win?
   a. yes
   b. no
   c. I don't know.
5. Which of the following would you most likely associate with the name Clint Eastwood?
   a. the American West
   b. Rio de Janeiro
   c. the high seas
   d. outer space
6. Which of the following would you most likely associate with the name Clint Eastwood?
   a. Colt .45
   b. Smith and Wesson .38
   c. .25 Beretta
   d. Magnum .357

Background Knowledge Questions
"J'ai vécu dans la maison de l'An 2000"

Answer these questions on the computer-scorable answer sheet <u>before</u> you begin reading:

1. Which of the following can a computer <u>not</u> do?
   a. answer telephones

  b. sound alarms

  c. enforce laws

  d. open doors

2. A modem is used with

  a. a telephone

  b. a television

  c. a typewriter

  d. an antenna

3. An electronic eye can be used to

  a. see long distances

  b. light delicate surgical operations

  c. open and close doors

  d. photograph star systems

4. Acoustics refers to the sense of

  a. smelling

  b. hearing

  c. seeing

  d. touching

5. RAM means

  a. "random access memory"

  b. "read and access memory"

  c. "read accessory memory"

  d. "random adjunct memory"

6. 500 grams equals about

  a. a pound

  b. a half-pound

  c. an ounce

  d. a ton

APPENDIX E

"Clint Eastwood sur les traces de Reagan"

par J. J. Jonas

Alors, c'est le premier pas(15) vers la Maison-Blanche? Sourire. Un sourire et un éclair (16) des yeux bleus de Clint Eastwood. A faire fondre 3.765.801 Américaines, toutes admiratrices de l'acteur, qui, lors d'un gigantesque référendum effectué (17) par le "National Enquirer" auprès (18) de ses lectrices, l'ont choisi comme partenaire en répondant à la question: Avec qui aimeriez-vous passer le jour de votre anniversaire?

Clint a gagné. Il a été élu maire de Carmel: 2.116 électeurs de cette petite ville de Californie, non loin de San Francisco, où il vit depuis quatorze ans, l'ont préféré au maire sortant, Charlotte Townsend, soixante et un ans. A cinquante-cinq ans, ayant laissé le Magnum 357 dans l'étui (19) des personnages de ses films, Clint Eastwood a gagné son plus difficile combat. Convaincre de vieilles dames vêtues (20) de rose ou de vert pâle, de riches et paisibles (21) retraitées (22) qui ne se déplacent qu'en Bentley ou en Volvo, qu'il n'était pas un danger public. Qu'il aimait cette ville où ses deux enfants, Kile, dix-sept ans, son garçon, l'aîné, et Alison, treize ans, sa fille, ont suivi les cours de l'école publique. Qu'en dépit de (23) son auberge La Laine de Porc installée au coeur de la ville et fréquentée par ses admiratrices, son entrée au City Hall (la mairie) ne signifiait pas pour ses concitoyens la fin de leur tranquillité.

En deux mois, moyennant (24) une mise de fonds de 34.000 dollars (270.000 F), soit 8 dollars par électeur (64 F), de multiples discours devant des auditoires d'Américaines fondant de bonheur, il s'est révélé un leader.

Cinquante-cinq ans. A cet âge, un certain Ronald Reagan était élu gouverneur de Californie en 1966. Le mari de Nancy ne devenait président des Etats-Unis qu'à soixante-neuf ans, en 1980. Après avoir échoué (25) une première fois en 1976.

Il reste donc deux septennats à la française pour qu'un deuxième cow-boy ait des chances d'entrer à la Maison-Blanche! Si telle est sa volonté. Il s'en défend. Mais, il y a six mois à peine (26) , il avait déclaré n'être candidat à rien, pas même à la mairie.(27)

Tout à son bonheur et à celui de ses proches(28), Clint Eastwood a donné sa première conférence de presse de vainqueur, mardi soir à 22h30, au Sunset Center. Pour la grande joie des centaines de journalistes venus du monde entier: "J'ai été surpris". Il se ravise (29) et poursuit fièrement: "Non, je n'ai pas été surpris par ma victoire. Ce n'est pas moi la star. Carmel est devenu une star". Pour amuser son public, devant les innombrables caméras de télévision braquées (30)sur lui, il se coiffe d'une casquette (31) de joueur de base-ball à large visière(32) bleue, frappée de son slogan: "Clint for mayor ". Applaudissements, hourras, congratulations.

J'ai vu Clint se conduire constamment en leader dans cette incroyable campagne à l'américaine. Dans une petite salle de campagne, sur fond de bannière étoilée, avec ballons rouges, blancs, bleus, guirlandes (33) dans la salle, j'ai eu le privilège d'assister à des réceptions privées de l'acteur. Devant parfois moins de cent personnes—mais toutes électrices à Carmel—, il déployait tout son charme pour convaincre. Il m'avait accueilli par un "Vive la France", les seuls mots de français qu'il connaissait. En mentionnant aussi l'hommage que lui avait rendu la Cinémathèque. Il m'a d'ailleurs confié, après son élection, qu'il envisageait de jumeler (34) Carmel à une ville du sud de la France. Maires intéressés, prière d'adresser votre candidature à "France-Soir Magazine". Je transmettrai.

France-Soir Magazine, du 12 au 18 avril 1986

"J'ai vécu dans la maison de l'An 2000"

Un ingénieur français a participé au programme Apollo. Il en a rapporté des astuces techniques. Elles lui ont permis de réaliser une singulière maison.

par Albert Zarca

La maison de l'an 2000 existe. Elle se trouve dans la banlieue de Bruxelles, à Rhode-Sainte-Genèse, mais c'est un Français, Pierre Sarda, qui la conçue et réalisée. Je l'ai visitée et ce que j'ai découvert défie toute imagination, inquiète quelque peu et fait en même temps rêver.

En fait, Pierre Sarda, son épouse et leurs trois enfants pourraient, s'ils le voulaient, vivre, sans bouger le petit doigt, 24 heures sur 24. Une femme de service est à demeure pour le ménage et la cuisine. Quand au reste, IHS 175 s'en chargerait (15) à chaque instant, de jour comme de nuit.

Au cours de la journée, pas de problème pour M. Sarda si Mme Claessens, sa secrétaire, est absente et si personne n'est à la maison. De quelque endroit où il se trouve, il peut appeler l'ordinateur et lui demander s'il y a eu des appels, si le facteur est passé, s'il y a du courrier ou non. Grâce à un petit appareil de 530g, muni (16) d'un coupleur acoustique qui s'adapte sur n'importe quel téléphone, il peut, quelle que soit la distance, converser avec l'ordinatuer. Celui-ci, d'une voix un peu métallique, répond par des chiffres-code qu'il suffit de traduire.

Non seulement l'ordinateur renseigne, (17) mais encore il veille (18:) si une inondation ou un incendie se produisent, il appelle de lui-même les pompiers. Et si quelqu'un cherche à pénétrer par effraction(19), il avertit (20) le commissariat de police le plus proche, dont les coordonnées téléphoniques ont été confiées à sa mémoire.

Par ailleurs, si de jeunes enfants sont seuls à la maison, pas d'inquiétude à avoir. Il ne risquent pas de se noyer (21) dans la piscine. A moins de le prévenir (22) d'abord, quand on veut s'y plonger, l'ordinateur déclenche une alarme stridente et prévient les pompiers dès qu'une onde (23) provoquée par le moindre mouvement de l'eau parvient à un micro-ultra sensible installée au fond de la piscine.

Enfin, Pierre Sarda n'a pas de <u>souci</u> (24) à se faire pour le jardin quand il est en vacances: des capteurs d'humudité dissimulés dans le <u>sol</u> (25) enregistrent le degré de <u>sécheresse</u> (26) qu'ils communiquent à l'ordinateur. Celui-ci décide alors, quand il le juge nécessaire, de déclencher <u>l'arrosage</u> (27). Quant à la <u>tondeuse</u> (28), elle sort tranquillement de son garage, tend la pelouse, à l'anglaise--en déposant le gazon tondu pour enrichir le sol--et rentre au bercail son ouvrage terminé. Si elle <u>bute contre</u> (29) un obstacle, elle essaie de se dégager une ou deux fois par ses propres moyens. En cas d'<u>échec</u> (30), elle émet un signal à destination de l'ordinateur: lequel appelle au secours d'abord les occupants de la maison, puis le mécanicien.

IHS 175 est très méticuleux: la porte du garage ne s'ouvre que si l'oeil électronique, sensible au brillant de la <u>carrosserie</u> (31) juge celle-ci suffissamment propre. Dans le cas contraire, elle demeure obstinément fermée et des buses d'arrosage dissimulées dans les murs de chaque côté de la <u>pente</u> (32) accédante au garage entre en fonction pour laver la voiture. En hiver, toujours à l'aide de l'ordinateur, la pente est chauffée pour éliminer le <u>verglas</u>.(33) **Mais il en faut pas <u>sacraliser</u> (34) l'ordinateur et en devenir l'esclave, prévient Pierre Sarda. Tout est en double dans ma maison. L'ordinateur fonctionne, mais il peut être également déconnecté pour revenir aux commandes manuelles.**

APPENDIX F

Strategy-Use Choices

"Clint Eastwood sur les traces de Reagan"

Use this sheet to choose the words or phrases you think best express the
meanings of the underlined words in the article you have. [* marks correct
answer.]

15. a. negative

    b. pass

    *c. step

    d. peace

    e. office

16. a. dessert

    b. clarity

    *c. flash

    d. lightning

    e. blink

17. *a. performed
    b. chosen
    c. affected
    d. elected

    e. eliminated

18. a. near to
    b. after
    c. beside
    d. depending on

    *e. in the opinion of

19. a. shotgun

    *b. holster

    c. criminal

    d. victim

    e. imagination

20. a. invested

    *b. dressed

    c. voting

    d. discovering

    e. discovered

21. a. plausible

    b. suburban

    *c. peaceful

    d. pleasant

    e. activist

22. a. retired

    b. retracted

    c. restricted

    d. retreated

    e. restrained

23. a. in place of

    b. on the part of

    c. because of

    *d. in spite of

    e. on behalf of

24. a. saving

    b. bargaining

    c. finding

    d. despite

    *e. in return for

25. a. sneezed
    b. conquered
    c. abstained
    *d. failed
    e. departed

26. a. painful
    *b. scarcely
    c. badly
    d. mostly
    e. in prison

27. a. presidency
    b. husbandry
    *c. mayoralty
    d. municipality
    e. mayor

28. *a. friends
    b. approaches
    c. antagonists
    d. excitement
    e. nearest

29. *a. changes his mind
    b. revises his life
    c. renews his acquaintance
    d. withdraws himself
    e. controls himself

30. a. bracketed
    b. dropped
    c. ignored
    d. determined
    *e. pointed

31. a. bat
    b. ball
    *c. hat
    d. shirt
    e. casket

32. a. vise
    b. sign
    c. hat
    d. scarf
    *e. visor

33. a. flags
    *b. garlands
    c. girders
    d. performers
    e. activists

34. a. humble
    *b. join
    c. marry
    d. export
    e. include

Strategy-Use Choices

"J'ai vécu dans la maison de l'An 2000"

Use this sheet to choose the words or phrases you think best express the meanings of the underlined words in the article you have. [* marks correct answer.]

15. a. would change
   *b. would take care of
    c. would blame itself
    d. would devote itself
    e. would charge

16. a. fortified
   *b. equipped
    c. armed
    d. paid
    e. explained

17. a. reteaches
    b. accepts
    c. resigns
    d. protects
   *e. informs

18. a. wakes up
    b. goes rapidly
   *c. watches over
    d. covers up
    e. grows older

19. a. stealing
    b. difficulty
    c. infraction
   *d. breaking in
    e. cracking

20. a. averts
   *b. informs
    c. avoids
    d. ignores
    e. defends

21. a. swim
    b. dive into
   *c. drown
    d. fall into
    e. save

22. a. come before
    b. predict
    c. prevent
    d. jump into
   *e. inform

23. a. fire
   *b. wave
    c. swimmer
    d. explosion
    e. provocation

24. *a. worry
    b. fish
    c. insects
    d. anger
    e. complaint

25. a. sun
    b. salt
    *c. soil
    d. only person
    e. gardener

26. a. anger
    b. distress
    c. temperature
    d. humidity
    *e. dryness

27. a. flowers
    b. garden
    *c. watering
    d. fertilizing
    e. digging

28. *a. mower
    b. plow
    c. automobile
    d. horticulturist
    e. sprinkling system

29. a. starts against
    *b. bumps into
    c. runs over
    d. destroys
    e. fights against

30. a. success
    *b. failure
    c. disaster
    d. checker
    e. time

31. a. casserole
    b. carousel
    *c. car body
    d. car interior
    e. motorcycle

32. *a. slope
    b. garage
    c. anger
    d. delay
    e. sprinkler

33. a. soap
    b. dirt
    *c. ice
    d. blind spot
    e. incline

34. a. sacrifice
    b. sacrilege
    *c. sanctify
    d. plunder
    e. neglect

APPENDIX G

Pilot Study

"Clint Eastwood sur les traces de Reagan"

Comprehension Questions

[These questions followed the Background Knowledge Questions, Appendix D.]

7. The author has directed this article towards an audience consisting of

    a. Americans

    b. French

    c. residents of Carmel

    d. politicians

8. According to this article, we know that Clint Eastwood is popular because

    a. an article about him appeared in *The National Enquirer*

    b. American women held a referendum about him

    c. many women celebrate his birthday

    d. American women want to spend their birthday with him

9. Clint Eastwood was elected

    a. citizen of the year

    b. mayor of Carmel

    c. mayor of San Francisco

    d. governor of California

10. The author of this article

    a. predicts that Eastwood will become President of the United States

    b. thinks Eastwood is more popular than Reagan

    c. declares that Eastwood has no intention of running for President

    d. compares Eastwood's career to Reagan's

11. According to this article, what kind of voters did Eastwood **have to** convince?

    a. rich old women

    b. rich young women

c. indigent old women

d. young voters of both sexes

12. According to this article, Eastwood

a. plays baseball frequently with his children

b. will move into the White House when he is 69 years old

c. is popular with journalists

d. had difficulty winning the election

13. According to this author, Eastwood won because

a. his family has lived in Carmel for 14 years, and he is well known

b. he is charming, and his films are popular

c. he is an actor, like Ronald Reagan

d. his opponent was no good

14. What does Eastwood say about France?

a. He wants to live there

b. He thinks French women are beautiful

c. He wants to make his next film there

d. He is looking for a sister city there

15. What do think of the tone of this article?

16. How does the title relate to the contents of the article?

Pilot Study

"J'ai vécu dans la maison de l'An 2000"

Comprehension Questions

[These questions followed the Background Knowledge Questions, Appendix D.]

7. The author has directed this article towards an audience consisting of

a. computer programmers

b. meteorologists

c. scientists in general

d. the general public

8. The house described

 a. exists as a physical reality

 b. exists as a theoretical design

 c. is completely imaginary

 d. is described as an absurdity

9. Who is Pierre Sarda?

 a. an astronaut who worked in the Apollo program

 b. a computer analyst who works 24 hours a day

 c. an architect who designs modern houses

 d. an engineer whose house can be run by computer

10. IHS 175 is

 a. a robot

 b. a very sophisticated telephone system

 c. a computer

 d. a house in Brussels

11. Which one of the following can IHS 175 not do?

 a. alert rescuers to a possible drowning

 b. call the police in case of a break-in

 c. announce whether the mail has arrived

 d. weed the garden

 e. wash the car

12. To take care of the yard, IHS 175 does not

 a. water the grass

 b. mow the grass

 c. call a yardman to mow the grass

 d. call a repairman to fix the lawn mower if it gets stuck

13. According to the article, IHS 175 does not

 a. send mail automatically

    b.   speak on the telephone

    c.   monitor the house doors and windows

    d.   take phone messages

14. According to this article,

    a.   Sarda is marketing his design in France

    b.   Sarda thinks that computers are more efficient that human beings

    c.   Sarda no longer works, because of his computers

    d.   Sarda believes that we must keep computers in perspective

15. The main thrust of this article is

    a.   an analysis of recent computer technology

    b.   a description of what one computer can do

    c.   an architectural description of a modern house

    d.   a science-fiction adventure into the year 2000

Number these points according to the order in which they appear in the text:

_____ IHS 175 takes care of security

_____ IHS 175 functions with great precision

_____ IHS 175 takes care of the yard

_____ IHS 175 keeps the proprietor informed

Give details about how IHS 175
    a.   takes care of security:

    b.   keeps the proprietor of the house informed:

APPENDIX H

Questionnaire to Elicit Perceived Strategy Use
Strategies considered effective are marked with an asterisk (*).
WHAT DO YOU DO WHEN YOU READ?
In order for us to teach better, we need to know more about how you read French. Please complete each statement according to what you do as you read in French; your gut reaction to each question is the best you can give.

Mark on your red-and-white answer sheet the letter of the answer that best describes how you read. Mark only one letter for each statement, and complete every statement. You have 10 minutes to complete this questionnaire.

Thanks very much for your help!

1. When I read, I pay most attention to
   a. what individual words mean.

   b. what the reading passage means.*

   c. what the form or grammatical function of the words is.*

   d. what the structure of the passage is.

2. When I read French, I

   a. read the whole passage once and then reread it.*

   b. read part of the passage, then reread that part before going on.*

   c. reread only the difficult sections.

   d. read straight through or reread, depending on the passage.*

   e. read straight through the passage and do not reread.

3. I read a French reading passage because

   a. I find the topic interesting or I want to find out how the story ends.*

   b. I have questions to answer about it.

   c. it has been assigned.

   d. I want to find out what the author has to say.*

   e. I want to learn how to read in French.

4. When I begin reading a French passage, I

   a. don't usually consider how it relates to what I already know.

   b. think about what I know about the topic or source of the passage.*

    c.   think about what I know about the author's style or point of view.*

    d.   simply begin reading the text itself.

5.   I read different French passages

    a.   the same way because French passages are usually difficult.

    b.   the same way because they're in French.

    c.   differently depending on what I need to learn from them.*

    d.   differently depending on what kind of passages they are.*

6.   When I read in French, I hypothesize about what might come next
    a.   often.*

    b.   sometimes.*

    c.   hardly ever.

    d.   never.

7.   When I read in French, I

    a.   can't tell what the structure of the reading passage is.

    b.   expect certain things because of the reading passage structure.*

    c.   read each paragraph by itself.

    d.   look for a logical structure.*

    e.   try to relate the points or ideas mentioned together.*

8.   When a French reading passage has a title, I

    a.   read the title but don't consider it as I read the passage.

    b.   read it first and imagine what the passage might be about.*

    c.   think about what I already know and how it might relate to the title.*

    d.   read the title but don't think much about it.

9.   When a French reading passage has illustrations with it, I

    a.   imagine what the reading passage might be about, considering what
        the illustrations are.*

    b.   look at the illustrations without relating them to the reading passage.

    c.   look at the illustrations but don't think much about them.

    d.   expect the reading passage to reflect what is in the illustrations.*

    e.   compare what is in the illustrations to what I read.*

10. When I read in French, I think that

    a.   all the **words are** important.

    b.   I can **skip some** words and still understand.*

    c.   I don't know which words I can skip.

    d.   it is a mistake to skip any words.

    e.   I need to look in the dictionary for the words I don't know.

11. When I read in French, I

    a.   feel uneasy if I don't know what most of the words mean.

    b.   look up most of the words I don't know.

    c.   want to know exactly what is in the passage.

    d.   am willing to guess what some words mean.*

12. If I come to a word I don't know, I

    a.   skip the word and come back to it later.

    b.   guess what **the word** might mean and go on.*

    c.   guess **what the** word might mean and reread the sentence.*

    d.   look **the word** up in a glossary or dictionary and reread the sentence.

    e.   look the word up in a glossary or dictionary and write the English meaning on the page.

13. If a paragraph contains several words I don't know, I

    a.   guess what they all mean.*

    b.   look up the ones that seem most important and guess the others.*

    c.   look them all up in a glossary or dictionary.

    d.   skip that paragraph.

    e.   feel frustrated and stop reading **for a** while.

14. To figure out what an unfamiliar **word** might mean, I

    a.   consider what the rest of the sentence or paragraph says.*

    b.   note whether the word looks like an English or other French word I
         know.*

    c.   analyze the grammatical form of the word.*

    d.   consider any illustrations.*

    e.   don't do any of the above.

15. When I figure out what new words mean, I find that my guesses are

    a.   usually correct.*

    b.   sometimes correct.*

    c.   usually incorrect.

    d.   untrustworthy.

16. When an unfamiliar word looks like an English word or other French word,
    I

    a.   assume the unfamiliar word means the same thing as the similar word.

    b.   consider whether the unfamiliar word may mean the same thing as the
         similar word.*

    c.   consider how the two words might relate to each other.*

    d.   rarely see that type of similarity.

17. When I read in French, I

    a.   am often confused by what I read.

    b.   expect to be confused by what I'm reading.

    c.   don't often make much sense of what I read.

    d.   expect what I read to make sense.*

    e.   find that what I'm reading makes sense.*

APPENDIX I

Selections from Think-Aloud Protocols

Notes on transcriptions:
French words appear in italics.

? following a word means that the word was not completely clear on the tape.

... indicates a pause of about three seconds.

MB: indicates comments from the researcher.

From "Eastwood": beginning of Paragraph 2

The text in English:

Clint won. He was elected mayor of Carmel: 2,116 electors in this small California town not far from San Francisco, where he's lived for fourteen years, preferred him to the outgoing mayor, 71-year-old Charlotte Townsend. At 55, having left his Magnum 357 in the holster of his film characters, Clint Eastwood has won his most difficult battle: convincing the old ladies dressed in pink or light green, the rich and peaceful retirees who travel only in a Bentley or Volvo, that he wasn't a public danger.

Think-Aloud Protocol of JS

Clint won. He was *élu maire* de, oh! he was mayor of Carmel. I know that, but I'm not sure if that's what that says, but I do know that. Two thousand one hundred and sixteen electors of this small village in California not far from San Francisco where he lived for fourteen years, preferred him to his, ... I guess, the other candidate, Charlotte Townsend, sixty-one years old. To fifty-five, oh!, at fifty-five years, *ayante laissé le Magnum* ... after, no, after, *laisé*, I always forget this word, *laisez-faire*, and I was trying to think of that, hands-off. After leaving, sort of, the Magnum three fifty-seven in *l'étui* ... of, of people or of characters of his films, *l'étui* ... I would think ... it would be some sort of just expression. This whole thing is like an expression describing his acting career, what types of acting he did. I'm not really sure what *l'étui* is, but it's a noun or it's like, I would think it would be like part of a, part of the person like in, in the pocket or in something like that. I'm not sure. Clint Eastwood won many difficult ... *combat*, many difficult fights. I'm not, no, it's not fights, something to that effect. *Convaincre de vieilles dames vêtues de rose* or *de vert pâle*. I do not know what *convain-- convaincre* means. Of old women *vêtues de rose ou de vert pâle, vêtues,* I'm not sure what that means, of rose or of pale green. So I would assume it would be something on their person, maybe an article of clothing or, no, of old, no it doesn't have an article, so it wouldn't be .... It's probably an adjective or, 'cause it doesn't have an article, so it's not; I don't see an article, so I don't think it's a noun ... of the something of <u>riches</u> and <u>paisibles retraitées qui ne se déplacent qu'en Bentley ou en Volvo</u> .... I'm going back and rereading this sentence from the beginning to see if I ... can ... . My biggest problem is the vocabulary ... <u>qu'en Bentley ou en Volvo qu'il n'était pas un danger public</u>. ... I think what I should try to do is to read the whole sentence first, which I never do; I always try to translate word for word, and that usually doesn't work. Or not word for word, but from fragment to fragment, and sometimes when I read the whole sentence, it helps me make a little bit more sense of what I'm reading. This is really; I'm not sure what this is saying, though, because of the vocabulary, I'm just not sure....<u>convaincre de vieilles dames vêtues de rose ou de vert pâle, vert pâle, de riches et paisibles retraitées, retraitées qui ne se déplacent qu'en Bentley ou en Volvo qu'il n'était pas</u>, that he was not ... a danger, a public danger! OK! That he was not a public danger. ... I ... <u>Il</u> is Clint, I would assume. If I knew what <u>convaincre</u> was, that would help. Old women <u>vêtues de rose</u> ... <u>de riches</u> ... Maybe part of his appeal, I don't know, I'm not really certain, maybe part of his appeal was, uh, even old ladies who, I don't know where the Bentley or the Volvo cars come in, <u>qui ne se déplacent</u> ... ... uh, I'm not sure. Maybe, maybe it's talking about the inhabitants of Carmel and his appeal to even the, oh! maybe what, what, what's going on here is they're trying to tell that his mass appeal even extends to these older ladies who drive Bentley and Volvo. I'm not sure, who own Bentley or Volvo. That he can't be too harmful if he is going to convince them that he is not a danger to the public. I'm not sure.

Think-Aloud Protocol of TH

Clint won. He was elected mayor of Carmel, two thousand one hundred and sixteen electors of this small village in California not far from San Francisco where he lives, where he's lived about fourteen years .... He preferred to be, he preferred mayor ... ... left Charles Townsend sixty-one years .... At fifty-five years ... ... with a three fifty-seven Magnum ... ... and I don't know what <u>l'étui</u> is. [MB: Can you figure it out?] ... ... I hate for the tape to keep going. [MB: That's OK. There is plenty of tape.] ... I think it's something to do with his character that carries his 357 in all of his, all of the characters he plays in his films .... He uh, Clint won his hardest combat .... <u>Convaincre</u>, I don't remember what that means either, of [sic] old women <u>vêtues</u>, again, I don't know that one either, of rose or pale green, riches and ... <u>retraitées</u>, it's kind of like retreat, <u>plausible</u>, who ... did not deplace themselves in a Bentley or a Volvo, and he ... ... was not in public danger. I'm not making much sense of this.

Selections from Think-Aloud Protocols
From "An 2000": Paragraph 4

In English:

Not only does the computer inform the household, but it also watches over it: if a flood or fire occurs, it takes it on itself to call the firemen. And if someone tries to break in, it alerts the closest police station, whose telephone number has been placed in its memory.

Think-Aloud of AP

Not only does the computer <u>renseigne,</u> which we don't know, but ... also, <u>il vielle</u> [sic], which looks kind of like the word "old," but the word "old" really wouldn't make sense here. If <u>un idonnation</u> [sic], which I don't know, <u>ou une incendie,</u> which I don't know either, is produced. So two things we don't know what they are produced, <u>il</u> names ... the, the same <u>les pompières</u>. Well, I'm gonna move on cause I didn't understand that, and if something find, look for is penetrated, <u>pénétérère</u> [sic] by <u>effraction,</u> which we don't know, <u>il avertit le commissaire de police le plus proche</u>. Now I get the impression from <u>pénéterer,</u> which might mean penetrate, and the fact that they are involving what I think is the commissioner of the police, that perhaps the computer is used like an alarm system, and if what it's hooked up to is disturbed, it immediately calls the police station ... of <u>le plus proche dont les coordonnées téléphoniques ont été confies</u> [sic] <u>son, sa mémoire ... coordonnées ... téléphoniques</u>. We know <u>téléphone</u> but ... we don't know what <u>sa mémoire</u> means, a, a personal story, I guess, not really sure about that part of the sentence, so I'll move on, again.

Think-Aloud of RW

Not only the computer information, but ... but also it <u>vieille</u> [sic], I don't know, the day before, uh, if, if and something I can't make out or something else happens, it calls the same ... I can't make out that word either, I'm totally lost now. If someone looks to get in by effraction, ... uh, it, I don't know, it contacts the commissioner of police, I would guess, oh, it alerts, ... I think that's what it would mean, the police, the closest police of which the telephone coordinates have been put in its memory. Going back, let's see, and if someone, it looks like if someone tries to break in, it alerts the closest police of which it has the telephone number in memory.

APPENDIX J

How to Analyze Text Structure

An author may choose from several types of logical organization: a sequence of events (perhaps chronological), general statements supported by examples, main ideas and supporting details, descriptions, comparisons and/or contrasts, cause and effect relationships, arguments and counter-arguments. In any reading you will likely find some combination of these organizing patterns, and you can predict much of the direction of the text on the basis of the patterns guiding it. Function words will often help you recognize the structure(s) of a specific text. Consider the following when analyzing text structures:

Chronological: Many stories and tales are told chronologically, as the events take place. Chronological organization is perhaps one of the easiest to follow: it presents events in order and marks them with appropriate adverbs of time, for example: <u>first, next, then, already, before, after, later, always, finally</u>.

Flashbacks: As you know, a number of stories are not written in chronological order but contain flashbacks (the presentation of events that have already taken place) and/or visions into the future. The author may, for stylistic reasons, make these changes in time and perspective more or less clear. In addition, reading in a second language certainly makes such shifts harder to recognize. Sources of problems are varied: unfamiliar vocabulary; a lack of skill with key verb tense forms (past or future) or a lack of understanding about how they are used; uncertainty about what is really happening in the story.

To deal with such problems and follow flashbacks more easily, look for the following clues:

--expressions of time (e.g., <u>last, ago, before</u>)

--indications of moments, days, weeks (e.g., <u>that evening, at that moment, a week ago, during the day</u>)

--changes in verb tense

--cause and effect and logical progression; use your common sense: which of two actions would logically cause the other?

General statements supported by examples: General statements are often characterized by:

--their position at the beginning of paragraphs

--use of the the present tense

--few details

--expressions like <u>in general, in a general way</u>.

Examples are often characterized by:

--their appearance after a general statement

--a change of tense from present to past or conditional

--details of places, times, names, etc.

--expressions like <u>for example, another..., one of them, besides, like, in that case</u>

Main ideas and supporting details: Texts organized on main ideas and supporting details are clearly similar to those defined by general statement and examples; these two text structures often appear together in the same selection. The differences are subtle. To decide which sort of structure(s) you have, ask yourself whether the supporting details are generally examples or simply more details about the main statement.

Descriptions: Descriptions most often contribute to another, larger text structure, such as those just discussed. A poem or short essay may be primarily descriptive, however. Look for adjectives and adverbs.

Comparisons and/or contrasts: Of course, a reading organized around comparisons and/or contrasts will contain a good deal of description. To read the comparative/contrastive structure effectively, ask yourself questions like the following:

What is being described?
What is being compared and/or contrasted?
Are there more similarities or differences?
What do these comparisons/contrasts show?

Useful function words describe:

a) **Similarity or Addition**		b) **Contrast**	
likewise	similarly	although	though
following	nevertheless	however	but
also	moreover	contrarily	otherwise
besides	furthermore	on the other hand	in contrast
in addition	beyond	still	conversely
as well as	at the same time		
in the same way			

Cause and effect relationships: Many nonfiction, explanatory essays and articles present the causes of a situation and the effects it has or might have. Here are some typical adverbs and conjunctions used to express:

a) **Cause**		b) **Effect/Result**	
why	because (of)	to have an effect	
since	given	in consequence	the consequence of
owing to	on account of	to result (in)	as a result
due to	thanks to	following	outcome
by virtue of	by reason of	to bring about	development

Arguments and counter-arguments: Selections organized around two or more points of an argument present different sides of a question either objectively or subjectively. As you read, look for different points of view and positive and negative remarks; decide whether the author is objective, openly arguing a certain position, or subtly supporting one point of view.

APPENDIX K
Basic English Prefixes

Prefix	Meaning	English ex.
a-,an-	not, without	anonymous
ab-,abs-	away from	abduction
ad-,ap-,ac-	towards, to	adherence
ana-	1)again	Anabaptist
	2)back, backward	anachronism
cata-	down	catastrophe
circon-, circum-	around	circumflex
co-,col-, com-,con-,cor-	with	collaborator
de-	1)reduce	devalued
	2)remove	decapitate
de-,dis-	separated from	disburse
di-	double	dissyllabic
di(a)-	1)separate, distinct	diacritical
	2)through	diagonal
ex-	1)out	export
	2)former	ex-husband
extra-	1)outside, beyond	extraordinary
	2)extremely	extra-fine
il-,im-,in-,ir-	1)in	infiltrate
	2)deprived of	irrelevant

Prefix	Meaning	English ex.
meta-	1)later, in succession	metaphysical
	2)change, transformation	metabolism
ob-	inversely, in the way	object
par-,para-	1)against, faulty	paradox
	2)related, resembling	paraphrase
per-	through	perforate
post-	after	postnatal
pre-	before, in advance, in front-preposition	
pro-	1)forward	prolong
	2)in favor of	pro-French
r-,re-	1)again	reexamine
	2)back, backward	recall (as in "remember")
sub-,sup-	under	subordinate
super-,supra-	over, above	superstructure
syl-,sym-	with, together	symmetry
syn-,sy- trans-	1)beyond	transatlantic
	2)through	transparent
	3)across	transport

References

Adams, S. J. (1982). Scripts and the recognition of unfamiliar vocabulary: Enhancing second language reading skills. *Modern Language Journal, 66* (2), 155-59.

Adamson, D. (1980). Prediction and reflection in reading in a foreign language. *Papers in language learning and language acquisition.* (ERIC Document Reproduction Service, No. ED 269 978).

Alderson, C., & Alvarez, G. (1978). The development of strategies for the assignment of semantic information to unknown lexemes in text. *Lenguas para Objetivos Específicas, 5,* 24 (ERIC Document Reproduction Service, No. ED 177 863).

Alderson, J. C. (1984). Reading in a foreign language: A reading problem or a language problem? In J. C. Alderson & A. H. Urquhart (Eds.), *Reading in a foreign language* (pp.1-27). New York: Longman.

Alderson, J. C., & Urquhart, A. H. (Eds.). (1984). Introduction: What is reading? *Reading in a foreign language* (pp. xv-xviii). New York: Longman.

Alderson, J. C., & Urquhart, A. H. (1985). This test is unfair: I'm not an economist. In P. Hauptman, R. Leblanc, & M. Bingham Wesche (Eds.), *Second language performance testing.* Ottawa: University of Ottawa Press. (Reprinted in: P. L. Carrell, J. Devine, & D. E. Eskey (Eds.), *Interactive approaches to second language reading* (pp.168-182). Cambridge: Cambridge University Press, 1988).

Allen, E. D. (1976). Miscue analysis: A new tool for diagnosing reading proficiency in foreign languages. *Foreign Language Annals, 9,* 563-67.

Allen, E. D., Bernhardt, E. B., Berry, M. T., & Demel, M. (1988). Comprehension and text genre: An analysis of secondary school foreign language readers. *Modern Language Journal, 72* (2), 163-72.

Allen, V. F. (1975). Some insights from linguistics for the teaching of literature. In M. K. Burt & H. C. Dulay (Eds.), *On TESOL '75: New directions in second language learning, teaching and bilingual education.* (pp. 319- 26) Los Angeles: Teachers of English to Speakers of Other Languages. (ERIC Document Reproduction Service, No. ED103 912).

Allerson, S., & Grabe, W. (1986). Reading assessment. In F. Dubin, D. E. Eskey, & W. Grabe (Eds.), *Teaching second language reading for academic purposes* (pp. 161-181).

Reading, MA: Addison-Wesley.

Anderson, R. C., & Pearson, P. D. (1984). A schema-theoretic view of basic processes in reading comprehension. In P. D. Pearson (Ed.), *Handbook of Reading Research* (pp.252-295). New York: Longman (ERIC Document Reproduction Service, No. ED 239 236).

Aron, H. (1979, September). *Comparing reading comprehension in Spanish and English by adult Hispanics entering a two-year college.* Paper presented at the international Conference on Frontiers in Language Proficiency and Dominance Testing, Carbondale, IL. (ERIC Document Reproduction Service, No. ED 184 307).

Aronson-Berman, R. (1978, August). *How hard it is to read? Syntactic complexity as a cause of reading difficulty.* Paper presented at the AILA Congress, Montreal.

Aspatore, J. V. (1984). But I don't know all the words! *Foreign Language Annals, 17,* 297-99.

Au, K. H. (1979). Using the experience-text-relationship method with minority children. *The Reading Teacher, 32,* 677-79.

Baker, L., & Brown, A. L. (1984). Metacognitive skills and reading. In P. D. Pearson (Ed.), *Handbook of reading research.* (pp. 353-394). New York: Longman (ERIC Document Reproduction Service, No. 195 932).

Bar-Lev, Z. (1980). *Exolexia.* (ERIC Document Reproduction Service, No. ED 231 217).

Barnett, M. A. (1986). Syntactic and lexical/semantic skill in foreign language reading: Importance and interaction. *Modern Language Journal, 70,* 343-49.

Barnett, M. A. (1988a). *Following reference words: One aspect of reading comprehension.* Unpublished manuscript.

Barnett, M. A. (1988b). Reading through context: How real and perceived strategy use affects L2 comprehension. *Modern Language Journal, 72* (2), 150-62.

Barnett, M. A. (1988c). Teaching reading strategies: How methodology affects language course articulation. *Foreign Language Annals, 21* (2), 109-19.

Barnitz, J. G. (1985). *Reading development of nonnative speakers of English.* Washington, DC: Center for Applied Linguistics (ERIC Document Reproduction Service, No. 256 182).

Beatie, B. A., Martin, L., & Oberst, B. S. (1984). Reading in the first-year college textbook: A syllabus for authors, publishers, reviewers, and instructors. *Modern Language Journal, 68*, 203-11.

Beebe, L. M. (Ed.) (1988). *Issues in second language acquisition: Multiple perspectives.* New York: Newbury House.

Been, S. (1979). Reading in the foreign language teaching program. In R. Mackay, B. Barkman, & R. R. Jordan (Eds.), *Reading in a second language: Hypotheses, organization, and practice* (pp. 91-105). Rowley, MA: Newbury House.

Benedetto, R. A. (1984). *A psycholinguistic investigation of the top-level organization strategies in first and second language reading: Five case studies.* Unpublished dissertation, New York University. Order No. DA8421427.

Benedetto, R. A. (1985, December). *Language ability and the use of top-level organizational strategies.* Paper presented at the Annual Meeting of the National Reading Conference. (ERIC Document Reproduction Service, No. ED 266 437).

Bensoussan, M. (1986). Beyond vocabulary: Pragmatic factors in reading comprehension—culture, convention, coherence and cohesion. *Foreign Language Annals, 19*, 399-407.

Bensoussan, M., & Laufer, B. (1984). Lexical guessing in context in EFL comprehension. *Journal of Research in Reading, 7*, 15 - 32.

Bensoussan, M., & Rosenhouse, J. (1984, August). *Using discourse analysis to diagnose difficulties in Arabic and Hebrew speaking EFL students' translations in comprehending a narrative text.* Paper presented at the 7th World Congress of the International Association of Applied Linguistics, Brussels.

Bereiter, C., & Bird, M. (1985). Use of thinking aloud in identification and teaching of reading comprehension strategies. *Cognition and Instruction, 2*, 131-56.

Berman, R. (1979). Analytic syntax: A technique for advanced level reading. In R. Mackay, B. Barkman, & R. R. Jordan (Eds.), *Reading in a second language: Hypotheses, organization, and practice* (pp. 178 - 186). Rowley, MA: Newbury House, 1979.

Berman, R. A. (1984). Syntactic components of the foreign language reading process. In J. C. Alderson & A. H. Urquhart (Eds.), *Reading in a Foreign Language.* (pp. 139-156). New York: Longman.

Bernhardt, E. B. (1983). Testing foreign language reading comprehension: The immediate recall protocol. *Die Unterrichtspraxis, 16*, 27-33.

Bernhardt, E. B. (1984). Toward an information processing perspective in foreign language reading. *Modern Language Journal 68* (4), 322-31.

Bernhardt, E. B. (1986a). A model of L2 text reconstruction: The recall of literary text by learners of German. In A. Labarca (Ed.), *Issues in L2: Theory as practice, practice as theory.* Norwood: Ablex.

Bernhardt, E. B. (1986b). Proficient texts or proficient readers? *ADFL Bulletin, 18,* 25-28.

Bernhardt, E. B. (1986c). Reading in the foreign language. In B. H. Wing (Ed.), *Listening, reading, and writing: Analysis and application* (pp. 93-115). Middlebury, VT: Northeast Conference.

Bernhardt, E. B. (1987a). Cognitive processes in L2: An examination of reading behaviors. In J. Lantolf & A. Labarca (Eds.), *Research on second language acquisition in classroom settings: Delaware symposium 6.* (pp. 35 - 50). Norwood, NJ: Ablex.

Bernhardt, E. B. (1987b). The text as a participant in instruction. *Theory into Practice, 26,* 32-37.

Bernhardt, E. B., & James, C. J. (1987). The teaching and testing of comprehension in foreign language learning. In D. Birckbichler (Ed.), *Proficiency, policy, and professionalism in foreign language education. Selected papers from the 1987 Central States Conference.* (pp.65-81). Lincolnwood, IL: National Textbook Co.

Bertin, C. (1987). L'exploitation des médiateurs de la compréhension pour la lecture des textes en langue étrangère. *Canadian Modern Language Review, 43* (3), 471-78.

Bialystok, E. (1979). The role of conscious strategies in second language proficiency. *Canadian Modern Language Review, 35,* 372-94. (Reprinted in *Modern Language Journal, 65,* 24-35).

Bialystok, E. (1983). Inferencing: Testing the "Hypothesis-Testing" hypothesis. In H. W. Seliger & M. H. Long (Eds.), *Classroom oriented research in second language acquisition* (pp. 104-133). Rowley, MA: Newbury House.

Bialystok, E., & Howard, J. (1979). *Inferencing as an aspect of cloze test performance. Working Papers on Bilingualism no. 17* (April). Toronto: Ontario Institute for Studies in Education. 24-36. (ERIC Document Reproduction Service, No. ED 169 774).

Biederman, I., & Tsao, Y.C. (1979). On processing Chinese ideographs and English words: Some implications from Stroop- test results. *Cognitive Psychology, 11,* 125-32.

Birckbichler, D., & Muyskens, J. (1980). A personalized approach to the teaching of literature at the elementary and intermediate levels of instruction. *Foreign Language Annals, 13,* 23-27.

Block, E. (1986). The comprehension strategies of second language readers. *TESOL Quarterly, 20* (3), 463-94.

Bramski, D., & Williams, R. (1984). Lexical familiarization in economics text, and its pedagogic implications in reading comprehension. *Reading in a Foreign Language, 2* (1), 169-81.

Bransford, J. D., & Johnson, M. K. (1973). Considerations of some problems of comprehension. In W. G. Chase, *Visual information processing* (pp. 383-438).New York: Academic Press.

Bransford, J. D., Stein, B. S., & Shelton, T. (1984). Learning from the perspective of the comprehender. In J. C. Alderson & A. H. Urquhart (Eds.), *Reading in a Foreign Language* (pp. 28-44). New York: Longman.

Bretz, M. L., & Persin, M. (1987). The application of critical theory to literature at the introductory level: A working model for teacher preparation. *Modern Language Journal, 71* (2), 165-70.

Brooks, G. (1984). Nineteenth and twentieth-century models of L2 reading. In A. K. Pugh & J. M. Ulijn (Eds.), *Reading for professional purposes: Studies and practices in native and foreign languages* (pp. 27-34). London: Heinemann.

Burling, R. (1982). An introductory course for reading French. In R. W. Blair (Ed.), *Innovative approaches to language teaching* (pp. 77-94). Rowley, MA: Newbury House.

Byrnes, H. (1985). Teaching toward proficiency: The receptive skills. In A. C. Omaggio (Ed.), *Proficiency, curriculum, articulation: The ties that bind* (pp. 77-107). Middlebury, VT: Northeast Conference.

Byrnes, H. (1988, August). *Looking behind the scenes: Images of America in texts.* Paper presented at the ACTFL Symposium on Teaching Foreign Languages to Adult Professionals: Approaches for the 1990's, Linthicum, MD.

Byrnes, H. & Canale, M. (Eds.). (1986). *ACTFL Proficiency Guidelines, 1986. Defining and developing proficiency: Guidelines, implementations and concepts.* Lincolnwood,

IL: National Textbook.

Byrnes, H., & Fink, S. (1985, April). *Read on: Developing reading strategies in German.* Paper presented at the Northeast Conference on the Teaching of Foreign Languages, New York.

Canale, M. (1984). Considerations in testing of reading and listening proficiency. *Foreign Language Annals, 17* (4), 349-57.

Capelle, G., & Grellet, F. (1979-81). *Ecritures: Textes et documents; Exercices de compréhension et de production écrites.* 3 vols. Paris: Hachette.

Carrell, P. L. (1981). Culture-specific schemata in L2 comprehension. In R. Orem & J. Haskell (Eds.), *Selected papers from the ninth Illinois TESOL/BE annual convention and the first midwest TESOL conference.* Chicago (123-132). IL: TESOL/BE.

Carrell, P. L. (1982). Cohesion is not coherence. *TESOL Quarterly, 16,* 479-88.

Carrell, P. L. (1983a). Some issues in studying the role of schemata, or background knowledge, in second language comprehension. *Reading in a Foreign Language, 1* (2), 81-92.

Carrell, P. L. (1983b). Three components of background knowledge in reading comprehension. *Language Learning, 33,* 183-207.

Carrell, P. L. (1984a). The effects of rhetorical organization on ESL readers. *TESOL Quarterly, 18* (3), 441-69.

Carrell, P. L. (1984b). Evidence of a formal schema in second language comprehension. *Language Learning, 34,* 87-112.

Carrell, P. L. (1984c). Schema theory and ESL reading: Classroom implications and applications. *Modern Language Journal, 68,* 332-43.

Carrell, P. L. (1985). Facilitating reading comprehension by teaching text structure. *TESOL Quarterly, 19* (4), 727-52.

Carrell, P. L. (1987a). Content and formal schemata in ESL reading. *TESOL Quarterly, 21* (3), 461-81.

Carrell, P. L. (1987b). ESP in applied linguistics: Refining research agenda. Implications and future directions of research on second language reading. *English for Specific Purposes, 6,* 233-43.

Carrell, P. L. (1987c). Introduction. In J. Devine, P. L. Carrell, & D. E. Eskey (Eds.), *Research in reading in English as a second language.* (pp.1-7). Washington, DC:

Teachers of English to Speakers of Other Languages.

Carrell, P. L. (1988a). Interactive text processing: Implications for ESL/second language reading classrooms. In P. L. Carrell, J. Devine, & D. E. Eskey (Eds.), *Interactive approaches to second language reading* (pp.239-259). Cambridge: Cambridge University Press.

Carrell, P. L. (1988b). Introduction. In P. L. Carrell, J. Devine, & D. E. Eskey (Eds.), *Interactive approaches to second language reading.* (pp.1-7). Cambridge: Cambridge University Press.

Carrell, P. L. (1988c). Some causes of text-boundedness and schema interference in ESL reading. In P. L. Carrell, J. Devine, & D. E. Eskey (Eds.), *Interactive approaches to second language reading* (pp.101-113). Cambridge: Cambridge University Press.

Carrell, P. L., Devine, J., & Eskey, D. E. (Eds.). (1988). *Interactive approaches to second language reading.* Cambridge: Cambridge University Press.

Carrell, P. L., & Eisterhold, J. C. (1983). Schema theory and ESL reading pedagogy. *TESOL Quarterly, 17* (4), 553-73.

Carton, A. S. (1971). Inferencing: A process in using and learning language. In P. Pimsleur & T. Quinn (Eds.), *The psychology of second language learning: Papers from the second international congress of applied linguistics* (pp. 45-58). Cambridge: Cambridge University Press.

Carver, R. (1977-78). Toward a theory of reading comprehension and rauding. *Reading Research Quarterly, 13,* 8-64.

Casanave, C. P. (1988). Comprehension monitoring in ESL reading: A neglected essential. *TESOL Quarterly, 22,* 283-302.

Cates, G. T., & Swaffar, J. K. (1979). *Reading a second language. Language in education: Theory and practice, 20.* Arlington, VA: Center for Applied Linguistics. (ERIC Document Reproduction Service, No. ED 176 588).

Chall, J. & Jacobs, V. (1983). Writing and reading in the elementary grades: Developmental trends among low SES children. *Language Arts, 60* (5), 617-26, 660.

Child, J. R. (1986). Language proficiency levels and the typology of texts. In H. Byrnes & M. Canale (Eds.), *Defining and developing proficiency.* (pp. 97-106). Lincolnwood, IL: National Textbook.

Chu-Chang, M., & Loritz, D. J. (1977). Even Chinese ideographs are phonologically encoded in short-term memory. *Language Learning, 27,* 341-52.

Clarke, D. F., & Nation, I. S. P. (1980). Guessing the meaning of words from context: Strategy and techniques. *System, 8* (3), 211-20.

Clarke, M. A. (1980). The short circuit hypothesis of ESL reading—or when language competence interferes with reading performance. *Modern Language Journal, 64,* 203-09.

Clarke, M. A., & Silberstein, S. (1977). Toward a realization of psycholinguistic principles in the ESL reading class. *Language Learning, 27* (1), 135-54.

Coady, J. (1979). A psycholinguistic model of the ESL reader. In R. Mackay, B. Barkman, & R. R. Jordan (Eds.), *Reading in a second language: Hypotheses, organization, and practice.* Rowley, MA: Newbury House. 5-12.

Cohen, A. D. (1984). The use of mentalistic measures in determining LSP reading problems. In A. K. Pugh & J. M. Ulijn (Eds.), *Reading for professional purposes: Studies and practices in native and foreign languages.* London: Heinemann. 177-89.

Cohen, A. D. (1986). Mentalistic measures in reading strategy research: Some recent findings. *English for Specific Purposes, 5* (2), 131-45.

Cohen, A. D. (1987). Studying learner strategies: How we get the information. In A. Wenden & J. Rubin (Eds.), *Learner strategies in language learning.* Englewood Cliffs, NJ: Prentice- Hall. 31-39.

Cohen, A., & Hosenfeld, C. (1981). Some uses of mentalistic data in second language research. *Language Learning, 31,* 285-313.

Connor, U. (1978). *A study of reading skills among English as a second language learners. Technical report No. 471.* Madison, WI: Wisconsin Univ. Research and Development Center for Individualized Schooling. Alexandria, VA: (ERIC Document Reproduction Service, No. ED 162 281)

Connor, U. (1981). The application of reading miscue analysis to diagnosis of English as a second language learner's reading skills. In C. W. Twyford, W. Deihl, & K. Feathers (Eds.), *Reading English as a second language: Moving from theory. Monograph in Language and Reading Studies.* Bloomington, IN: Indiana University School of Education. 47-55.

Connor, U. (1984). Recall of text: Differences between first and second language readers. *TESOL Quarterly, 18,* 239-56.

Connor, U. (1987). The Eclectic Synergy of Methods of Reading Research. In J.

Devine, P. L. Carrell, & D. E. Eskey (Eds.), *Research in reading in English as a second language* (pp. 9-20). Washington, DC: Teachers of English to Speakers of Other Languages.

Connor, U., & McCagg, P. (1983). Crosscultural differences and perceived quality in written paraphrases of English expository prose. *Applied Linguistics 4 (3)*, 259-68.

Cowan, J. R. (1974). Lexical and syntactic research for the design of EFL reading materials. *TESOL Quarterly, 8*, 389-99.

Cowan, J. R. (1976). Reading, perceptual strategies, and contrastive analysis. *Language Learning, 26*, 95-109.

Crow, J. T. (1986). Receptive vocabulary acquisition for reading comprehension. *Modern Language Journal, 70*, 242-50.

Cziko, G. A. (1978). Differences in first- and second-language reading: The use of syntactic, semantic and discourse constraints. *Canadian Modern Language Review, 34* (3), 473-89.

Cziko, G. A. (1980). Language competence and reading strategies: A comparison of first- and second-language oral reading errors. *Language Learning, 30*, 101-14.

Dandonoli, P. (1987). ACTFL's current research in proficiency testing. In H. Byrnes & M. Canale (Eds.), *Defining and developing proficiency* (pp. 75-96). Lincolnwood, IL: National Textbook Company.

Dank, M., & McEachern, W. (1979). A psycholinguistic description comparing the native language oral reading behavior of French immersion students with traditional English language students. *Canadian Modern Language Journal, 35* (3), 366-71.

Davis, J. N. (1988). Facilitating effects on foreign-language reading of marginal glosses. Unpublished manuscript.

Deemer, H. B. (1978). *The transfer of reading skills from first to second language: The report of an experiment with Spanish speakers learning English.* Alexandria, VA: ERIC Clearinghouse on Languages and Linguistics. (ERIC Document Reproduction Service, No. ED 172 532)

Deese, J. (1984). *Thought into speech: The psychology of a language.* Englewood Cliffs, NJ: Prentice Hall.

Dever, S. Y. (1986). Computer-assisted reading instruction. In F. Dubin, D. E. Eskey,

& W. Grabe (Eds.), *Teaching second language reading for academic purposes* (pp. 183-216). Reading, MA: Addison-Wesley.

Devine, J. (1981). Developmental patterns in native and non- native reading acquisition. In S. Hudelson (Ed.), *Learning to read in different languages. Linguistics and literacy series* (pp. 103-114). Washington, DC: Center for Applied Linguistics.

Devine, J. (1984). ESL readers' internalized models of the reading process. In J. Handscombe, R. A. Orem, & B. P. Taylor (Eds.), *On TESOL '83: The question of control* (pp. 95-108). Washington, DC: Teachers of English to Speakers of Other Languages.

Devine, J. (1987). General language competence and adult second language reading. In J. Devine, P. L. Carrell, & D. E. Eskey (Eds.), *Research in reading in English as a second language.* Washington, DC: Teachers of English to Speakers of Other Languages.

Dixon, C. N., & Nessel, D. (1983). *Language experience approach to reading (and writing).* Hayward, CA: Alemany (ERIC Document Reproduction Service, No. 236 933).

Dubin, F. (1986). Dealing with texts. In F. Dubin, D. E. Eskey, & W. Grabe (Eds.), *Teaching second language reading for academic purposes* (pp.127-160). Reading, MA: Addison-Wesley.

Dubin, F. (1987). Comments on Sarig, "High-level reading in the first and in the foreign language: Some comparative process data." In J. Devine, P. L. Carrell, & D. E. Eskey (Eds.), *Research in reading in English as a second language* (pp.127-160). Washington, DC: Teachers of English to Speakers of Other Languages.

Dubin, F., Eskey, D. E., & Grabe, W. (Eds.) (1986). *Teaching second language reading for academic purposes.* Reading, MA: Addison-Wesley.

Elias, J. A. (1975). Predicting your way through written English: An approach to teaching advanced reading to ESL students. In M. K. Burt, & H. C. Dulay (Eds.), *On TESOL '75: New directions in second language learning, teaching, and bilingual education* (pp. 307-18). Washington, DC: Teachers of English to Speakers of Other Languages.

Ericsson, K. A., & Simon, H. A. (1980). Verbal reports as data. *Psychological Review, 87,* 215-51.

Ervin, G. L. (October, 1988). *How many per dozen? Some thoughts on changing a light bulb.* Paper presented at the 27th Annual Virginia Foreign Language Conference, Virginia Beach.

Eskey, D. (1971). Advanced reading: The structural problem. *English Teaching Forum, 9* (5), 15-19.

Eskey, D. (1973). A model program for teaching advanced reading to students of English as a second language. *Language Learning,* 23 (2), 169-84. (Reprinted in R. Mackay, B. Barkman, & R. R. Jordan (Eds.), *Reading in a second language: Hypotheses, organization, and practice.* (pp. 66-78). Rowley, MA: Newbury House, 1979).

Eskey, D. E. (1976, July). *Toward a theory of second language reading.* Paper presented at the Conference on Second Language Learning and Teaching, Oswego, NY. (ERIC Document Reproduction Service, No. ED 132 845).

Eskey, D. E. (1988). Holding in the bottom: An interactive approach to the language problems of second language readers. In P. L. Carrell, J. Devine, D. E. Eskey (Eds.), *Interactive approaches to second language reading* (pp. 93-100). Cambridge: Cambridge Univ. Press.

Everson, M. (1987, November). *Spatial manipulation of characters.* Paper presented at the ACTFL Annual Meeting, Atlanta.

Faerch, C., & Kasper, G. (Eds.). (1987). *Introspection in second language research.* Clevedon, Avon/Philadelphia: Multilingual Matters ,Ltd.

Field, M. L. (1987). Comments on Parry, "Reading in a second culture." In P. L. Carrell, J. Devine, & D. E. Eskey (Eds.), *Research in reading in English as a second language* (pp. 71-72). Washington, DC: Teachers of English to Speakers of Other Languages.

Flavell, J. H. (1981). Cognitive monitoring. In W. P. Dickson (Ed.), *Children's oral communication skills* (pp.35-60). New York: Academic Press.

Floyd, P., & Carrell, P. L. (1987). Effects on ESL reading of teaching cultural content schemata. *Language Learning, 37,* 89-108.

Fransson, A. (1984). Cramming or understanding? Effects of intrinsic and extrinsic motivation on approach to learning and test performance. In J. C. Alderson & A. H. Urquhart (Eds.), *Reading in a Foreign Language* (pp. 86-115). New York: Longman.

Garrett, N. (1987, December). *Using the computer for data elicitation, collection, and analysis in second-language-acquisition research.* Paper presented at the Modern Language Association Convention, San Francisco.

Gipe, J. (1979). Investigating techniques for teaching word meanings. *Reading Research Quarterly, 14,* 624-44.

Goldman, S. R., & Reyes, M. (1983, April). *Use of prior knowledge in understanding fables in first and second languages..* Paper presented at the Annual Meeting of the American Educational Research Association, Montreal. (ERIC Document Reproduction Service, No. ED 233 571).

Goodman, K. S. (1967). Reading: a psycholinguistic guessing game. *Journal of the Reading Specialist, 6,* 126-135.

Goodman, K. S. (Ed.). (1968). *The psycholinguistic nature of the reading process.* Detroit: Wayne State University Press.

Goodman, K. S. (1975). The reading process. In S. Smiley & J. Towner (Eds.), *Language and reading: Sixth western symposium on learning.* Bellingham, WA: Western Washington State College.

Goodman, K. S. (1981). Miscue analysis and future research directions. In S. Hudelson (Ed.), *Learning to read in different languages. Linguistics and literacy series* (pp. ix-xiii). Washington, DC: Center for Applied Linguistics.

Goodrich, H. C. (1977). Vocabulary development with contextual clues. *Zielsprache Englisch, 3,* 18-20.

Gough, P. B. (1972). One second of reading. In J. F. Kavanagh & I. G. Mattingly (Eds.), *Language by Ear and by Eye* (pp.331-358). Cambridge, MA: MIT Press.

Greenewald, M. J. (1979, March). *Teaching basic reading comprehension skills.* Paper presented at the Central States Conference. (ERIC Document Reproduction Service, No. ED 184 362)

Grellet, F. (1981). *Developing reading skills: A practical guide to reading comprehension exercises.* Cambridge: Cambridge University Press (ERIC Document Reproduction Service, No. .207 347).

Gremmo, M. J. (1980). *Apprenant en langue ou apprenti lecteur?* Nancy, France: Université de Nancy Centre de Recherches et d'Applications Pédagogiques en Langages. (ERIC Document Reproduction Service, No. ED 201 194).

Groebel, L. (1981). Reading: The students' approach as compared to their teachers' recommended approach. *English Language Teaching Journal, 35* (3), 282-87.

Grove, M. P. (1981). Psycholinguistic theories and ESL reading. In C. W. Twyford, W. Diehl, & K. Feathers (Eds.), *Reading English as a second language: Moving from theory* (pp. 3-20). Bloomington, IN: Indiana University School of Education.

Guarino, R., & Perkins, K. (1986). Awareness of form class as a factor in ESL reading comprehension. *Language Learning, 36,* 77-82.

Hagboldt, P. (1926). On inference in reading. *Modern Language Journal, 11,* 73-78.

Hague, S. A. (1987). Vocabulary instruction: What L2 can learn from L1. *Foreign Language Annals, 20* (3), 217-25.

Halliday, M. A. K., & Hasan, R. (1976). *Cohesion in English.* London: Longman.

Harri-Augstein, S., & Thomas, L. F. (1984). Conversational investigations of reading: The self-organized learner and the text. In J. C. Alderson & A. H. Urquhart (Eds.), *Reading in a Foreign Language* (pp.250-276). New York: Longman.

Hatch, E. (1974). Research on reading a second language. *Journal of Reading Behavior, 6* (1), 53-61.

Hatch, E., Polin, P., & Part, S. (1974). Acoustic scanning and syntactic processing: Three experiments—first and second language learners. *Journal of Reading Behavior, 6,* 275-85.

Hauptman, P. C. (1979). A comparison of first and second language reading strategies among English-speaking university students. *Interlanguage Studies Bulletin, Utrecht State Univ.ersity, 4* (2), 173-201. (ERIC Document Reproduction Service, No. ED 207 324)

Hayes, E. (1988). Encoding strategies used by native and non-native readers of Chinese Mandarin. *Modern Language Journal, 72* (2), 188-95.

Haynes, M. (1984). Patterns and perils of guessing in second language reading. In J. Handscombe, R. Orem, & B. P. Taylor (Eds.), *On TESOL '83* (pp. 163-177). Washington, DC: Teachers of English to Speakers of Other Languages.

Hellgren, P. (1986). *Thinking in a foreign language. Research report 44.* Helsinki: Helsinki Univ. Dept. of Teacher Education. (ERIC Document Reproduction Service, No. ED 283 371).

Henning, G. W. (1975). Measuring foreign language reading comprehension. *Language Learning, 25,* 109-14.

Henry, R. (1984). Reader-generated questions: A tool for improving reading comprehension. *TESOL Newsletter, 18* (3), 29.

Hill, L. A. (1978). Practice in intelligent guessing of meaning from context. *Zielspra-*

che Englisch, 3, 1-2.

Hinds, J. L. (1983). Contrastive rhetoric: Japanese and English. *Text 3* (1), 183-95 (ERIC Document Reproduction Service, No. 217 720).

Hirsch, E. D. (1987). *Cultural literacy: What every American needs to know.* Boston: Houghton Mifflin.

Holley, F. (1973). A study of vocabulary learning in context: The effect of new-word density in German reading materials. *Foreign Language Annals, 6,* 339-47.

Honeyfield, J. (1977). Word frequency and the importance of context in vocabulary learning. *RELC Journal, 8* (2), 35-42.

Hosenfeld, C. (1976). Learning about learning: Discovering our students' strategies. *Foreign Language Annals, 9,* 117-29.

Hosenfeld, C. (1977a). *A learning-teaching view of second-language instruction: The learning strategies of second-language learners with reading-grammar tasks.* Dissertation, Ohio State University.

Hosenfeld, C. (1977b). A preliminary investigation of the reading strategies of successful and nonsuccessful second language learners. *System, 5* (2), 110-23.

Hosenfeld, C. (1979). Cindy: A learner in today's foreign language classroom. In W. C. Born (Ed.), *The foreign language learner in today's classroom environment* (pp. 53-75). Middlebury, VT: Northeast Conference (ERIC Document Reproduction Service, No. ED 185 837).

Hosenfeld, C. (1984). Case studies of ninth grade readers. In J. C. Alderson & A. H. Urquhart (Eds.), *Reading in a foreign language* (pp. 231-234). New York: Longman.

Hosenfeld, C., Arnold, V., Kirchofer, J., Laciura, J., and Wilson, L. (1981). Second language reading: A curricular sequence for teaching reading strategies. *Foreign Language Annals, 14* (5), 415-22.

Hudelson, S. (Ed.). (1981). *Learning to read in different languages. Linguistics and literacy series.* Washington, DC: Center for Applied Linguistics (ERIC Document Reproduction Service, No. ED 198 744).

Hudelson, S. (1984) Kan yu ret and rayt en Ingles: Children become literate in English as a second language. *TESOL Quarterly, 18* (2), 221-38.

Hudson, T. (1982). The effects of induced schemata on the "short circuit" in L2 reading: Non-decoding factors in L2 reading performance. *Language Learning, 32*, 1-31.

Hummel, R. D. (1985). Evaluating proficiency in comprehension skills: How can we measure what we can't observe? *ADFL Bulletin, 16*, 13-16.

James, M. O. (1987). ESL reading pedagogy: Implications of schema-theoretical research. In J. Devine, P. L. Carrell, & D. E. Eskey (Eds.), *Research in reading in English as a second language* (pp. 175-188). Washington, DC: Teachers of English to Speakers of Other Languages.

Jarvis, G. (1979). The second language teacher: Reconciling the vision with the reality. In W. Born (Ed.), *The foreign language learning in today's classroom* (pp. 77-104). Middlebury, VT: Northeast Conference.

Jensen, L. (1986). Advanced reading skills in a comprehensive course. In F. Dubin, D. E. Eskey, & W. Grabe (Eds.), *Teaching second language reading for academic purposes* (pp. 103-124). Reading, MA: Addison-Wesley.

Jew, V. (1986, April) *Literacy skills development and the Asian LEP students.* Paper presented at the Annual International Bilingual/Bicultural Conference of the National Association for Bilingual Education, Chicago. (ERIC Document Reproduction Service, No. ED 272 036).

Johnson, D. D. (1983). *Three sound strategies for vocabulary development* (No. 3 of Ginn Occasional Papers). Lexington, MA: Ginn and Co. (Xerox Corp.).

Johnson, D. D., & Pearson, P. D. (1984). *Teaching reading vocabulary.* (2nd ed.). New York: Holt, Rinehart, & Winston.

Johnson, P. (1981). Effects on reading comprehension of building background knowledge. *TESOL Quarterly, 16*, 503-16.

Johnson, P. (1982). Effects on reading comprehension of language complexity and cultural background of text. *TESOL Quarterly, 15*, 169-81.

Johnston, P. (1983). *Reading comprehension assessment: A cognitive basis.* Newark, DE: International Reading Association (ERIC Document Reproduction Service, No. ED 226 338).

Jones, R. L. (1984). Testing the receptive skills: Some basic considerations. *Foreign Language Annals, 17* (4), 365-67.

Just, M. A., & Carpenter, P. A. (1980). A theory of reading: From eye fixations to comprehension. *Psychological Review, 87*, 329-54.

Kamil, M.L. (1984). Current traditions of reading research. In P.D. Pearson, R. Barr, M.L. Kamil, P. Mosenthal (Eds.), *Handbook of reading research.*(pp.39-62). New York: Longman.

Kamil, M. L. (1986). Reading in the native language. In B. H. Wing (Ed.), *Listening, reading, and writing: Analysis and application* (pp. 71-91). Middlebury, VT: Northeast Conference.

Kaplan, R. B. (1966). Cultural thought patterns in inter-cultural education. *Language learning, 16,* 1-20. (Reprinted in K. Croft (Ed.), *Readings on English as a second language* (pp. 399-418). 2nd ed. Cambridge, MA: Winthrop, 1980).

Kaplan, R. B. (1967). Contrastive rhetoric and the teaching of composition. *TESOL Quarterly, 1,* 10-16.

Kaya-Carton, E., & Carton, A. S. (1986). Multidimensionality of foreign language reading proficiency: Preliminary considerations in assessment. *Foreign Language Annals, 18,* 95-102.

Kellerman, M. (1981). *The forgotten third skill.* Oxford, Pergamon (ERIC Document Reproduction Service, No. ED 213 269).

Kern, R. G. (1988). *The role of comprehension strategies in foreign language reading.* Unpublished dissertation, University of California, Berkeley.

Kintsch, W., & Greene, E. (1978). The role of culture-specific schemata in the comprehension and recall of stories. *Discourse Processes, 1* (1), 1-13.

Kintsch, W., & van Dijk, T. (1978). Toward a model of text comprehension and production. *Psychological Review, 85,* 363-94.

Knight, S. L., Padron Y. N., Waxman, H. C. (1985). The cognitive reading strategies of ESL students. *TESOL Quarterly, 19* (4), 789-92.

Koda, K. (1987). Cognitive strategy transfer in second language reading. In J. Devine, P. L. Carrell, & D. E. Eskey (Eds.), *Research in reading in English as a second language (pp. 125-144).* Washington, DC: Teachers of English to Speakers of Other Languages.

Kozminsky, E., & Graetz, N. (1986). First vs. second language comprehension: Some evidence from text summarizing. *Journal of Research in Reading, 9* (1), 3-21.

Kramsch, C. (1985). Literary texts in the classroom. *Modern Language Journal, 69,* 356-66.

Krashen, S. D. (1981). *Second language acquisition and second language learning.* Oxford: Pergamon (Reprinted: New York: Prentice Hall, 1988.).

Krashen, S. D. (1988). Do we learn to read by reading? The relationship between free reading and reading ability. In D. Tannen (Ed.), *Linguistics and context: Connecting observation and understanding* (pp. 269-298). Norwood, NJ: Ablex.

Kreeft, H., & Sanders, P. (1983). Model responses for examinations with open-ended questions. *Practice and Problems in Language Testing* 5. Alexandria, VA: ERIC Document Reproduction Service, No. ED 282 424.

Kruse, A. F. (1979). Vocabulary in context. *English Language Teaching Journal, 33* (3), 207-13.

LaBerge, D. & Samuels, S. J. (1974). Toward a theory of automatic information processing in reading. *Cognitive Psychology, 6,* 293-323.

Lange, D. L., & Lowe, Jr., P. (1988). Rating reading passages according to the ACTFL reading proficiency standard: Can it be learned? *Foreign Language Annals, 21* (3), 227-39.

Langer, J. A. (1981). From theory to practice: A pre-reading plan. *Journal of Reading, 25,* 152-58.

Laroche, J. M. (1979). Readability measurement for foreign language materials. *System, 7,* 131-35.

Laufer, B., & Sim, D. D. (1982, November). *Does the EFL reader need reading strategies more than language? Some experimental evidence.* Paper presented at the Annual Meeting of the American Council on the Teaching of Foreign Languages, New York. Alexandria, VA: ERIC Document Reproduction Service, No. ED 228 848.

Laufer, B., & Sim., D. D. (1985) Measuring and explaining the reading threshold needed for English for academic purposes texts. *Foreign Language Annals, 18* (5), 405-11.

Lee, J. F. (1986). Background knowledge & L2 reading. *Modern Language Journal, 70* (4), 350-54.

Lee, J. F. (1987a). Comprehending the Spanish subjunctive: An information processing approach. *Modern Language Journal, 71* (1), 50-57.

Lee, J. F. (1987b, November). *The impact of reading on writing.* Paper presented at the ACTFL/AAT Joint Annual Meeting, Atlanta.

Lee, J. F. (1988a, August). *An input approach to reading*. Paper presented at the ACTFL Symposium on Teaching Foreign Languages to Adult Professionals: Approaches for the 1990's, Linthicum, MD.

Lee, J. F. (1988b, October). *Models for exploring non-native reading*. Paper presented at the Conference on Research Perspectives in Adult Language Learning and Acquisition, Columbus, OH.

Lee, J. F. (1988c). Toward a modification of the "proficiency" construct for reading in a foreign language. *Hispania, 71* (4), in press.

Lee, J. F., & Musumeci, D. (1988). On hierarchies of reading skills and text types. *Modern Language Journal, 72* (2), 173- 87.

Levine, M. G., & Haus, G. J. (1985). The effect of background knowledge on the reading comprehension of second language learners. *Foreign Language Annals, 18* (5), 391-97.

Liskin-Gasparro, J. E. (1984). Practical considerations in receptive skills testing. *Foreign Language Annals, 17* (4), 369-73.

Littlewood, W. T. (1975). Literature in the school foreign language course. *Modern Languages, 56* (3), 127-31.

Loew, H. Z. (1984). Developing strategic reading skills. *Foreign Language Annals, 17,* 301-303.

Lowe, Jr., P. (1984). Setting the stage: Constraints on ILR receptive skills testing. *Foreign Language Annals, 17* (4), 375-79.

Lundberg, I. (1984, August). *Reading process*. Paper presented at the IRA Symposium on Reading and Linguistics of the 7th World Congress of the International Association of Applied Linguistics, Brussels.

Mackay, R. (1979). Teaching the information-gathering skills. In R. Mackay, B. Barkman, & R. R. Jordan (Eds.), *Reading in a second language: Hypotheses, organization, and practice* (pp.79-90). Rowley, MA: Newbury House.

Mackay, R., & Mountford, A. (1979). Reading for information. In R. Mackay, B. Barkman, & R. R. Jordan (Eds.), *Reading in a second language: Hypotheses, organization, and practice* (pp. 106-141). Rowley, MA: Newbury House.

MacNamara, J. (1967). *Comparative studies of reading and problem solving in two languages*. McGill University: Language Research Group (ERIC Document Reproduction Service, No. ED 038 635).

Mahon, D. (1986). Intermediate skills: Focusing on reading rate development. In F. Dubin, D. E. Eskey, & W. Grabe (Eds.), *Teaching second language reading for academic purposes* (pp. 77-102). Reading, MA: Addison-Wesley.

Mandler, J. M., Scribner, S., Cole, M., & DeForest, M. (1980).Cross-cultural invariance in story recall. *Child Development, 51* (1), 19-26.

McLeod, B., & McLaughlin, B. (1986). Restructuring or automaticity? Reading in a second language. *Language Learning, 36,* 109-23.

Meara, P. (1984). Word recognition in foreign languages. In A.K. Pugh & J. M. Ulijn (Eds.), *Reading for professional purposes: Studies and practices in native and foreign languages* (pp. 97-105). London: Heinemann.

Medley, F. W., Jr. (1977). Reading assignments versus reading instruction: Native language strategies and techniques for use in the foreign language classroom. In R. A. Schulz (Ed.), *Personalizing foreign language instruction: Learning styles and teaching options* (pp.29-42). Skokie, IL: National Textbook.

Melendez, E. J., & Pritchard, R. H. (1985). Applying schema theory to foreign language reading. *Foreign Language Annals, 18* (5), 399-403.

Meyer, B. J. F. (1975). *The organization of prose and its effects on memory.* Amsterdam: North Holland.

Meyer, B. J. F. (1977). What is remembered from prose: A function of passage structure. In R. O. Freedle (Ed.), *Discourse production and comprehension* (pp. 307-336). Norwood, NJ: Ablex.

Meyer, B. J. F. (1979). Organizational patterns in prose and their use in reading. In M. L. Kamil & A. J. Moe (Eds.), *Reading research: Studies and applications* (pp.109-117). Clemson, SC: National Reading Conference.

Meyer R. M., & Tetrault, E. W. (1986). Open your CLOZEd minds: Using cloze exercises to teach foreign language reading.*Foreign Language Annals,19* (5), 409-15.

Meyer, R. M., & Tetrault, E. W. (1988). Getting started: Reading techniques that work from the very first day. *Foreign Language Annals, 21,* 423-31.

Moirand, S. (1979). *Situations d'écrit (compréhension, production en langue étrangere).* Paris: CLE International.

Moody, K. W. (1976). A type of exercise for developing prediction skills in reading. *RELC Journal, 7* (1), 13-20.

Muchisky, D. (1983). Relationship between speaking and reading among second language learners. *Language Learning, 33,* 77- 102.

Munby, J. (1979). Teaching intensive reading skills. In R. Mackay, B. Barkman, & R. R. Jordan (Eds.), *Reading in a second language: Hypotheses, organization, and practice* (pp. 142-158). Rowley, MA: Newbury House.

Muylaert, W., Nootens, J., Poesmans, D., & Pugh, A. K. (1983). Design and utilisation of subtitles on foreign language television programmes. In P. H. Nelde (Ed.), *Theorie, Methoden und Modelle der Kontaktlinguistik.* Bonn: Dummler.

Nuttall, C. (1983). *Teaching reading skills in a foreign language.* London: Heinemann.

Oller, J. W., Jr. (1972). Assessing competence in ESL reading. *TESOL Quarterly, 6* (4), 313-23.

Oller, J. W., Jr. (1973) Cloze tests of second language proficiency and what they measure. *Language Learning, 23,* 105-18.

Olshavsky, J. E. (1976-77). Reading as problem solving: An investigation of strategies. *Reading Research Quarterly, 12* (4), 654-74.

Omaggio, A. C. (1979). Pictures and second language comprehension: Do they help? *Foreign Language Annals, 12* (2), 107-16.

Omaggio, A. C. (1984). Making reading comprehensible. *Foreign Language Annals, 17,* 305-308.

Omaggio, A. C. (1986). *Teaching language in context: Proficiency-oriented instruction.* Boston: Heinle.

Ozete, O. (1978). *Assessing reading comprehension in Spanish for bilingual children. Bulletin no. 9533.* Madison: Wisconsin State Dept. of Public Instruction. (ERIC Document Reproduction Service, No. ED 157 667).

Padron, Y. N., & Waxman, H. C. (1988). The effect of ESL students' perception of their cognitive strategies on reading achievement. *TESOL Quarterly, 22* (1), 146-50.

Pak, J. (1986). The effect of vocabulary glossing on ESL reading comprehension. Unpublished experiment report.

Pakenham, K. J. (1984). Developing expectations for text in adult beginning ESL readers. In J. Handscombe, R. Orem, & B. P. Taylor (Eds.), *On TESOL '83* (pp. 149-161). Washington, DC: Teachers of English to Speakers of Other Languages.

Palmberg, R. (1987). On lexical inferencing and the young foreign-language learner. *System, 15* (1), 69-76.

Parry, K. J. (1987). Reading in a second culture. In J. Devine, P. L. Carrell, & D. E. Eskey (Eds.), *Research in reading in English as a second language* (pp. 59-70). Washington, DC: Teachers of English to Speakers of Other Languages.

Pearson, P. D., & Tierney, R. (1984). On becoming a thoughtful reader: Learning to read like a writer. In A. Purves & O. Niles (Eds.), *Becoming a reader in a complex society*. Chicago, IL: Chicago University Press.

Perkins, K. (1983). Semantic constructivity in ESL reading comprehension. *TESOL Quarterly, 17,* 19-27.

Perkins, K., & Brutten, S. (1983). The effects of word frequency and contextual richness on ESL students' word identification abilities. *Journal of Research in Reading, 6* (2), 119-28.

Peters, C. W. (1978). Assessing reading performance at a second level through the utilization of a cognitive self-rating scale. In P. D. Pearson & J. Hansen (Eds.), *Reading: Disciplined inquiry in process and practice* (pp. 161-165). Clemson, SC: National Reading Conference.

Phifer, S. J., & Glover, J. A. (1982). Don't take students' word for what they do while reading. *Bulletin of the Psychonomic Society, 19,* 194-96.

Phillips, J. K. (1975). Second language reading: Teaching decoding skills. *Foreign Language Annals, 8,* 227-32.

Phillips, J. K. (1984). Practical implications of recent research in reading. *Foreign Language Annals, 17,* 285-96.

Phillips, J. K. (1985, April). *Proficiency-based instruction in foreign language reading: A teacher education model*. U. S. Department of Education International Research and Studies Program, #G008402271. (Also, *Teaching foreign language reading: A five-step plan*. Paper presented at the Northeast Conference, New York.).

Phillips, J. K., & Dandonoli, P. (1986, April). *Testing receptive skills in a proficiency mode*. Paper presented at the Northeast Conference, Washington, DC.

Pierce, M. E. (1979). Teaching the use of formal redundancy in reading for ideas. In R. Mackay, B. Barkman, & R. R. Jordan (Eds.), *Reading in a second language: Hypotheses, organization, and practice* (pp. 159-177). Rowley, MA: Newbury

House.

Plaister, R. (1968). Reading instruction for college level foreign students. *TESOL Quarterly, 2* (3), 164-68.

Prince, G. (1984). Literary theory and the undergraduate curriculum. *Profession 84,* 37.

Pugh, A. K., & Ulijn, J. M. (Eds.) (1984). *Reading for professional purposes: Studies and practices in native and foreign languages.* London: Heinemann.

Pusack, J. P. (1984). The interactive computer testing of reading proficiency. *Foreign Language Annals, 17* (4), 415-19.

Rathmell, George. (1984). *Bench marks in reading: A guide to reading instruction in the second language classroom.* Hayward, CA: Alemany Press.

Renault, L. (1981). Theoretically based second language reading strategies. In C. W. Twyford, W. Diehl, & K. Feathers (Eds.), *Reading English as a second language: Moving from theory* (pp. 64-80). Bloomington: Indiana University School of Education.

Rigg, P. (1977). The miscue-ESL project. In H. D. Brown, C. Yorio, R. Crymes (Eds.), *On TESOL '77: Teaching and learning English as a second language: Trends in research and practice* (pp. 106-118). Washington, DC: Teachers of English to Speakers of Other Languages.

Rivers, W. (1968). *Teaching foreign language skills.* (2nd ed., 1981). Chicago: University of Chicago Press (ERIC Document Reproduction Service, No. ED 205 037).

Rizzardi, M. C. (1980). Reader and text in comprehension. In G. Cortese (Ed.), *Reading in a foreign language* (pp. 449-458). Milan: Franco Angeli.

Robinett, B. W. (1980). Reading English as a second language. In K. Croft (Ed.), *Readings on English as a second language* (pp. 355-366). Cambridge, MA: Winthrop.

Robinson, F. P. (1962). *Effective Reading.* New York: Harper.

Rogers, C. V., & Medley, Frank W., Jr. (1988). Language with a purpose: Using authentic materials in the foreign language classroom. *Foreign Language Annals, 21,* 467-78.

Royer, J. M., Bates, J. A., & Konold, C. E. (1984). Learning from text: Methods of affecting reader intent. In J. C. Alderson & A. H. Urquhart (Eds.), *Reading in a Foreign Language* (pp. 65-81). New York: Longman.

Rumelhart, D. E. (1977a). Toward an interactive model of reading. In S. Dornic (Ed.), *Attention and Performance VI* (pp. 573-603). Hillsdale, NJ: Lawrence Erlaum.

Rumelhart, D. E. (1977b). Understanding and summarizing brief stories. In D. LaBerge & S. J. Samuels (Eds.), *Basic processes in reading: Perception and comprehension* (pp.265-303). Hillsdale, NJ: Erlbaum.

Rumelhart, D. E., McClelland, J. L., & the PDP Research Group. (1986). *Parallel distributed processing: Explorations in the microstructure of cognition.* 2 vols. Cambridge, MA: MIT Press.

Sacco, S. J. (1987). Crap detecting: An approach to developing critical reading and thinking skills in the foreign language curriculum. *Foreign Language Annals, 20* (1), 57-62.

Samuels, S. J. (1977). Introduction to theoretical models of reading. In W. Otto (Ed.), *Reading Problems.* Boston: Addison-Wesley.

Samuels, S. J., & Kamil, M. L. (1984). Models of the reading process. In P. D. Pearson (Ed.), *Handbook of Reading Research* (pp.185-224). New York: Longman.

Samuels, S. J., & LaBerge, D. (1983). A critique of "A theory of automaticity in reading": Looking back: A retrospective analysis of the LaBerge-Samuels reading model. In L. Gentile, M. Kamil, & J. Blanchard (Eds.), *Reading research revisited.* Columbus, OH: C. E. Merrill.

Saragi, T., Nation, I. S. P., & Meister, G. F. (1978). Vocabulary learning and reading. *System, 6* (2), 72-78.

Sarig, G. (1987). High-level reading in the first and in the foreign language: Some comparative process data. In J. Devine, P. L. Carrell, & D. E. Eskey (Eds.), *Research in reading in English as a second language* (pp.107-120). Washington, DC: Teachers of English to Speakers of Other Languages.

Saville-Troike, M. (1979). Reading and the audio-lingual method. In R. Mackay, B. Barkman, & R. R. Jordan (Eds.), *Reading in a second language: Hypotheses, organization, and practice* (pp. 24-35). Rowley, MA: Newbury House.

Schatz, E. K., & Baldwin, R. W. (1986). Context clues are unreliable predictors of word meanings. *Reading Research Quarterly, 21,* 439-53.

Schulz, R. A. (1981). Literature and readability: Bridging the gap in foreign language reading. *Modern Language Journal, 65,* 43-53.

Schulz, R. A. (1983). From word to meaning: Foreign language reading instruction after the elementary course. *Modern Language Journal, 67* (2), 127-34.

Segalowitz, N. (1986). Skilled reading in the second language. In J. Vaid (Ed.), *Language processing in bilinguals: Psycholinguistic and neuropsychological perspectives* (pp.3-19). Hillsdale, NJ: Erlbaum.

Seliger, H. W., & Long, M. H. (Eds.). (1983). *Classroom oriented research in second language acquisition.* Rowley, MA: Newbury House.

Shanahan, T. (1984). The nature of the reading-writing relationship: A multivariate analysis. *Journal of Educational Psychology, 76,* 466-77.

Siebert, L. C. (1945). A study of the practice of guessing word meanings from a context. *Modern Language Journal, 29,* 296- 323.

Singer, H. & Ruddell, R. B. (Eds.). (1985). *Theoretical Models and Processes of Reading.* (3rd ed.). Newark, DE: International Reading Association (ERIC Document Reproduction Service, No. ED 269 749).

Smith, F. (1982). *Understanding Reading.* (3rd ed.). New York: Holt, Rinehart & Winston.

Smith-Burke, M. T. (1982). Extending concepts through language activities. In J. A. Langer & M. T. Smith-Burke (Eds.), *Reader meets author/bridging the gap: A psycholinguistic and sociolinguistic perspective.* Newark, DE: International Reading Association. (ERIC Document Reproduction Service, No. ED 217 395)

Spack, R. (1985). Literature, reading, writing, and ESL: Bridging the gap. *TESOL Quarterly, 19* (4), 703-25.

Spinelli, E., & Siskin, H. J. (1987). Activating the reading skill through advance organizers. *Canadian Modern Language Review, 44* (1), 120-33.

Stanovich, K. E. (1980). Toward an interactive-compensatory model of individual differences in the development of reading fluency. *Reading Research Quarterly, 16,* 32-71.

Stansfield, C. (1980). The cloze procedure as a progress test. *Hispania, 63,* 715-18.

Stansfield, C., & Hansen, J. (1983). Field dependence as a variable in second language cloze test performance. *TESOL Quarterly, 17,* 29-38.

Stauffer, R. G. (1980). *The language experience approach to the teaching of reading.* New York: Harper & Row.

Steffensen, M. S. (1988). Changes in cohesion in the recall of native and foreign language texts. In P. L. Carrell, J. Devine, & D. E. Eskey (Eds.), *Interactive approaches to second language reading* (pp.140-151). Cambridge: Cambridge Univ. Press.

Steffensen, M. S., & Joag-Dev, C. (1984). Cultural knowledge and reading. In J. C. Alderson & A. H. Urquhart (Eds.), *Reading in a Foreign Language* (pp.48-61). New York: Longman.

Steffensen, M. S., Joag-Dev, C., & Anderson, R. C. (1979). A cross-cultural perspective on reading comprehension. *Reading Research Quarterly, 15*, 10-29.

Stoller, F. (1986). Reading lab: Developing low-level reading skills. In F. Dubin, D. E. Eskey, & W. Grabe (Eds.), *Teaching second language reading for academic purposes* (pp.51-76). Reading, MA: Addison-Wesley.

Strother, J. B., & Ulijn, J. M. (1987). Does syntactic rewriting affect English for science and technology (EST) text comprehension? In J. Devine, P. L. Carrell, D. E. Eskey (Eds.), *Research in reading in English as a second language* (pp.89-101). Washington, DC: Teachers of English to Speakers of Other Languages.

Swaffar, J. K. (1981). Reading in the foreign language classroom: Focus on process. *Unterrichtspraxis, 14*, 176-94.

Swaffar, J. K. (1985). Reading authentic texts in a foreign language: A cognitive model. *Modern Language Journal, 69* (1), 15-34.

Swaffar, J. K. (1988a, August). *The interactive reader: Implications for the second language classroom*. Paper presented at the Symposium on Teaching Foreign Languages to Adult Professionals: Approaches for the 1990s, Linthicum, MD.

Swaffar, J. K. (1988b) Readers, texts, and second languages: The interactive process. *Modern Language Journal, 72* (2), 123-49.

Swaffar, J. K., & Arens, K. (forthcoming). *Reading as language learning: Integrating reader and cultural meanings*. Englewood Cliffs, NJ: Prentice-Hall.

Swaffar, J. K., & Woodruff, M. S. (1978). Language for comprehension: Focus on reading: A report on the University of Texas German Program. *Modern Language Journal, 62* (1-2), 27-32.

Swann, W. (1981). *The gothic cathedral*. New York: Park Lane.

Tierney, R. J., & Pearson, P. D. (1983). Toward a composing model of reading. *Language Arts, 60*, 568-80.

Tuttle, H. G. (1981). Helping students to make inferences about location. *Foreign Language Annals, 14* (5), 427-28.

Twaddell, W. F. (1973). Vocabulary expansion in the TESOL classroom. *TESOL Quarterly, 7* (1), 61-78.

Tyacke, M. (1981). Alice through the looking glass: Reading in another language. In C. W. Twyford, W. Deihl, & K. Feathers (Eds.), *Reading English as a second language: Moving from theory* (pp.56-63). Bloomington, IN: Indiana University School of Education.

Ulijn, J. M. (1977). An integrated model for first and second language comprehension. *System, 5* (3), 187-99.

Ulijn, J. M. (1980). Foreign language reading research: Recent trends and future prospects. *Journal of Research in Reading, 3* (1), 17-37.

Ulijn, J. M. (1981). Conceptual and syntactic strategies in reading a foreign language. In E. Hopkins & R. Grotjahn (Eds.), *Studies in language teaching and language acquisition* (pp.129-166). Bochum: Brockmeyer.

Ulijn, J. M. (1984). Reading for professional purposes: Psycholinguistic evidence in a cross-linguistic perspective. In A. K. Pugh & J. M. Ulijn (Eds.), *Reading for professional purposes: Studies and practices in native and foreign languages* (pp.66-81). London: Heinemann.

Valette, R. M. (1977). *Modern language testing.* (2nd ed.). New York: Harcourt, Brace, Jovanovich (ERIC Document Reproduction Service, No.ED 153 489).

van Parreren, C. F., & Schouten-van Parreren, M. C. (1981). Contextual guessing: A trainable reader strategy. *System, 9,* 235-41.

VanPatten, B., Dvorak, T. R., & Lee, J. F. (Eds.). (1987). *Foreign language learning: A research perspective.* Cambridge, MA: Newbury House.

Walker, L. (1983). Word identification strategies in reading a foreign language. *Foreign Language Annals, 16* (4), 293-99.

Wardhaugh, R. (1969) *Reading: A linguistic perspective.* New York: Harcourt, Brace, & World.

Weible, D. M. (1980). Teaching reading skills through linguistic redundancy. *Foreign Language Annals, 13,* 487-93.

Wells, D. R. (1986). The assessment of foreign language reading comprehension: